NATIONAL PARKS

Explore America's 60 National Parks

Contents

Park Locations

Alaska

Hawaii

U.S. Virgin Islands

American Samoa

America's national parks inspire wonder and awe, restore our souls, and often renew our faith in the nation. The sight of rushing rivers, snowcapped peaks, steaming volcanoes, vibrant coral reefs, shimmering deserts, and lush forests reminds us of America's amazing spirit and its astonishing beauty.

Behind it all is the National Park Service, which oversees 417 units that include not only the 60 national parks covered in this book but also national preserves, monuments, lakeshores, seashores, recreation areas, scenic rivers and trails, memorials, parkways, battlefields, and historic parks and sites. In addition, the park service plays an advisory role for 49 National Heritage Areas: regions and/or communities whose landscapes, structures, trails, and byways have earned a chapter in the American story.

And all of this is yours to discover.

Opposite Page: Mount Rainier National Park, WA

Parks 101

Plan Ahead

It's important to check on park conditions, closures, and lodge or campground availability—before *and* during your visit. Access to entrances, roads, trails, visitors centers, and attractions can be affected by seasonality, weather, crowd-management measures, conservation works, or even, sadly, budget cuts.

And nature can be as devastating as it is devastatingly beautiful. The effects of eruptions and earthquakes (2018) in Hawai'i Volcanoes National Park, of hurricanes Irma and Maria (2017) in the U.S. Virgin Islands National Park, and of larger-than-usual forest fires in and Glacier (2017) and Great Smoky Mountains (2016) national parks will be evident for years to come.

Learn Something New

The park service encourages you to learn as well as to sightsee. Many parks have amazing (and often free) ranger-led tours and other programs. Institutes and field schools offer courses on a vast array of topics from astronomy, biology, botany, and conservation to photography, storytelling, art, crafts, music, yoga—even mountaineering and survival skills.

Take a Pass

Several cost-saving America the Beautiful passes make your national parks even more accessible. The recommended **Annual Pass**, available to everyone, offers admission to national parks and other federal lands for 12 months from date of purchase. Note, too, that this pass is available free to active-duty military personnel *and* their dependents.

To introduce youngsters to the parks, the **Every Kid in a Park Pass** offers free entry to fourth graders—and their family members and friends—for the duration of the school year. The **Annual Senior Pass**, available for a nominal fee, and the **Lifetime Senior Pass** are options for U.S. citizens or permanent residents age 62 and up; the **Access Pass** is free to U.S. citizens or permanent residents with permanent disabilities; and the **Volunteer Pass** costs nothing for those with 250 service hours at federal agencies participating in the Interagency Pass Program.

Part-Time Park Time?

Enroll in the **Volunteers-in-Parks** (www.nps.gov/getinvolved/volunteer.htm) program, and you'll join about 315,000 dedicated souls who work side-by-side with more than 20,000 NPS employees by contributing their time in more than 400 park sites, programs, and offices.

Many parks or their official concessionaires hire paid part- or full-time employees to work in hotels, restaurants, gift shops, and other guest services. Check **USAjobs.gov**, the federal government's official employment site, or the **national parks site**, which has sections on **jobs/careers** (www.nps.gov/aboutus/workwithus.htm) and a searchable list of **authorized concessioners** (www.nps.gov/subjects/concessions/index.htm) big and small.

You can also check out the websites of several large private companies that manage select park-based hotels, restaurants, and stores. These include **Aramark** (www.aramark.com), **Delaware North** (www.delawarenorth.com), and **Xanterra** (www.xanterra.com).

The Contact List

National Heritage Areas: www.nps.gov/heritageareas or www.nationalheritageareas.us

National Park Service: www.nps.gov

National Park Foundation: www.nationalparks.org

National Parks Conservation Association: www.npca.org

Recreation.gov: 877/444-6777, www.recreation.gov; trip-planning assistance, park campground reservations, attraction and event tickets

Opposite Page: Bryce Canyon National Park, UT

Acadia National Park

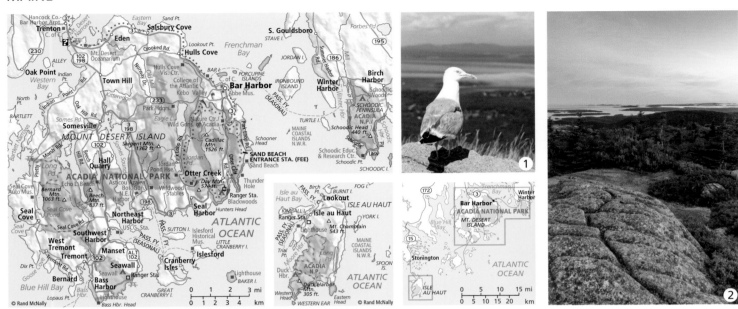

New England's only national park represents the region well. As you wind your way to Mount Desert Island, home to most of the park, the magic of Maine begins to enchant you.

Acadia itself has breathtaking coasts, with granite boulders, tidal pools, moss-covered rocks, and sandy beaches. The park's interior—peppered with lakes, ponds, and overlooks—is no less spectacular. So, too, are its separate, less-congested areas: the craggy Schoodic Peninsula and Isle au Haut, a remote islet that's partially under park stewardship yet also has a year-round population of less than 75 hardy souls.

From atop 1,526-foot Cadillac Mountain, all of Maine seems to spread out before you. Head to the summit early for one of the nation's first sunrises. Then head back down to charming Bar Harbor for a hearty New England breakfast before returning to the park to hike, bike, paddle, or enjoy a carriage ride—and lunch or afternoon tea at Jordan Pond House.

Park Basics

Established: July 8, 1916 (as Sieur de Monts National Monument); February 26, 1919 (as Lafayette National Park); January 19, 1929 (renamed Acadia National Park).
Area: 76.6 square miles/49,052 acres, including 47.3 square miles/30,300 acres on Mount Desert Island, 4.3 square miles/2,728 acres on Isle au Haut, and 3.7 square miles/2,366 acres on the Schoodic Peninsula.
Best For: Bird-Watching (eagles, falcons, hawks, owls); Canoeing; Cross-Country Skiing; Cycling; Fishing; Hiking; Snowmobiling; Snowshoeing.
Contact: 207/288-3338, www.nps.gov/acad.
Getting Oriented: Bangor, Maine, is 45 miles inland and northwest of the park; Portland is 160 miles to its southwest along the coast. The nearest major airport, though, is Logan International in Boston, Massachusetts (260 miles southwest). From Boston, follow I-95 north to Augusta, then ME 3 (aka Route 3) east to Ellsworth and south to Mount Desert Island, the location of most of Acadia. **The Hulls Cove Visitor Center** (25 Visitor Center Rd., 207/288-3338)—where there's access to the Park Loop Road and Carriage Road network—is just north of the town of **Bar Harbor** (www.barharbormaine.gov).

The smaller but no less charming **Northeast Harbor** (www.mountdesertchamber.org) and **Southwest Harbor** (www.southwestharbor. org), each just 1 mile from a park entrance, also make good bases. Seasonal **Island Explorer** (207/667-5796, www.exploreacadia. com) shuttle buses will scoot you around the island for free.

Acadia National Park, ME

1. Gull in the park. 2. Sunset view from atop Cadillac Mountain. 3. Bass Harbor Head Lighthouse. **Opposite Page:** Rocky shoreline.

Park Highlights

Natural Attractions. Although Acadia is one of the smaller national parks (Yellowstone, for instance, is 46 times bigger), there's still a lot to see and do. Exploring Maine's evocative coast is a must. Peek at tidal pools teeming with life, gaze at striated granite boulders, flex your toes in the sand, or (if you're really brave) dip those same toes in the frigid Atlantic.

A hike through the woods is also a must. Acadia's impossibly green groundcover of ferns is always picture-worthy, as are the "reveals" when you happen upon a secluded pond or lake. Canoeing, boating, or fishing in these inland waters are popular pastimes.

Mainers spend a great deal of time on the ocean—for work, pleasure, or often a little of both—and you should, too. Hop a ferry, book a cruise, or rent a motorboat or sailboat to see not only the coastal scenery but also lighthouses and spectacular summer homes.

Trails, Drives & Viewpoints. The 27-mile **Park Loop Road** passes Jordan Pond, Sand Beach, Thunder Hole, and other sights, giving you a great orientation to much of the Mount Desert Island portion of the park. Be sure to hike, bike, or drive to the summit of **Cadillac Mountain**, the park's signature viewpoint. Intrepid folks do this very early to watch one of the nation's first sunrises (*the* first from early October through early March).

Another quirky, lovely aspect of Acadia is its network of **Carriage Roads**—a gift from John D. Rockefeller Jr.—that weaves almost imperceptibly through the park. Built between 1913 and 1940, the 45 miles of elegant pathways were originally designed for horse-drawn vehicles and feature a series of slightly curvaceous stone bridges. Today, wheelchairs aside, motorized vehicles are still prohibited.

Although horseback riding is allowed, you need your own horse; there are no riding outfitters in or near the park. Most folks have an equine experience (May–Oct.) with **Carriages of Acadia** (207/276-5721, acadiahorses.com), which offers narrated carriage rides that depart from Wildwood Stables, near the town of Seal Harbor on the southeastern side of Mount Desert Island.

The park is also loaded with trails—everything from short, level hikes to the shoreline, like the 1.4-mile roundtrip **Wonderland Trail**, to lakeside trails such as the moderate 3.2-mile **Jordan Pond Path** loop, to extreme trails like the aptly named **Perpendicular Trail** (2.2 miles, with stairs and iron rungs) and **Precipice Trail** (2.5 miles, for experienced climbers only). The **Friends of Acadia Village Connector Trails** (www.friendsofacadia.org) enable you to walk from Mount Desert Island's various towns directly into the park itself; the Duck Brook Connector access, for example, is right beside the Acadia Inn on Route 3 in Bar Harbor.

To escape peak-season crowds on Mount Desert Island, head over to Acadia's **Schoodic Peninsula**—about 39 miles from the Hulls Cove Visitor Center via Route 3 and US 1 north. Here you'll find still more (and more peaceful) Maine woods and rocky shore. The 6-mile, one-way **Schoodic Loop Road** will take you to **Schoodic Point**, a coastal outcrop with stunning views of crashing waves and Mount Desert Island.

Museums & Sites. The **Islesford Historical Museum** (www.islesfordhistoricalmuseum.info), outside the park on Little Cranberry Island, gives you a true sense of the connection that Mainers have with the sea; the lobstering exhibit is particularly interesting. You can get to the Cranberry Isles (both Great and Little) by

A DAY ON ISLE AU HAUT

You can't leave Maine without taking a ferry ride. It's a rule. If you have time for only one, make it the ferry to **Isle au Haut** (www.isleauhaut.org), one of many remote Maine islands with incredibly small year-round populations and maybe a town or two. The islet, half of which is part of Acadia National Park, has just 73 full-time residents and a general store, aptly named **The Island Store** (near the Town Landing, 207/335-2008, www.theislandstore.net, closed Sun. except July–Sept.), which sells everything from groceries and beer/wine to sundries and souvenirs.

Isle au Haut Boat Services (207/367-5193, www.isleauhautferryservice.com) ferries passengers, freight, and mail to Isle au Haut's Town Landing (year-round) or Duck Harbor Boat Landing (summer only), which is in the park. The boats depart from the picturesque fishing village of **Stonington** (www.deerisle.com), roughly 58 miles southwest of Bar Harbor. A hike between the two landings is a great way to explore Isle au Haut for a few hours, as Jerusalem Mountain looms over one side and Isle au Haut Lighthouse (Robinson Point) is on the other. Cycling is also a great way to explore the island in one day, and bikes are allowed on the ferries.

Although The Island Store sells picnic items, for a day trip, it's probably best to pack a meal or at least some snacks—unless you're lucky enough to catch the **Maine Lobster Lady** (207/669-2751, www.mainelobsterlady.com). She serves delicious lobster rolls from a food truck (which heads to Arizona every October).

If you want to stay a little longer, lodging options include the park's small **Duck Harbor Campground** (mid-May–mid-Oct.; reservations required), with five primitive sites; a few private house rentals; and **The Keeper's House** (Isle au Haut Lighthouse, 207/335-2990, keepershouse.com), an all-inclusive inn with four rooms and two private cottages. Note that it's open seasonally from June 1 to October (Columbus Day weekend).

③

ferry from Southwest Harbor, mail boat from Northeast Harbor, or water taxi from either port; check schedules at the Hulls Cove Visitor Center. The incredibly informative **Mount Desert Oceanarium** (off ME-3 just past Mount Desert Island Bridge, 207/288-5005, www.theoceanarium.com) has a great lobster touch tank that kids love.

Programs & Activities. Night talks and other ranger-led events happen at both Blackwoods and Seawall campgrounds. There are also guided sunrise strolls, cruises to Baker Island to spot seabirds and (of course) lighthouses, and plenty of family activities—including a children's story hour.

In summer, hikers and bikers hit the trails, and paddlers and rowers take to the lakes and ponds. In winter, cross-country skiers, snowshoers, and snowmobilers descend on the park. **Cadillac Mountain Sports** (26 Cottage St., Bar Harbor, 207/288-4532, www. cadillacsports.com) is a great general outfitter.

Acadian Boat Tours (119 Eden St., Bar Harbor, 207/801-2300, acadianboattours. com) offers daily sightseeing/nature cruises and fishing or puffin/seabird excursions. To sail, kayak, or canoe on area ponds and lakes, contact **Acadia Boat Rental** (Apple Ln., Southwest Harbor, 207/370-7663, www. acadiaboatrental.com) or **National Park Canoe & Kayak Rentals** (145 Pretty Marsh Rd., northern tip of Long Pond, 207/244-5854, www.nationalparkcanoerental.com). Tired yet?

Lodging. Other than the nearly 600 sites (mostly for small tents) in the park's **Blackwoods**, **Seawall**, and **Schoodic Woods campgrounds**, all booked through Recreation.gov, there are no in-park lodging options. Acadia is surrounded, however, by classic Maine coastal towns and villages, so the number of nearby inns, B&Bs, hotels, and motels—as well as private campgrounds and home rentals—is fairly astounding.

So, where to stay? Let's start with the area's grand hotels. Consider the shake-shingle **Asticou Inn** (15 Peabody Dr., 207/276-3344, www.asticou.com) in Northeast Harbor, the giant **Bar Harbor Inn** (1 Newport Dr., 207/288-3351, barharborinn.com), or the historic **Claremont Hotel** (22 Claremont Rd., 207/244-5036, theclaremonthotel.com) in Southwest Harbor. All are on the water and have good restaurants.

For a more intimate experience, try Bar Harbor's Tudor-style **Atlantean Cottage** (11 Atlantic Ave., 207/288-5703, www. atlanteancottage.com) or porch-wrapped **Yellow House Bed & Breakfast** (15 The Field, 207/288-5100, www.yellowhousemaine. com). Southwest Harbor has the lovely, Victorian **Inn at Southwest** (371 Main St., 207/244-3835, www.innatsouthwest.com).

1. Walking along the shore at Sand Beach. **2.** The Keeper's House. **3.** Bar Harbor Inn.

JORDAN POND HOUSE

When you think "national park," you don't generally think, "Oh . . . what a perfect place for high tea!" But that's just another way in which Acadia National Park is its own special world. Between mid-May and mid-October, few folks visit Acadia without swinging by the Jordan Pond House, if only to browse in its gift shop and enjoy the view. But we suggest making your stop here an event by partaking in a time-honored tradition.

Although Jordan Pond House serves lunch and dinner, with both indoor and "lawn" seating, it also serves afternoon tea—offered since the late 1800s, well before Acadia National Park was established. We can't think of a better late-afternoon break than enjoying Prosecco and popovers while gazing at Jordan Pond. You can also chow down on a fresh Maine lobster roll at lunch or tuck into a New York strip steak or full-on boiled Maine lobster for dinner. Just remember . . . like many things in this very popular national park, reservations are recommended. *2928 Park Loop Rd., 7.6 miles from Hulls Cove Visitor Center, 207/276-3316, jordanpondhouse.com.*

Arches National Park

UTAH

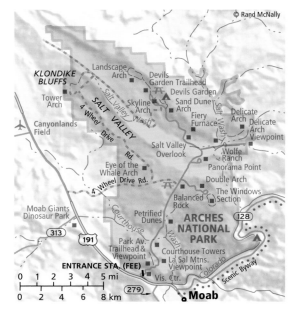

In museums, sculptures are artfully placed around a room so that you can fully appreciate their forms and aesthetics. In Arches, this happens on a grand, natural scale—it's America's greatest sculpture garden, featuring ancient rock formations.

At night, these shapely natural sculptures created over millions of years become the backdrop to an expansive sky filled with the twinkling lights of the Milky Way. Bring your own telescope or make friends with the astronomy enthusiasts, who swap their cameras for some serious astral hardware at nightfall.

There's plenty to experience here, from viewing the magnificent geologic formations carved from desert sandstone to biking, climbing, hiking, off-roading, and horseback-riding. Add to this the lively nightlife in the nearby town of Moab, and it's easy to appreciate why a visit to Arches National Park, no matter what the season, is on many a bucket list.

Park Basics

Established: April 12, 1929 (national monument); November 12, 1971 (national park).
Area: 120 square miles; 76,679 acres.
Best For: Astronomy, Climbing, Geology, Hiking.
Contact: 435/719-2299, www.nps.gov/arch.
Getting Oriented: Arches is in eastern Utah, and the nearest large airports are Salt Lake City International (235 miles northwest of entrance) in Utah and Denver International (379 miles east) in Colorado. The entrance to Arches is 28 miles south of I-70 on US 191 from Crescent Junction if you're coming from the west, and 46 miles south of I-70 on UT 128 from Cisco if you're coming from the east; **Arches Visitor Center** is at the park entrance. **Moab** (discovermoab.com), 5 miles south of the

Arches National Park, UT

entrance, is one of America's coolest towns, with good restaurants and lodgings, so you won't need any other town during your visit.

Park Highlights

Natural Attractions. Arches, arches everywhere: The park has more than 2,000 of them by most counts, all formed primarily by erosion. Double arches, long arches, partial arches, fins, spires, buttes (isolated hills with flat tops and steep sides), and simply wacky-looking formations fill the park from end to end. Trails lead up to, through, around, under, and over these terrestrial marvels.

It's not just the shape of the arches that will astound you. It's also their multi-colored layers and angles that appear to glow especially bright in the Utah sunsets, when the rock turns from pale rust to a red-and-orange wash of colors. So stay in the park until well past nightfall, as the view changes with the angle of the sun, rising of the moon, and brilliance of the stars.

Trails, Drives & Viewpoints. The park's **scenic drive** takes about three hours if you stop at all the amazing viewpoints; be sure to turn off for the **Windows Section** and the **Delicate Arch Viewpoint** especially. For intrepid drivers, there are four-wheel-drive-only roads through **Willow Flats**, **Salt Valley**, and **Klondike Bluffs**. Even though irascible naturalist author Edward Abbey, the park's most famous ex-ranger, may rebel at these scenic drives (he wanted the park empty of cars), you can assuage his soul by buying a copy of his classic *Desert Solitaire* at the visitors center.

Hiking in Arches will almost *always* bring you to some amazing arch, pinnacle, or canyon. Always pack water, even for short hikes, since there's extremely limited access to water in the park, where temperatures soar in summer. Short hikes to both the seemingly impossible **Balanced Rock**, off the main road, and the giant **Double Arch** in the Windows Section are relatively flat; the 1.6-mile round-trip hike to **Landscape Arch** in Devils Garden is a good intermediate hike. The 3-mile round-trip, uphill hike to iconic **Delicate Arch** may be one of the most sublime experiences—just be fit for

the challenge, since rangers rate this trail as difficult.

Programs & Activities. Arches has a fabulous night sky, and generally it has great **stargazing programs**. Check ahead, though; roadwork can lead to closures at night. Otherwise, ranger-led **geology talks** or short **guided hikes** are fun options (park rangers are *the* coolest).

One special program is the strenuous **Fiery Furnace Guided Hike**, a 2.5-hour loop that will have you scrambling up and sliding down sandstone cliffs and squeezing through narrow slot canyons. It's great fun for (in-shape) families; kids must be five or older. Spots fill quickly; generally you can book in advance,

but sometimes it's first-come, first served. Arches also always has an artist-in-residence who leads **Art in the Parks** programs that offer artistic perspectives on park wonders.

The park isn't the best place for mountain biking, but the surrounding area is world famous for this sport. Moab has plenty of outfitters and equipment-rental shops.

Lodging. There are few lodging options within Arches but many choices nearby. Note, too, that there has been a moratorium on backcountry camping, and the 50-site, in-park **Devils Garden Campground** has only two group campsites (reserve through Recreation. gov). Just outside the park are plenty of camping options—in fact, more than 400 campsites across 20 locations are listed on the Arches Campground Map on the park website.

Head to quirky, outdoorsy Moab for a variety of lodging options. You can enjoy a spa treatment at the upscale **Sorrel River Ranch** (HC 64, Mile 17, UT 128, 435/259-4642, www.sorrelriver.com), 29 miles outside town; or hang out at the pool and hot tub at downtown's **Gonzo Inn** (100 W. 200 South St., 435/259-2515, www. gonzoinn.com). B&Bs, such as **Sunflower Hill** (147 N. 300 East St., 435/259-2974, www.sunflowerhill.com) with 12 rooms and a pool, are popular too.

1. Sorrel River Ranch. **2.** Delicate Arch. **3.** Fiery Furnace hike. **4.** Landscape Arch in the Devils Garden area of the park.

Badlands National Park

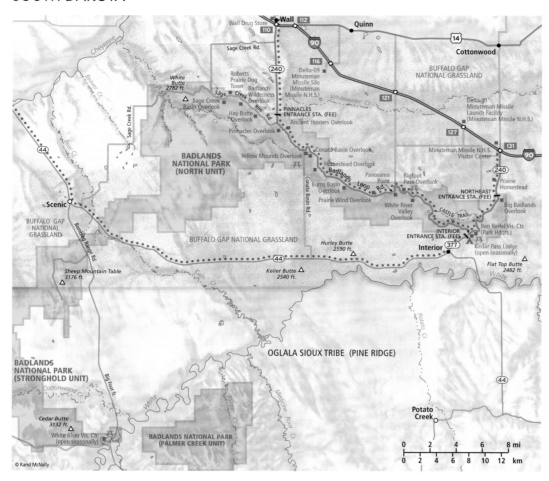

1

2

The magic of Badlands is hidden in the high prairies of southwestern South Dakota: Initially, you see only seemingly endless miles of grassland. Then, the pale-pink and tan buttes appear, at which point you can't stop staring.

Badlands National Park's two varied treasures—its sandstone buttes (isolated hills with steep sides and flat tops) and its mixed-grass prairie—form a wonderful natural interplay. Stripes of green grass wend and weave their way into the narrow slot canyons formed over millions of years by erosion. To fully absorb the scenery, drive the loop road, but don't miss the chance for a hike and a glimpse of wildlife among the buttes.

When night falls, don't go anywhere—a completely different kind of show begins, this one featuring thousands of stars shining brightly in the dark South Dakota sky. Although reaching the Badlands might be a bit of an odyssey, being here is worth the travel time.

Park Basics

Established: January 29, 1939 (national monument); November 10, 1978 (national park).

Area: 379 square miles; 242,756 acres.

Best For: Astronomy; Geology; Hiking; Paleontology; Wildlife Watching (bighorn sheep, bison, prairie dogs).

Contact: 605/433-5361, www.nps.gov/badl.

Getting Oriented: Badlands is in southwestern South Dakota; the closest major airport is Colorado's Denver International, 370 miles southwest. South Dakota's Rapid City Regional is about 65 miles west. You can access the main drive of the park, SD Highway 240, from two entrances—Pinnacles and Northeast—20 miles apart on I-90 from Exits 110 and 131, respectively. **Ben Reifel Visitor Center** (Badlands Loop Rd.) is 5 miles south

Badlands National Park, SD

of the Northeast Entrance. The nearest towns with lodging options are **Wall** (www.wallsd.us), 8 miles north of the Pinnacles Entrance, and **Rapid City** (www.visitrapidcity.com).

Park Highlights

Natural Attractions. The unforgettable sandstone buttes of the Badlands—first given that name by the Lakota people for the ruggedness of this land—were formed more than 50 million years ago by the twin geologic forces of deposition and erosion. Different-hued layers of rock, such as the dark Rockyford Ash, the brown Brule Formation, and the gray Chadron Formation, show the deposits of various types of sediment and ash that were compressed into vivid layers. The surrounding mixed-grass prairie, one of the largest undisturbed tracts of its kind in America, is composed of western wheatgrass as well as more than 400 additional plant species. The prairie runs straight up to the cliffs and sometimes slips into the slot canyons.

Bighorn sheep and 2,000-pound bison are starring attractions, especially if you hit one of the park's backcountry trails. Keep an eye out for bobcats, pronghorns (resembles an antelope), and prairie dogs, too. The park's fossil beds are protected from fossil hunting, but exhibits at the visitors center and a short interpretive trail might slake your paleontological thirst. At night, the sky is clear enough that you can see more than 7,500 stars, so do linger after dark, and maybe catch an evening ranger program.

Trails, Drives & Viewpoints. No matter which way you enter the **Badlands Loop Road (SD Highway 240)**—from the west, where you hit Pinnacles Overlook, or from the east, where you encounter Big Badlands Overlook—the buttes seem to rise up out of nowhere. Another dozen or so overlooks, including Panorama Point with its view of both the geology of the buttes and the swaths of prairie, are along a 26-mile stretch between Pinnacles and Big Badlands. Allow at least an hour, excluding any hiking time, to get from one end to the other.

The signature hiking trail in Badlands is the moderate, 1.5-mile round-trip **Notch Trail**. It starts with a walk through a canyon before you climb a nearly vertical (and totally cool) 50-step log ladder; at the top is a view of the sprawling White River Valley. In contrast, the easy 4-mile **Medicine Root Loop** gets you up close to the mixed-grass prairie, with the buttes in the distance. Both trails are in the Cedar Pass area.

Programs & Activities. The Badlands are known for their rich cache of plant and animal fossils, and you can watch paleontologists work at the **Fossil Prep Lab** at the Ben Reifel Visitor Center every day during summer. Families can download the park's **GPS Adventure Activity Book** from the Kids & Youth/Teens section of the Badlands website; it's perfect for the naturalists and geocachers in the backseat.

At night, full-moon hikes and stargazing programs with telescopes are essential and fun for the whole family; the night sky, with the buttes as a backdrop, is truly incredible. The park's annual 3-day **Astronomy Festival**, generally held in late June or early July, features guest speakers, planetarium shows, telescope viewings, and evening programs.

Lodging. Inside the park, **Cedar Pass Lodge** (20681 SD Hwy. 240, Interior, 605/433-5460, www.cedarpasslodge.com; closed mid-Oct. to mid-Apr.) has 22 cabins, 96 tent and RV sites, and 4 group campground sites. It's 5 miles south of the Northeast Entrance. The park's windswept, generally uncrowded **Sage Creek Campground** (off Sage Creek Rd., 13 miles west of Pinnacles Entrance), good for tents and RVs (no hookups), has a dozen or so free sites (first come, first served) on the high prairie.

Wall, north of the park, has the sprawling, famous **Wall Drug Store** (510 Main St., 605/279-2175, www.walldrug.com) and a decent number of motels, including locally owned **Welsh's Motel** (312 South Blvd., 605/279-2271). Farther afield, Rapid City (en route to Mount Rushmore, 23 miles southwest of Rapid City) has dozens of hotels and motels, including **Rushmore Hotel & Suites** (445 Mt. Rushmore Rd., 605/348-8300, www.therushmorehotel.com).

1. Bison. **2.** Wall Drug Store. **3.** Ladder on Notch Trail. **4.** Badlands landscape.

Big Bend National Park

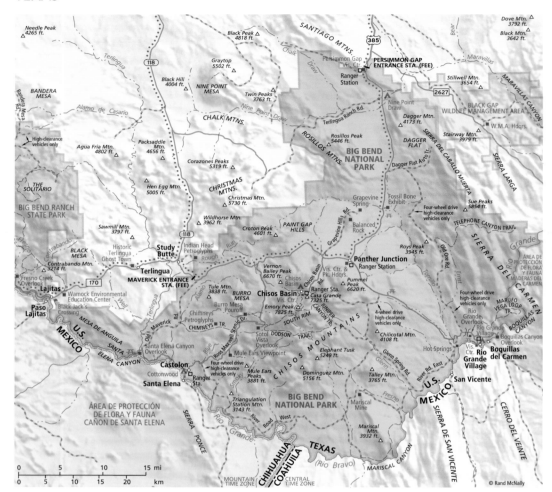

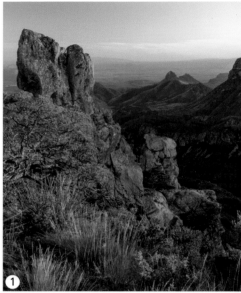

Vast, brash, and unforgiving, this park is definitively Texan. Big Bend offers the desert untouched, where seemingly endless cactus-studded plains give way to mountains, canyons, and river.

It's a place where just about everything will scratch, stick, or bite you. Yet it's also a place to truly get away from it all: Deep in West Texas on the United States–Mexico border, the park is exceedingly remote but well worth the time it takes to get here.

Big Bend owes its name to the gentle curve of the Rio Grande—accessible primarily to those who paddle its flows—on the park's southern edge. Rising from the scorching plain in the heart of the park, the forested Chisos Mountains are an oasis of cool. The hiking here is some of the state's best, with trails culminating in sweeping

views. Come sunset, the earthen hues darken into shadows, and the desert night offers a spectacular lens into the Milky Way, spinning in the infinite sky.

Park Basics

Established: June 12, 1944.
Area: 1,252 square miles; 801,163 acres.
Best For: Astronomy; Hiking; Whitewater Rafting; Wildlife Watching (bears, javelinas, tarantulas).
Contact: 432/477-2251, www.nps.gov/bibe.
Getting Oriented: Big Bend is just north of the U.S.–Mexico border in West Texas. The closest major airports are Midland, 235 miles north of park headquarters at Panther Junction, and El Paso International, 330 miles west. The main **Panther Junction Visitor Center** is in the park's interior at the intersection of TX 118 and US 385. Other visitors centers are **Persimmon Gap** (at the northern entrance on US 385), **Rio Grande Village** (on the river along the park's east

Big Bend National Park, TX

side, 50 miles from the western entrance), **Castolon** (on the west side, along Ross Maxwell Scenic Dr.), and **Chisos Basin** (in the park's center at the end of Basin Junction Rd.).

Nearby towns with dining and lodging options include **Terlingua** and **Study Butte** (visitbigbend.com for both), 3 miles west of the western entrance; **Alpine** (visitalpinetx. com), 103 miles north of the western entrance; and **Marathon** (visitbigbend. com), 40 miles north of the northern entrance. Hip **Marfa** (visitmarfa.com), 129 miles northwest of the western entrance, has a lively contemporary art scene.

Park Highlights

Natural Attractions. At 5,400 feet in elevation, scenic **Chisos Basin** is a circular valley with lodging, camping, and numerous trailheads. The basin offers a base for exploring the **Chisos Mountains**, the park's highest peaks. The mountain trails include a fabled route on the South Rim, favored by backcountry campers.

The park's southern boundary, the **Rio Grande**, known as Rio Blanco in Mexico, is a rafting mecca. Over the eons, the slow, snaking flow of the river has cut three dramatic **canyons** in the park: Mariscal, Santa Elena, and Boquillas canyons. The latter two are accessible by paved road; Mariscal is accessible only by river or dirt road.

Trails, Drives & Viewpoints. Emory Peak Trail takes you to the park's high point—7,825 feet above sea level—on a difficult 9.3-mile round-trip. **Lost Mine Trail**, a moderate hike, offers great views as it climbs 1,000 feet over 2.3 miles. **Window View Trail** is an easy 0.3-mile round-trip with a spectacular sunset view of the desert below framed by its namesake.

Ross Maxwell Scenic Drive, a 22-mile paved road on the park's west side, features several panoramic vistas of the desert wilderness and

ends at the trailhead into Santa Elena Canyon; expect to spend two to three hours on the round-trip. **Chisos Basin Road** leads 6 miles from the main park road to Chisos Basin and offers a number of scenic overlooks on a 15-minute drive.

Museums & Sites. Accessible via Ross Maxwell Scenic Drive and a short walk, **Hot Springs** is an abandoned resort in Big Bend's southeastern corner that still has natural pools where you can take a soak. In the **Castolon Historic District**, in the park's southwest, you can see a 1901 house that's the park's oldest structure and a store built to house troops during the Mexican Revolution.

Petroglyph sites include the Chimneys on the park's west side and Indian Head Mountain northeast of Study Butte. Just west of the park, **Historic Terlingua Ghost Town** is a formerly abandoned mining town that's been revitalized by artists. Another option, if you have a valid passport, is to cross the border to Mexico to explore the small town of **Boquillas del Carmen**.

Programs & Activities. Ranger programs include campfire talks and guided hikes; for a fee, rangers will guide you for a half-day or more. Rafting the Rio Grande is a big draw: Check in with **Far Flung Outdoor Center** (432/371-2633, bigbendfarflung.com) or **Big Bend River Tours** (432/371-3033, www.bigbendrivertours.com) for guided trips that may also include other activities.

Lodging. Big Bend has one lodging and some camping. There are also numerous options outside the park in Terlingua, Study Butte, Alpine, Marfa, and Marathon that range from roadside motels to grand historic hotels. In Chisos Basin, **Chisos Mountains Lodge** (432/477-2291, www.chisosmountainslodge.com) has 66 basic motel rooms as well as 6 rustic stone cottages.

In the park's southeastern corner, **Rio Grande Village** has two campgrounds: one with 100 tent sites (Recreation.gov for reservations) and another with 25 RV hookups, as well as laundry facilities and a small store. Reservations for the RV hookups are handled through Chisos Mountains Lodge. The park also has campgrounds (84 sites in all; Recreation.gov) in Chisos Basin and near Castolon; these don't have hookups, but RVs are permitted.

On the site of a reclaimed ruin in quirky Terlingua, **La Posada Milagro** (100 Milagro Rd., 432/371-3044, www.laposadamilagro.net) has four distinctively West Texan rooms with ornate rockwork. In Marathon, the 45-room, redbrick **Gage Hotel** (102 N.W. 1st St., 432/386-4205, gagehotel.com) is a historic property from 1927 that's been updated for the new millennium, with a restaurant, day spa, and pool perfect for escaping the heat.

1. Lost Mine Trail at sunset. **2.** Cactus blossoms. **3.** Jeep tour with Far Flung Outdoor Center.

③

Biscayne National Park

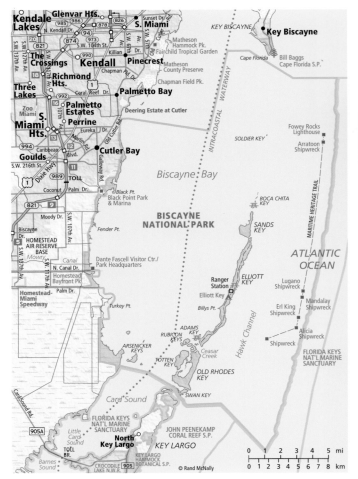

National parks evoke visions of broad valleys, towering mountains, and endless forests. Biscayne Bay, though, has none of these. It's also missing one other component: land.

Biscayne, in southeastern Florida, is a celebration of the sea. Of its roughly 173,000 acres, fewer than 10,000 consist of small sandy islands or mangrove swamps along the shore. The park's aquatic nature draws half a million visitors a year—400,000 of them via watercraft, with others from the mainland visitors center.

What the park contrasts with magnifies its appeal: To the north, the Miami skyline reveals a commercial empire. Indeed, just as Miami Beach was on the verge of again becoming a trendy resort, Biscayne National Park was established. It preserves not only an area but also an era, one in which

savoring the state's natural wonders was an affordable tradition. Here, you'll experience Old Florida in all its diverse beauty.

Park Basics

Established: October 18, 1968 (national monument); June 28, 1980 (national park).
Area: 270 square miles; 172,971 acres.
Best For: Bird-Watching (herons, ospreys, warblers); Boating; Diving/Snorkeling; Fishing; Kayaking.
Contact: 305/230-1144, www.nps.gov/bisc.
Getting Oriented: Biscayne is near major airports in southeastern Florida: Miami International is 35 miles north of the park entrance in Homestead, and Fort Lauderdale International is 60 miles north. Boaters access the park from four marinas at the park's boundaries, and the **Dante Fascell Visitor Center** (9700 S.W. 328th St., Sir Lancelot Jones Way, Convoy Point, Homestead) is the mainland's only access point, a few miles east of US 1 and the Florida Turnpike.

Biscayne National Park, FL

Dining and lodging options abound in **Homestead** (www.cityofhomestead.com), 8 miles west of the park entrance, and also in **Coral Gables** (30 miles north), **Miami** (35 miles north), and **Miami Beach** (45 miles northeast), all at www.miamiandbeaches.com.

Park Highlights

Natural Attractions. Primarily a broad, shallow lagoon, **Biscayne Bay** has a blend of fresh and salt water that creates the perfect environment for a forested shoreline and deep swamp of red, black, and white mangrove

(3)

trees. This provides birds with well-protected nesting spots, and waters teeming with fish offer meals in abundance. A portion of the **Great Florida Birding Trail** (floridabirdingtrail.com) skims over Biscayne National Park, attracting bird-watchers in search of seasonal and year-round residents including elusive mangrove cuckoos and several species of warblers. Sharing the shoreline and barrier islands are yellow-crowned night herons, black skimmers, and raptors such as hawks and bald eagles. On and over the waters, look for pelagic seabirds: pelicans, gulls, and loons.

Florida's famous manatees can be seen in Biscayne Bay, along with crocodiles that have adapted to the saltier estuarine waters. Dolphins playfully break the surface that conceals an undersea world that thrills divers and snorkelers with views of sponges, corals, and 500 species of tropical fish. Dive shops can lead you to the best sites, where you might see parrotfish, loggerhead sea turtles, goliath grouper, and green moray eels.

Although land is in short supply, three keys attract visitors. **Adams Key** is a recreation

area open dawn to dusk; **Elliott Key** has a 6-mile highway to an abandoned community (Islandia) that is now a pleasant, easy trail. The most-visited key is **Boca Chita**, in the 1930s a "party island" for its wealthy owner (Mark Honeywell of heating and cooling fame); his ornamental lighthouse is a highlight.

Museums & Sites. An art gallery at **Dante Fascell Visitor Center** celebrates the park's natural beauty with changing exhibits. The museum here explores the park's history and ecosystems. You can watch two orientation films and view displays on birds, fish, wildlife, reefs, and mangrove swamps.

Rangers lead snorkeling tours through the **Maritime Heritage Trail**, the park system's only underwater archaeological trail, to visit wreck sites in shallow waters. Markers at each site have information about the ship.

Programs & Activities. If you arrive unequipped, a concessionaire at the visitor center can set you up with gear for snorkeling, paddling, and sailing. You can also choose among a wide selection of **Biscayne National Park Institute** (786/335-3644, www.biscaynenationalparkinstitute.org) trips and tours, among them half- and full-day sailing excursions; 3-hour tours aboard a 40-passenger pontoon boat; and snorkeling and paddling tours that explore open waters and might stop at Adams Key, Elliott Key, and Boca Chita. Depending on the concessionaire, tours depart from the visitor center or a marina near the park's boundaries.

This watery park is great for fishing, and you can sail about to look for crab, shrimp, lobster

and designated sport fish at favorite fishing spots. A recreational saltwater fishing license, available at bait and tackle shops and online (www.myfwc.com) is required. Adventurous folks snorkel and dive among tropical fish and float beside the sunken remnants of boats and ships that got too close to the water's sharp coral.

Lodging. Although choices in the park are limited to campgrounds, Miami and its suburbs have every level of lodging. Biscayne's **Elliott Key and Boca Chita campgrounds** (786/335-3644, www.biscaynenationalparkinstitute.org) are accessible only by boat; a shuttle service ferries you to the islands. Elliott Key's campground has 33 slips for boats and room for an abundance of campers. Drinking water, restrooms with sinks, and cold-water showers are available. Boca Chita's grassy camping area by the water has picnic tables, grills, and toilets. What's missing? Sinks, showers, and drinking water. Boats tie up along the lagoon (first-come, first-served), and campers find room on a grassy camping area.

La Flora (1238 Collins Ave., Miami Beach, 305/531-3406, www.laflorahotelsouthbeach.com) is a colorful boutique hotel in the Art Deco district. More in keeping with Biscayne's slower pace, the **Redland Hotel** (5 S. Flagler Ave., Homestead, 305/246-1904, www.hotelredland.com) has an Old Florida feel—not surprising since it's the town's oldest hotel.

1. Red mangrove trees. 2. Fishing near Elliott Key. 3. Yellow-crowned night heron. 4. Boca Chita Key lighthouse.

(4)

Black Canyon of the Gunnison National Park

COLORADO

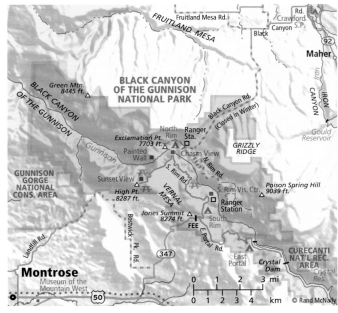

Looking down from the rim to the frothy blue Gunnison River a half-mile below is like peering into a different universe, one populated by gliding birds, gravity-defying flora, and cliffs cut by water and wind over the eons.

This southwestern Colorado gorge is one of the country's most dramatic. Other canyons are bigger and deeper, but none are steeper and narrower relative to their depth. The 14 miles of the crevasse within the park's boundaries range from 1,730 to 2,722 feet. At its most slender, the canyon is just 40 feet across.

The forested North and South rims and surrounding West Elk Mountains complement dizzying views of the river, rock outcroppings, and canyon-wall buttresses. Most people visit the park's South Rim, but it's worth spending an extra couple of hours on an ultra-scenic drive to the lesser-seen North Rim. You're likely to have the overlooks and trails all to yourself.

Black Canyon of the Gunnison National Park, CO

Park Basics

Established: March 2, 1933 (national monument); October 21, 1999 (national park).
Area: 47 square miles; 30,750 acres.
Best For: Bird-Watching (golden eagles, red-tailed hawks, white-throated swifts); Climbing; Hiking.
Contact: 970/641-2337, www.nps.gov/blca.
Getting Oriented: Major airports close to Black Canyon of the Gunnison in southwestern Colorado are Denver International (285 miles northeast of South Rim entrance) and Utah's Salt Lake City International (359 miles northwest). From US 50, take CO Highway 347 to the park entrance and the **South Rim Visitor Center** (South Rim Rd.).

On the other side of the canyon, by way of US 50 and CO Highway 92, the **North Rim Ranger Station** is about 65 miles away from the South Rim (some of the route is not paved); it's open intermittently from late May to early September. **Montrose** (www.visitmontrose.com), 14 miles southwest of the more-used South Rim entrance, and **Crawford**, (www.crawfordcountry.org), 9 miles north of the North Rim entrance, are nearby towns with lodging options.

Park Highlights

Natural Attractions. The park is defined by the **Gunnison River** on the canyon floor, more than 1,700 feet below the North and South rims. Steep canyon walls mean that shadows can cover the rock, giving the Black Canyon its name. The tallest cliff in Colorado, multihued **Painted Wall** is 2,250 feet tall, a full 1,000 feet taller than New York's Empire State Building. **Pulpit Rock** on South Rim Drive offers a panoramic view of the rock walls and more than a mile of the wild river on the canyon floor. Visible from the North Rim, **Balanced Rock** looks as if it is bound to tumble into the river, any millennia now.

The birds that live in the canyon are especially impressive to watch from above, and include red-tailed hawks, golden eagles, and white-throated swifts. Mule deer, elk, and yellow-bellied marmots are some of the most visible wild animals on the rims.

Trails, Drives & Viewpoints. An easy hike of less than a mile on the South Rim, **Cedar Point Nature Trail** delivers incredible views of Painted Wall and the river more than 2,000 feet down. More experienced hikers can venture out on the moderate 2-mile **Oak Flat Loop** through forested areas near the South Rim, or the more difficult **North Vista Trail**, a 7-mile round-trip on the North Rim that offers stunning views from the aptly named

Exclamation Point before a more difficult stretch that climbs Green Mountain.

Only the hardiest adventurers make it down to the river: The difficult **Gunnison Route** drops more than 1,800 feet from the Oak Flat Loop. Although it's only a mile long, the round-trip requires about 4 hours, and the ascent is extremely strenuous.

Those with less time can stop at the overlooks on paved **South Rim Road**, a 7-mile route with 12 overlooks, including **Chasm View** above the narrowest part of the canyon (the 40-foot-wide and aptly named **Narrows**) and an end-of-day stunner at **Sunset View**. Expect to spend 2 to 3 hours on the drive. Closed in winter, unpaved **North Rim Road**, with 6 overlooks, can be accessed by car on the 204-mile **West Elk Loop Scenic Byway**, one of the most sublime ribbons of roadway in the Rockies. It takes about 90 minutes to drive here from the South Rim.

Museums & Sites. Ute Indian Museum (17253 Chipeta Rd., Montrose, 970/249-3098, www.historycolorado.org), 14 miles southwest of the park, celebrates Ute culture with exhibits and a memorial to the legendary Chief Ouray. **Museum of the Mountain West** (68169 E. Miami Rd., 970/240-3400, www.museumofthemountainwest.org), 2 miles east of Montrose, offers a look at the area's fascinating history with artifacts and original buildings.

Programs & Activities. Ranger programs include guided hikes and campfire programs in summer and snowshoe and cross-country ski tours in winter. Just downstream from the park in the **Curecanti National Recreation Area** (970/641-2337, www.nps.gov/cure), the 1.5-hour boat tour to Morrow Point is a different look at the canyon.

Lodging. The park has no hotels. Montrose has numerous national chains and a few independent lodgings. **Country Lodge** (1624 E. Main St., Montrose, 970/249-4567, www.countrylodgecolorado.com) provides well-kept rooms and cabins and space to spread out on grassy lawns out front.

For those going to the North Rim, the **Last Frontier Lodge** (40300 D Ln., 970/921-5150, www.lastfrontierlodge.com) outside Crawford is off the beaten path with sublime views of Needle Rock and the West Elk's snow-capped peaks. In Crawford proper, the **Hitching Post Hotel and Feed Store** (313 CO Hwy. 92, 970/921-5040, www.hitchingposthotel.com) is a unique budget choice that offers both farm supplies and rooms for the night.

In the park, the **South Rim Campground** (Recreation.gov for reservations) has 88 sites for tents and RVs; the first-come, first-served **North Rim Campground** has 13 sites for tents only.

1. Gunnison River on the canyon floor. **2.** View to the canyon below. **3.** Ute Indian Museum.

Bryce Canyon National Park

UTAH

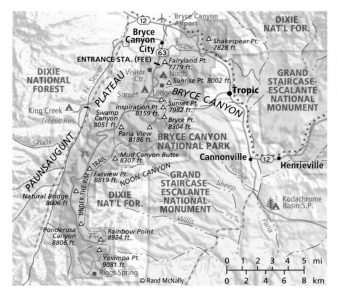

Hoodoos rise, hawks soar. The setting sun turns the canyon crimson. The stars emerge, and all is still and quiet. In the clear morning light, the colorful rock formations seem to glow. Welcome to Bryce Canyon, Utah's remote, magical masterpiece.

Bryce technically isn't a canyon. Rather, the park is a set of natural amphitheaters with tall, reddish rock spires called hoodoos that rise up from its floor. Nevertheless, it's quite possibly the single most spectacular, ornate, and awe-inspiring geologic formation on planet Earth. But do tear yourself away from the view at the top, because following a trail down through the hoodoos really shouldn't be missed.

You might also want to plan an overnight stay. Bryce's sky is so clear that more than three times as many

stars can be seen here than in most urban locations. When you wake up in the park, you can greet the day with a sunrise view of its colorful rock treasures.

Park Basics

Established: June 8, 1923 (national monument); February 25, 1928 (national park).
Area: 56 square miles; 35,835 acres.
Best For: Astronomy, Backcountry Camping, Geology, Hiking, Horseback Riding, Snowshoeing.
Contact: 435/834-5322, www.nps.gov/brca.
Getting Oriented: Bryce is in southwestern Utah, and the closest major airports are Salt Lake City International (272 miles north of entrance) in Utah, and McCarran International (270 miles southwest) in Las Vegas, Nevada. The park's sole entrance is on UT 63, a few miles south of its junction with Scenic Byway UT 12; the helpful **Bryce Canyon Visitor Center** (UT 63) is 1 mile south of the entrance. In summer, use the park shuttle bus to enjoy

Bryce Canyon National Park, UT

the scenery and avoid adding to the traffic. The towns of **Escalante** (www.escalanteut.com), 49 miles east of the entrance, and **Panguitch** (www.panguitch.com), 28 miles northwest, have more lodging options than places closer to the park.

Park Highlights

Natural Attractions. The fantastic-looking hoodoos in the world's largest collection have variable thicknesses (like totem poles) and were formed by rain, erosion, and "frost wedging"—a process that occurs when water

(3)

freezes overnight and then expands in the morning, splitting rock.

The park itself is arranged in a "line" of natural amphitheaters along the edge of the Paunsaugunt Plateau. Walking *among* the hoodoos is as cool as gazing at them from above, with more chances to spot wildlife.

About 175 species of birds—and plenty of mammals, insects, and reptiles—inhabit the park year-round or seasonally. The other real show is the night sky: Bryce is hundreds of miles from the nearest large city. Pull up a chair at Bryce Canyon Lodge or peer from your tent to see more than 7,500 stars on a moonless night. You'll understand why Bryce is one of America's Dark Sky–certified parks.

Trails, Drives & Viewpoints. Sunrise Point, Sunset Point, Inspiration Point, Bryce Point, Natural Bridge, and Rainbow Point are all must-see **viewpoints** along the sole park road (UT 63), which runs for 17 miles between the visitors center and the terminus at Rainbow Point. If you are into photography or want to stop at every viewpoint, it will take half a day to travel fully out and back. Sunset Point is, indeed, the best stop for sunsets, but every stop has postcard-worthy vistas.

The strenuous, backcountry 23-mile **Under-the-Rim Trail** (a full-day hike or more) and

the strenuous 8.6-mile **Riggs Spring Loop Trail** (half a day, minimum) are excellent diversions from gawking crowds at the top of the plateau, and the park shuttle (summer only) is handy if you want to hike only part of the Under-the-Rim Trail—just be prepared, and mind the elevation.

Programs & Activities. Attending a geology talk or the park's annual two-day **Geology Festival** in July is a must to fully comprehend how the hoodoos came into existence. At night, full-moon hikes and stargazing programs, including the annual **Astronomy Festival** in June, are fun for the whole family. You can also join a 1-mile **Rim Walk**, and let a park ranger point out wonders that your eye might have missed.

In spring, summer, and fall, a horseback-riding excursion with **Canyon Trail Rides** (435/679-8665, www.canyonrides.com) is a classic way to explore Bryce's geology and terrain. In winter, try a 1- to 2-mile, ranger-guided **snowshoe hike**—the park will provide the snowshoes. When the snow is deep enough, rangers also lead full-moon snowshoe hikes.

Lodging. Bryce Canyon Lodge (435/834-8700, www.brycecanyonforever.com; closed mid-Nov. to late Mar.), designed by Gilbert Stanley Underwood and opened in 1925, is the only lodging inside the park. It has more

than a hundred rooms and some stand-alone cabins, and it's the last remaining lodge designed for Utah's parks in the early 20th century.

Bryce has two campgrounds (reserve through Recreation.gov), both near the visitors center. **Sunset Campground** has 20 tent-only sites, and 80 RV and tent sites (no RV hookups). **North Campground** has 13 reservation RV-only sites and 86 RV and tent sites available first-come first-served (also no RV hookups); it also has more nearby amenities. Twelve **backcountry campsites** are along the Under-the-Rim and Riggs Spring Loop trails; permits are required and water is scarce, but the experience of camping among the hoodoos is unforgettable.

Plenty of motels are just outside the park, along UT 12 and UT 63, and some have heated outdoor pools in summer, like **Bryce Canyon Resort** (13500 E. UT 12, Bryce Canyon City, 435/834-5351, www.brycecanyonresort.com). The two nearest towns of any size, Escalante and Panguitch, offer a larger range of lodging (and dining) options. But if it's at all possible, book ahead and stay in the park—there's nothing quite like it.

1. View from Rainbow Point. **2.** Thor's Hammer. **3.** Bryce Canyon Amphitheater at sunrise.

Canyonlands National Park

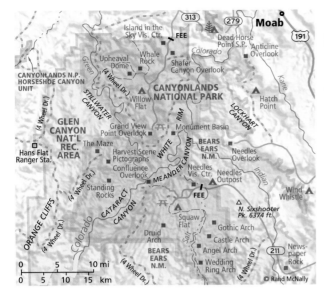

A ranger leads hikers to ancient rock art. Rafters scream excitedly on the mighty Colorado's rapids. A canoeist paddles the tranquil Green River. Whatever the adventure, Canyonlands will stay burned in your memory.

Of course, just soaking in the vistas from Grand View Point isn't a bad way to go about experiencing this park, either. Massive canyons stretch out before you, with giant spires of windswept rocks poking out from the enormous valley bowl. The overall silence and majesty draw you in to the magic of Canyonlands, deep in southeastern Utah.

The park spreads across four districts: the popular (and nearest to Moab) Island in the Sky District; the Needles District in the southeast; the Maze District in the park's almost inaccessible western section; and the two mighty rivers that flow through this beautiful area—the Green and the famous Colorado.

Park Basics

Established: September 12, 1964.
Area: 527 square miles; 337,598 acres.
Best For: Climbing, Geology, Hiking, Mountain Biking, Rafting.
Contact: 435/719-2313, www.nps.gov/cany.
Getting Oriented: Canyonlands is in eastern Utah. The nearest major airports are Utah's Salt Lake City International (247 miles northwest of the park's northern entrance) and Colorado's Denver International (386 miles east). **Island in the Sky Visitor Center** (Grand View Point Rd., 435/259-4712) is 21 miles southwest on UT 313 (aka Route 313) from its junction with US 191 (aka Route 191). In the southeast corner is **Needles Visitor Center** (435/259-

Canyonlands National Park, UT

4711) on UT 211 (aka Route 211); the remote Maze District has the **Hans Flat Ranger Station** (Recreation Rd. 777, 435/259-2652), which is 82 miles and over a 2-hour drive south from Green River and I-70.

Towns with a good variety of restaurants and lodgings include **Moab** (discovermoab.com), 32 miles northeast of Island in the Sky Visitor Center, and **Monticello** (www.monticelloutah.org), 48 miles southeast of the Needles Visitor Center. Keep your gas tank and water bottles filled when exploring this remote corner of Utah.

Park Highlights

Natural Attractions. If you're looking for one place to encapsulate all the wonders of Utah's five national parks, Canyonlands is that place. Arches? Check. Colorful rocks in bizarre shapes, including hoodoos, spires, pinnacles, and needles? Check. Amazing canyons? Check. River adventures? Check.

It's hard to pick one attraction, but if you've never seen a giant canyon in the West, its reddish-brown sandstone sides lit by the setting sun and carved by the twin forces of erosion and river water, the canyon views are essential experiences. Soak in the vistas of majestic **Monument Basin** from Grand Point View before exploring some of the park's smaller offerings, like the narrow, curvaceous slot canyon that is **Holeman Slot**; both are in the Island in the Sky District.

Trails, Drives & Viewpoints. Miles of hiking trails thread Canyonlands, many leading to canyon viewpoints. In Island in the Sky, take the easy loop hike to the elongated **Mesa Arch** (0.5 mile) and explore the awe-inspiring **White Rim Overlook** (an easy 1.8 miles). If you're in the Needles District, check out short, easy **Pothole Point Trail** (0.6 mile), which leads to seasonally filled slickrock potholes and a canyon view, or gear up for one of two stunning long hikes: the difficult 10-mile **Peekaboo Trail**, with some ladder climbing; or the moderate but long 11-mile **Chesler Park Trail**, a loop hike past some of the park's best geologic features.

Scenic paved roads in the Island in the Sky (34 miles round-trip) and the Needles (13 miles round-trip) districts have awesome overlooks. Canyonlands also has hundreds of miles of unpaved four-wheel-drive trails, many of which are ideal for mountain biking. Unpaved roads feature hairpin turns, cliff-edge views, rocky descents and ascents, and plenty of solitude. The signature unpaved drive, the 100-mile **White Rim Road** loop, can take many brave souls two (by 4WD) to four (by mountain bike) days to complete, camping along the way. Drivers need permits for 4WD roads, and bike rentals are available in Moab; try **Chile Pepper Bike Shop** (702 S. Main St., 435/259-4688, chilebikes.com).

Programs & Activities. Canyonlands has everything from **ranger-led hikes** to nighttime **stargazing programs** (indeed, it's been named an International Dark Sky Park). The strenuous **Horseshoe Canyon Guided Hike**, a 7-mile, 5-hour trip, takes you past prehistoric rock art.

Hiking, mountain biking, horseback riding, and rock climbing can be experienced across the park's districts, but some of the most distinctive experiences are on the Green and Colorado rivers. You can rent canoes or kayaks through **Tex's Riverways** (435/259-5101, www.texsriverways.com) or try a single-day or multi-day rafting adventure with **Tag-A-Long Expeditions** (435/259-8946, www.tagalong. com) through the exciting Class III–V Cataract Canyon on the Colorado.

Lodging. Canyonlands doesn't have any hotels, motels, inns, or cabins, but the town of Moab has all of these. The park has two small campgrounds: **Needles (Squaw Flat) Campground** (3.4 miles southwest of the Needles Visitor Center), with 27 sites—booked through Recreation.gov or as first-come, first-served, depending on the season—and **Island in the Sky (Willow Flat) Campground** (7.7 miles south of Island in the Sky Visitor Center), with 12 first-come, first-served sites.

In addition, Canyonlands allows backcountry camping; check with the park about locations and permits. Just outside the park, near the Needles Visitor Center, there's also the privately owned **Needles Outpost Campground** (www.needlesoutpost.com, 435/459-0777).

Enjoy a spa treatment at the upscale **Sorrel River Ranch** (HC 64, Mile 17, UT 128, 435/259-4642, www.sorrelriver.com), 20 miles outside of Moab, or relax at a bed-and-breakfast such as **Sunflower Hill** (147 N. 300 East St., Moab, 435/259-2974, www.sunflowerhill.com). If you're exploring the Needles District first, you might stay in Monticello; affordable motels include the **Inn at the Canyons** (533 N. Main St., 435/587-2458, www.monticellocanyonlandsinn.com). Families can opt for the houses and large cabins rented by **Canyonlands Lodging** (435/220-1050, www.canyonlandslodging.com).

1. Camping. **2.** Canyonlands landscape. **3.** Sunrise at Mesa Arch.

Capitol Reef National Park

UTAH

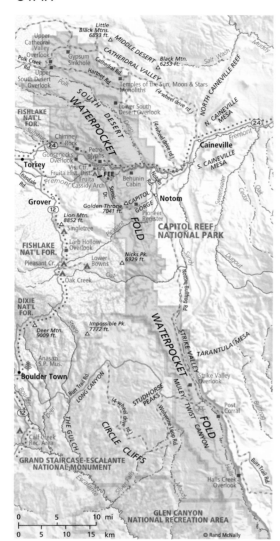

In the center of southern Utah lies the Waterpocket Fold, a 100-mile-long geologic masterpiece with colorfully striated layers of rock that look like brushstrokes from a master painter.

Our advice: Don't skip or just quickly pass through less-visited Capitol Reef when touring Utah's five national parks. This park's features are just as stunning as Bryce's hoodoos, Zion's cliffs, and the arches and canyons to the east. If you're heading east from Torrey on Route 24, chances are your first glimpse of the Waterpocket Fold's white-and-rust-layered sandstone cliffs, spires, canyons, and monoliths will make you toss out any plans for simply driving on to Moab.

Capitol Reef has petroglyphs dating back 1,000 years; a campground surrounded by orchards first planted by Mormon pioneers; a historic homestead, schoolhouse, and blacksmith's shop; nearly 200 miles of marked trails and backcountry routes for hiking, mountain biking, and horseback riding; and an utterly sublime night sky hours away from the nearest large city. This is Utah's hidden-in-plain-sight jewel of a national park.

Park Basics

Established: August 2, 1937 (national monument); December 18, 1971 (national park).
Area: 378 square miles; 241,904 acres.

Capitol Reef National Park, UT

Best For: Astronomy, Climbing, Geology, Hiking, Horseback Riding, Mountain Biking.
Contact: 435/425-3791; www.nps.gov/care.
Getting Oriented: Although Capitol Reef is Utah's most geographically "central" national park, it's one of the state's least visited because it's far from Zion and Bryce in southwest Utah and Arches and Canyonlands in the southeast. Salt Lake City International Airport is 227 miles north of the park entrance via I-15, US 50, and UT 24. UT 24, which bisects the park, makes

a 175-mile loop off I-70 between Green River and Aurora.

The main visitors center is off Route 24, 11 miles east of **Torrey** (www.torreyutah.gov), a small town that is the gateway to Capitol Reef and also makes a great base. The park itself is narrow and long, running north to south, and envelops the Waterpocket Fold. You'll find few paved roads, almost no water, and one developed campground.

Park Highlights

Natural Attractions. As with Arizona's Grand Canyon, a single geologic feature—here, the **Waterpocket Fold**—dominates Capitol Reef. The feature is a monocline, essentially a bend or wrinkle in rock strata that has, at some point, a steep dip in its formation. When you're driving east from Torrey on Route 24, this stunning sight more than lives up to its evocative name. Also visible are dome-like shapes of white sandstone that resemble a capitol building's dome and influenced the park's name.

Exploring the Waterpocket Fold is what you do in Capitol Reef—from narrow slot canyons and deep washes (usually dry riverbeds) to majestic panoramic viewpoints at the top. Many of the fold's walls have deep, circular, pockmarks—"waterpockets" formed by millions of years of erosion in the sedimentary rock—that look as if they were notched out with an extremely powerful shotgun. If you have extra time for exploring, the park's **Cathedral Valley** is a great natural counterpoint to the fold, featuring reddish-orange, freestanding sandstone monoliths of striking form.

Trails, Drives & Viewpoints. The park's only paved road, the 8-mile, aptly named **Scenic Drive**, follows Waterpocket Fold south from the visitors center to the beginning of a slot canyon at the **Capitol Gorge** parking lot. The fold's photo-friendly features—caves,

②

spires, bends, outcroppings—will be on your left the entire way.

Two unpaved roads (4WD vehicle recommended) reach the monoliths of **Cathedral Valley**, the park's remote northern section. A spectacular, mostly unpaved, 102-mile loop surrounding the park involves driving Route 12 south from Torrey through the Fishlake and Dixie national forests; turning east on the Burr Trail Road into the park, featuring the Burr Trail Switchbacks once in the fold; and heading north on the Notom-Bullfrog Road to Route 24.

Even a short hike on one of the park's 15 "day" trails, such as the easy 4.4-mile **Grand Wash Trail** and the moderate 3.4-mile **Cohab Canyon Trail**, can put you in a pocket of the fold with seemingly no one around for miles. The moderate 2.5-mile **Lower Cathedral Valley Overlooks Route**, in the Cathedral Valley section, offers views of the Temples of the Sun and Moon monoliths. In the southern part of the park, the strenuous **Upper Muley Twist Canyon Trail**—9 miles round-trip with a good 4WD vehicle taking you partway; otherwise, a 14.8-mile round-trip hike from the trail's start—will definitely help you get away from it all.

Programs & Activities. The daily **Geology Talk** at the visitors center is a half-hour introduction to what you can see in the fold and how it all came about. **Ranger-led hikes** over, around, and under the fold are fun

and informative, as are folksy **Porch Talks** on various topics.

Make time for programs about the area's petroglyphs and its Mormon settlers, such as the daily **Fremont Culture Talk** and the **Orchard Chat**. During the daily **Astronomy Talk**, you can view the sun through a solar telescope. Then, after dark, join the informal **star-gazing** activities at the Fruita Campground amphitheater; the night sky here is dazzling.

Lodging. The park's **Fruita Campground** (Recreation.gov) is just off Scenic Drive a mile east of the main visitors center. This beautiful spot sits within a small, green valley filled with fruit trees and surrounded by the rust-colored sandstone of the Waterpocket Fold. Fruita has 64 first-come, first-served RV/tent sites and 7 walk-in tent sites. Two additional campgrounds (11 primitive sites, in total) are in more remote areas.

Otherwise, delightfully green (more trees!) Torrey has a range of lodgings and restaurants on or near Route 24. One relatively high-end choice is the amenities-laden **Cougar Ridge Lodge** (580 E. Cougar Ridge Ln., 435/979-7824, cougarridgelodge.com). For a less expensive pick, try **Austin's Chuckwagon Motel** (12 W. Main St., 435/425-3335, www.austinschuckwagonmotel.com).

③

1. Strike Valley Overlook. **2.** Temple of the Moon monolith, Cathedral Valley section. **3.** Fremont Petroglyphs.

Carlsbad Caverns National Park

NEW MEXICO

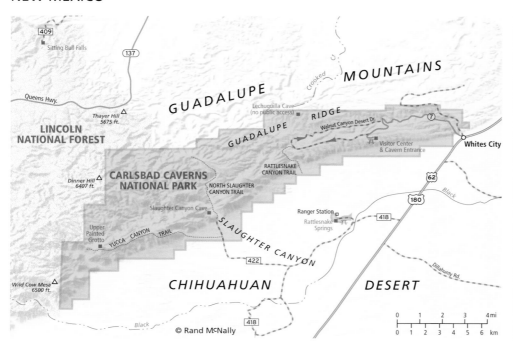

Deep underground in southeastern New Mexico, natural forces have shaped a brilliant labyrinth of caves, pools, stalagmites, and other formations that simply don't exist on the surface of the planet.

A journey into even one of the more than 119 caves collectively known as Carlsbad Caverns is unlike any you'll ever take above ground. The gaping entrance leads to a tunnel-like passage that winds down over 700 hundred feet into a vast cavern filled with every kind of curiously shaped

underground geologic formation. When you come up for air, don't leave the park: Thousands of resident bats and millions of stars are about to emerge into New Mexico's crystal-clear skies.

Photographers: Bring your tripods for those long exposures you'll want to shoot. Actually, bring everything you have. You might not like lugging equipment down to the caverns, and you'll like lugging it all back up even less, but photographing the dramatically lit formations here might be a once-in-a-lifetime opportunity.

Carlsbad Caverns National Park, NM

Park Basics

Established: October 5, 1923 (national monument); May 14, 1930 (national park).
Area: 73 square miles; 46,766 acres.
Best For: Astronomy; Geology; Hiking; Spelunking; Wildlife Watching (bats and more bats).
Contact: 575/785-2232; www.nps.gov/cave.
Getting Oriented: Carlsbad Caverns is tucked away in southeastern New Mexico, in the Guadalupe Mountain Range that straddles New Mexico and Texas. The nearest large airport is Albuquerque International Sunport, 304 miles northwest of the park using I-40, US 285, US 62/180, and NM 7.

The town of **Carlsbad** (www.carlsbadchamber. com) is 20 miles northeast of the park entrance on US 62/180, and 27 miles from the **Carlsbad Caverns National Park Visitor Center** on NM 7. There isn't much action on the park's surface during the day except for the gift shop, the visitors center,

and an amphitheater showing movies, but the underground magic of the caverns is a show-stopper. If you have time, also explore **Guadalupe Mountains National Park** (www.nps.gov/gumo) in West Texas, 37 miles southwest of the park via US 62/180.

Park Highlights

Natural Attractions. "Cave" and even "cavern" don't really convey the majesty of some of the spaces that you can walk through at Carlsbad Caverns, so let's go with "naturally formed underground cathedrals." UNESCO has declared these spectacular caves, created between 4 and 6 million years ago, a World Heritage Site.

There is no greater "cathedral" than the **Big Room**, an 8-acre underground expanse larger than a half-dozen football fields. The most exciting way to get here is on a 1.25-mile path leading down 750 feet from the **Natural Entrance**, though a wheelchair-accessible elevator is also an option. Once you're in the Big Room, speleothems, or cave formations, such as the **Rock of Ages** and the **Temple of the Sun** amaze you with their size and detail; many formations look as if a sculptor poured colored, quick-drying plastic resin into towering moulds.

After a full day at Carlsbad Caverns, you'll be talking like a spelunker, and you'll finally understand the difference between a stalagmite (a structure like an icicle rising up from the ground) and a stalactite (a structure hanging from the ceiling). You'll also know about formations such as soda straws, twig-like helictites, chandeliers, and totem poles. You'll learn that the caverns were formed by a process called speleogenesis, in which carbon dioxide–infused water produces carbonic acid that dissolves limestone's calcium carbonate, creating—essentially—space between rock.

Programs & Activities. The only thing better than taking the self-guided tour through Carlsbad Caverns is to take one with a park ranger: All guided tours require reservations (Recreation.gov) and have a fee. The 1.5-hour **Kings Palace Tour** and the 2-hour **Left-Hand Tunnel Tour** run daily most of the year and are utterly fascinating. The Left-Hand Tunnel tour has you wandering with candle-lit lanterns through delicate formations, and the rangers turn off all the lights briefly during the King's Palace Tour, plunging everyone into the complete darkness of the cave. Wear sturdy shoes and layered clothing (the caves are cool) for these excursions.

On longer tours, such as the **Hall of the White Giant Tour** and the **Spider Cave Tour**, the park provides helmets, pads, and gloves, as you'll be crawling your way in spots through this wondrous cave system. Several longer tours run only once a week, so book well in advance. If you have time between tours, take a short walk through the surrounding Chihuahuan Desert on one of the aboveground trails.

Stay in the park at dusk and later for two more shows. During the nightly (generally May–Oct.) **Bat Flight Program**, you can watch thousands of Brazilian free-tailed bats emerge at dusk from the caverns in search of food; an informal ranger talk afterward will answer all the questions you have. The night sky here, hundreds of miles from the nearest large city, is spectacular, and rangers run **Night Sky Programs** such as star parties and astronomy talks, as well as **Full Moon Walks**. After your evening program, head into Carlsbad for some Mexican food.

Lodging. There is no formal lodging inside the park except for **backcountry camping**, which requires a free permit from the visitors center. Campsites can be set up west of the Rattlesnake Canyon trailhead off the Walnut Canyon Desert Drive, and south of the Guadalupe Ridge Trail.

Whites City, just a mile east of the park, has only a few motels and an RV campground, so most people head to Carlsbad for a range of lodging options. The nine-room **Trinity Hotel** (201 S. Canal St., 575/234-9891, www.thetrinityhotel.com), in an 1890s bank building, makes a fun choice, as does the four-room **Fiddler's Inn Bed & Breakfast** (705 N. Canyon St., 575/725-8665, www.fiddlersinnbb.com). The Fiddler's Inn folks provide vouchers for you to start your day at **Blue House Bakery & Café** (609 N. Canyon St., 575/628-0555).

1. Visitors carry candle-lit lanterns on the Left-Hand Tunnel Tour. **2.** Bat Cave. **3.** Formations in the Big Room.

Channel Islands National Park

CALIFORNIA

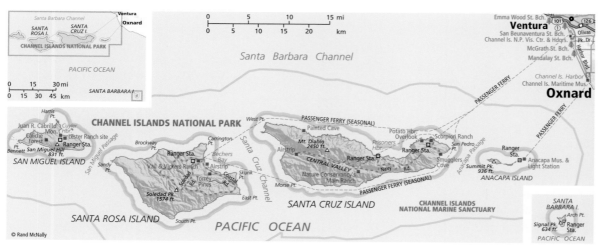

Only 75 miles west of downtown Los Angeles but worlds away, Channel Islands National Park includes five islands that are mostly devoid of modern development—and that's a beautiful thing.

Whereas California is known for its car culture, these islands are accessible exclusively by water or air. Just 12 miles from the coast, treeless Anacapa Island is an easy day trip. To its west, Santa Cruz Island—the largest of the park's five at 22 miles long—draws

kayakers to its natural harbors and sea caves. The Nature Conservancy owns the west side of Santa Cruz; only the eastern 25% is national parkland.

Santa Rosa Island, the park's second-largest, has a notable trail network and wildlife population. Windswept, wild San Miguel Island is the westernmost, about a four-hour boat trip from Ventura, on the mainland. To the south, tiny, less-visited Santa Barbara Island is a single square mile. Although it's closer to developed Santa Catalina Island (not in the

Channel Islands National Park, CA

park) than to the park's other islands, it's pier sustained severe damage in a 2016 storm and has been closed indefinitely (check ahead).

3

Park Basics

Established: April 26, 1938 (national monument); March 5, 1980 (national park).
Area: 390 square miles; 249,561 acres.
Best For: Bird-Watching (brown pelicans, cormorants, island scrub-jays, western gulls); Diving/Snorkeling; Kayaking; Hiking; Wildlife Watching (island foxes, sea lions, whales).
Contact: 805/658-5730, www.nps.gov/chis.
Getting Oriented: In Ventura, 65 miles north of Los Angeles via US 101, the **Robert J. Lagomarsino Visitor Center at Channel Islands National Park** (1901 Spinnaker Dr., 805/658-5730) is the park's headquarters and primary point of visitor contact. Ventura Harbor is the main embarkation port for island shuttles; boats also depart from Oxnard and Santa Barbara. The nearest major airport is Los Angeles International; John Wayne Airport–Orange County is 40 miles farther south. Shuttle vans between Ventura and either airport depart several times daily.

There are no shops or restaurants on the islands (bring your own provisions, including water), no public transportation, no bicycles allowed, no electricity for public use, and little (if any) cell service. Lodging and dining options abound in **Ventura** (visitventuraca.com), 15 miles northeast of Anacapa Island; **Oxnard** (visitoxnard.com), 12 miles east of Anacapa; and **Santa Barbara** (santabarbaraca.com), 25 miles north of Santa Cruz Island. Note that the Channel Islands also include three islands that are not part of the park—including well-developed Santa Catalina, which has amenities such as beach bars and marinas.

Park Highlights

Natural Attractions. Measuring about 80 miles long and 28 miles wide, the **Santa Barbara Channel** separates the park's four northernmost islands from the mainland. All of the islands feature rugged and wild coasts with tide pools and kelp forests. The highest peak, 2,450-foot **Mt. Diablo**, is on the west side of Santa Cruz on Nature Conservancy land. On the island's northwestern edge, **Painted Cave**, named for its colorful rocks, ranks among the world's largest (100 ft. wide) and deepest (more than 1,300 ft.) sea caves. Kayaking into the cave is popular, whether on your own or with an organized tour.

On remote San Miguel, a **caliche forest** consists of calcified remnants of long-gone trees, which remained after sandy earth eroded from their root systems. At **Point Bennett** on the island's far western tip, tens of thousands of seals and sea lions congregate during mating season. Visiting either location requires a ranger- or volunteer-led hike.

Nicknamed "North America's Galápagos," the islands are alive with **wildlife** found nowhere else, including the island scrub-jay and the diminutive island fox. These species evolved separately from their counterparts on the mainland. The boat trip out to the islands itself often provides spectacular sightings of marine mammals. In summer, the Santa Barbara Channel is a hot spot for migrating blue whales—the largest animals on the planet.

Trails & Viewpoints. On Anacapa, the 2-mile **Loop Trail** is an easy stroll with some great coastal views. Because of its size and accessibility, Santa Cruz offers several

moderately difficult day hikes, including the 1.2-mile (round trip) **Cavern Point Trail** (look for passing whales) and 4.6-mile (round trip) trek to magnificent **Potato Harbor Overlook**. On Santa Rosa, the strenuous hike along the **Lobo Canyon Trail** is about 9 miles round-trip.

Museums & Sites. The seafaring Chumash people inhabited these islands for thousands of years, as evidenced by artifacts found in numerous archaeological sites scattered around the area. On San Miguel, the **Cabrillo Monument** commemorates explorer Juan Rodríguez Cabrillo, the first European to "discover" California (1542); he was buried here the following year.

The **Anacapa Light Station and Museum** is at the foot of the lighthouse that has guided ships through the Santa Barbara Channel since 1932. On Santa Cruz and Santa Rosa, respectively, **Scorpion Ranch** and **Vail & Vickers Ranch** offer a look back at the cattle ranches that operated on the islands during the 19th and 20th centuries.

Programs & Activities. From Ventura and Oxnard harbors, **Island Packers Cruises** (805/642-1393, islandpackers.com) provides regularly scheduled boat service to the islands for day-trippers, campers, and whale-watchers. **Channel Islands Aviation** (805/987-1301, flycia.com) flies from Ventura's Camarillo Airport to Santa Rosa Island, a 25-minute flight, for day trips and overnight camping.

Truth Aquatics (805/962-1127, truthaquatics. net) runs dive trips from Santa Barbara Harbor. **Channel Islands/Santa Barbara Adventure Company** (805/884-9283, www. islandkayaking.com) in Santa Barbara offer guided sea kayaking trips and rentals, and so does **Island Packers**.

Lodging. Because the park has no lodgings except for tent campgrounds (reserve through Recreation.gov), Ventura makes a convenient base. Built in the Craftsman bungalow style in 1910, the **Wyndham Garden Ventura Pierpont Inn** (550 Sanjon Rd., 805/643-0245, www.pierpontinn.com) offers rooms, suites, and cottages—many with ocean views.

At Ventura Harbor, two reliable chain hotels are useful if you're catching an early morning boat: **Four Points by Sheraton Ventura Harbor Resort** (1050 Schooner Dr., 805/658-1212, www.fourpointsventuraharborresort. com) and **Holiday Inn Express & Suites Ventura Harbor** (1080 Navigator Dr., 805/856-9533, www.ihg.com).

1. Island fox. **2.** Sea cave kayak tour with Santa Barbara Adventure Company. **3.** Channel Islands National Park seascape.

Congaree National Park

SOUTH CAROLINA

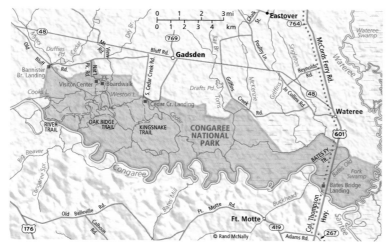

Congaree might not be the largest national park or the most visually dramatic, but it is one of the most essential—preserving 11,000 acres of old-growth bottomland hardwood forest, the Southeast's largest expanse.

Consider this: Prior to the late 1800s, from 35 to 50 *million* acres of floodplain forests covered wide areas from Florida to Texas and Maryland to Missouri. Some trees died naturally; some were used for building materials or fuel. But in many forests, trees were simply chopped down or went up in smoke as cities grew and highways emerged. In the 1960s, grassroots environmental groups got involved with Congaree. It would, however, take several decades to save a relatively modest slice of wilderness.

As a national park as well as a designated Wilderness Area, National Natural Landmark, International Biosphere Reserve, Ramsar Wetland, and Important Bird Area, Congaree does its job every day: reminding visitors that the natural world is worth saving.

Park Basics

Established: October 18, 1976 (national monument); November 10, 2003 (national park).
Area: 41 square miles; 26,276 acres.
Best For: Bird-Watching (orange-crowned warblers, pileated woodpeckers, wood thrushes, yellow-billed cuckoos); Canoeing; Forestry; Hiking; Kayaking.
Contact: 803/776-4396, www.nps.gov/cong.
Getting Oriented: Congaree is in central South Carolina, close to several major airports: Columbia Metropolitan, 25 miles northwest of the visitors center; Charleston International, 106 miles southeast; and, in North Carolina, Charlotte-Douglas International, 112 miles north. To get to the **Harry Hampton Visitor**

Congaree National Park, SC

Center (100 National Park Rd., Hopkins) from I-77, take SC Highway 48 East (aka Bluff Road) to Old Bluff Road and the park entrance.

The state capital, **Columbia** (www.experiencecolumbiasc.com), 20 miles northwest of the visitors center, has abundant restaurant and hotel choices. Towns with fewer options include **Eastover** (www.townofeastoversc.com), 13 miles northeast of the visitors center; Hopkins, 7 miles northwest; and **Santee** (santeetourism.com), 40 miles southeast.

Park Highlights

Natural Attractions. What draws people to Congaree is simple: nature. Even if you usually can't see the forest for the trees, dig a little deeper. At Congaree you are inside a marvel of biodiversity and natural engineering, surrounded by a spectacular world that sustains and recycles itself. It's a time machine that shows how the South once looked.

With the wilderness largely off limits to cars and motorized watercraft, Congaree is even more calming than most forests. It has one of the world's highest temperate deciduous forest canopies and North America's largest concentrations of **champion trees**—the largest known examples of a tree species within a geographic area. In Congaree, these are the cherrybark oak, sweetgum, American elm, swamp chestnut oak, common persimmon, and more than a dozen other towering giants.

Varied **wildlife** thrives in this old-growth forest: bobcats, deer, feral pigs, opossums, raccoons, coyotes, armadillos, turkeys, and more. In the waters of Congaree's creeks, wetlands, and oxbow lakes (created when a curve of a river becomes cut off from the main flow) are turtles, snakes, alligators, frogs, otters, and catfish. The Carolina Bird Club notes about 200 year-round and migrating species including the wild turkey, yellow-crowned night heron, barred owl, and rose-breasted grosbeak, as well as several species of warblers and woodpeckers.

Trails & Viewpoints. Congaree has no public roads. Between hiking and paddling, you can spend about half a day here, longer if you're ready to work your way into the backcountry. Pick up brochures in the visitors center that show 20 miles of hiking trails, including an easy tour through the wetlands via a 2.4-mile hike atop an **elevated boardwalk**. Maps mark trails leading to the oxbow lakes and old-growth trees most visitors see, but if you plan to delve deeper into the wilderness (more than half the park is a designated wilderness area), ask the rangers for a checklist of gear.

Canoeing or kayaking through a primeval old-growth forest on a 15-mile marked trail along **Cedar Creek** is an unforgettable experience as you paddle in the shade of some of the nation's tallest trees. One of the park's most popular trails for canoeists and kayakers is the 50-mile **Congaree River Blue Trail**, designated a National Recreation Trail by the U.S. Department of the Interior. Beginning in Columbia, it flows downriver and around the park's west perimeter. On the eastern side of the park, the **Wateree River Blue Trail** is another option. Note that Congaree has no concessionaires, so it's BYOC (Bring Your Own Canoe). Outfitters in Columbia such as **River Runner Outdoor Center** (905 Gervais St., 803/771-0353, shopriverrunner.com) can help you out with canoe and kayak rentals, and some companies also offer guided trips.

Museum. An orientation film at the **Harry Hampton Visitor Center** explains Congaree's story, and interpretive exhibits include artifacts and information on Native American history, forestry, logging, and the settlements that spelled opportunity for pioneers (and tragedy for the trees).

Programs & Activities. Bird-watching is popular: Even before Congaree became a national park, the National Audubon Society

designated it an Important Bird Area. Rangers and volunteers host **Nature Discovery Tours** to the park boardwalk and big trees each Saturday morning, and occasionally schedule guided canoe tours and evening programs celebrating owls (the **Owl Prowl**) and fireflies that, incredibly, synchronize their glow. Check ahead for details.

Lodging. Aside from tent camping at **Longleaf** and **Bluff** campgrounds (20 sites, booked through Recreation.gov), and primitive backcountry camping, the park has no lodging. Columbia, 20 minutes away, has chain hotels as well as a few bed-and-breakfasts. The 8-room **1425 Inn** (1425 Richland St., 803/252-7225, www.1425inn.com) downtown is within walking distance of the University of South Carolina, restaurants, museums, and nightlife. **The Chestnut Cottage Bed and Breakfast** (1718 Hampton St., 803/256-1718, www.chesnutcottage.com) has 5 rooms in a neighborhood of antebellum homes and mansions.

1. Hiking the elevated boardwalk through the park. **2.** Bald cypress trees. **3.** The 1425 Inn in Columbia. **4.** Entering the park. **5.** Barred owl.

Crater Lake National Park

OREGON

The impossibly blue surface of this wilderness-ringed lake is a vision from near and far. It was once the site of the long-gone volcanic Mt. Mazama in southern Oregon's Cascade Range.

Remote and legendary for its long winters, Crater Lake is the by-product of Mt. Mazama's eruption. The 12,000-foot peak collapsed and left behind a crater that filled with snowmelt. The park averages more than 44 feet of snow annually, so the lake has a good supply. And the water has little sediment, algae, or pollution. This purity is behind the lake's striking hue: A critical mass of pure water absorbs every color of light except for blue.

North America's deepest lake bottoms out at a remarkable 1,943 feet. In geologic terms, though, it's notably young—about 7,700 years old—and it takes up only 10% of the park. Soaring peaks, old-growth forests, and an abundance of wilderness surround it. See the lake, of course, but take time to experience the entire park.

Park Basics

Established: May 22, 1902.
Area: 286 square miles; 183,224 acres.
Best For: Boating (guided tours only), Cross-Country Skiing, Geology, Hiking, Snowshoeing.
Contact: 541/594-3000, www.nps.gov/crla.
Getting Oriented: Crater Lake is in

Crater Lake National Park, OR

southwestern Oregon; the nearest major airports are Portland International, 280 miles northwest of the North Entrance, and California's Sacramento International, 343 miles south of the Annie Springs (aka West) Entrance. The primary routes into the park are OR Highways 62 and 138; from I-5, these roads access the western and northern entrances, respectively.

The **Steel Visitor Center** is just south of the lake, off OR Highway 62; **Rim Visitor Center**, open seasonally, is in Rim Village. The towns of **Klamath Falls** (discoverklamath.com), 60 miles south of the park, and **Medford** (www.travelmedford.org), 60 miles southwest, have accommodations; **Prospect**, 21 miles southwest, is closer but has fewer choices.

Park Highlights

Natural Attractions. Due to its color, depth, and geologic history, **Crater Lake** is one of the true wonders of the West. It's about 5 miles across and almost 2,000 feet deep. Near Crater Lake's western shore, **Wizard Island** is the lake's largest island, and it, too, was the result of a volcanic eruption. It features its own crater at the summit. A second, much smaller island, **Phantom Ship**, is on the south side of the lake; its resemblance to a ghostly frigate, especially in fog, earned the island its name.

Layers of hot ash and pumice deposited north of the volcano created the barren landscape of the **Pumice Desert**, along the North Entrance Road. A by-product of the big eruption and thousands of years of erosion, the **Pinnacles**, southeast of the lake, are pillars of hardened ash that you can access by a short hike on one of the park's few bicycle-friendly trails. The park is also home to old-growth forest and numerous mountains including **Mt. Scott**, **Garfield Peak**, and **Union Peak**.

Trails, Drives & Viewpoints. An easy, 0.4-mile loop through a forest, **Castle Crest Wildflower Garden Trail** passes a meadow that's lush with colorful blooms well into the summer. **Mt. Scott Trail**, a difficult, 5-mile round-trip, climbs to the highest point in the park, the 8,929-foot summit. Still, the park's best hike might just be the trek to the **Wizard Island Summit**, a moderate trail that's just under a mile round-trip. Because it's accessible only by boat tour, this hike requires an entire day. It also involves hiking the difficult 1.1-mile **Cleetwood Cove Trail** between the boat dock and the parking lot.

Scenic, paved **East Rim Drive** and **West Rim Drive** circumnavigate the lake in 33 miles, and offer several excellent viewpoints, including **Watchman Overlook** and **Cloudcap Overlook**. Allow 2 to 3 hours for the drive and note that the roads close seasonally due to snow. The 115-foot **Vidae Falls**, south of the lake, is the park's only waterfall visible from the roadside.

Museums & Sites. Open year-round on the lake's south side, **Rim Village** merits a stop for a look at **Crater Lake Lodge**. Built in the park's early years, it's still the hub of visitor services. The **Sinnott Memorial Observation Station and Museum** behind the Rim Visitor Center offers superb views of Crater Lake as well as exhibits about the park's geology.

Programs & Activities. Rangers on **boat cruises** (www.craterlakelodges.com) provide narration about the lake's natural and cultural history. Some cruises stop to allow passengers to explore Wizard Island. Getting to the boat dock involves a difficult hike down a steep trail more than a mile long and then hiking out after the tour. Reservations are recommended; there's a fee for all cruises.

The park's program highlights include **ranger talks** covering the park's geology and ecology, **guided hikes**, and **campfire programs** in summer and snowshoe tours in winter. **Crater Lake Trolley** (541/882-1896, craterlaketrolley. net) offers 2-hour bus tours around the lake.

Lodging. Crater Lake is remote, but nearby Prospect and the Diamond Lake area have lodging and camping options, and there are two accommodations and camping within park boundaries. In Rim Village on the park's south side, stately **Crater Lake Lodge** (888/774-2728, www.craterlakelodges.com) is often sold out years in advance for its short summer season. Dating from 1915, it's one of the classic park lodges.

In Mazama Village, 5 miles south of the lake, the **Cabins at Mazama Village** (888/774-2728, www.craterlakelodges.com) offer spartan rooms near a restaurant. Just west of the park, **Union Creek Resort** (56484 Hwy. 62, Prospect, 866/560-3565, www.unioncreekoregon.com) offers rustic log cabins and rooms at a 1922 lodge in the Rogue River National Forest.

The park has two developed campgrounds, one in **Mazama Village** with 214 sites for tents and RVs (888/774-2728, www.craterlakelodges.com); and the first-come, first-served **Lost Creek Campground** with 16 sites for tents only, about 3 miles southeast of the lake just off the road to the Pinnacles.

1. Backcountry skiing. **2.** Vidae Falls. **3.** Crater Lake and Wizard Island.

Cuyahoga Valley National Park

OHIO

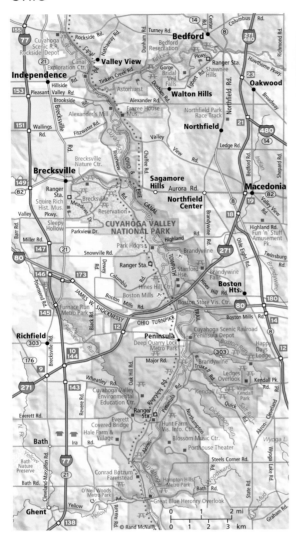

There's a distinctly Midwestern feel to northeastern Ohio's Cuyahoga Valley National Park. It might be spring's wildflowers; summer's cyclists; autumn's colorful foliage; or winter's picture-perfect snowy landscape, dotted with cross-country skiers.

At this four-season park, it is all of the above, along with the land the park preserves. Ohio's only national park frames one of the state's most picturesque regions. Its rivers, lakes, caves, cliffs, waterfalls, farmland, and forests capture the essence of the Buckeye State's natural beauty.

The area has come a long way. After industries filled the Cuyahoga River with enough chemical waste that it ignited in a well-publicized 1969 blaze (it actually caught fire more than once), the movement to save the land gained urgency. Thanks to the efforts of citizens and state and federal officials, in 1974 Gerald Ford signed a bill creating the Cuyahoga Valley National Recreation Area. Since then, new generations have recognized the importance of protecting Ohio's distinctive landscape, which makes Cuyahoga Valley National Park one of the state's most increasingly valuable assets.

Park Basics

Established: December 27, 1974 (national recreational area); October 11, 2000 (national park).
Area: 51 square miles; 32,571 acres.
Best For: Bird-Watching (bald eagles, blue

Cuyahoga Valley National Park, OH

herons, peregrine falcons, ruby-throated hummingbirds); Cycling; Cross-Country Skiing; Hiking.
Contact: 330/657-2752, www.nps.gov/cuva.
Getting Oriented: Cuyahoga Valley is sandwiched between Cleveland and Akron in northeastern Ohio, convenient to Cleveland Hopkins International Airport (25 miles northwest of the visitors center) and Akron Fulton International (22 miles south). Multiple interstates and the Ohio Turnpike (toll

road) pass near and even through the park, providing easy access.

The park's **Boston Store Visitor Center** (1550 Boston Mills Rd., Peninsula) makes a useful starting point for exploring. Besides **Cleveland** (thisiscleveland.com) and **Akron** (visitakron-summit.org), nearby towns include **Macedonia**, 5 miles east. The park surrounds **Peninsula**, which is 2 miles south of the visitors center.

Park Highlights

River & Canal. Although the **Cuyahoga River** is a natural centerpiece, the park's main attraction comes courtesy of a manmade marvel of engineering. Prior to the 1830s, Ohio was still a distant western frontier to most Americans. What began changing things was the creation of the Ohio & Erie Canal, opening a gateway from Lake Erie through Ohio and into the eastern United States. Running roughly parallel to the Cuyahoga River, the canal was essential to the creation of the **Ohio & Erie Canal Towpath Trail**.

Where barge-towing mules once trod a towpath, the park service established a recreational trail that follows the canal for about 85 of its once-active 308 miles. Open 24 hours a day, the largely ADA-accessible, multipurpose trail provides an easy route for cycling, hiking, cross-country skiing, or casual strolling through the Cuyahoga River Valley's diverse landscape of forests, fields, wetlands, historic sites, and former canal locks.

Trails, Drives & Viewpoints. Cuyahoga Valley's 125 miles of trails include segments added from municipal park trails and the statewide **Buckeye Trail** that passes through the park; other trails head out of the park toward Cleveland or Akron and to neighboring communities. Don't miss a walk on the boardwalk and steps by one of the park's most picturesque sights, 65-foot **Brandywine Falls**. Trail maps and rangers at the visitors center can direct you to wooded trails, old carriage trails, and paths leading to covered bridges, boardwalks, and historical structures.

Riverview Road, running north to south through the heart of the park, is perfect for a scenic drive. In season and for holidays, the privately operated **Cuyahoga Valley Scenic Railroad** (330/439-5708, www.cvsr.com) whistles its way up and down the valley on a three-hour round-trip excursion. "Hike Aboard" and "Bike Aboard" options are convenient for anyone who prefers a lift back after pedaling or hiking in the park. The nine stops include the main depots at Rockside Station and Peninsula Station.

Museums & Sites. Protecting the area's natural and cultural heritage includes the preservation of original and restored rural buildings, such as general stores and warehouses like the circa-1836 **Boston Store** (now the main visitors center in Peninsula) along the towpath. Exhibits in the visitors center explore boat building and life in a canal town, and the **Canal Exploration Center** (7104 Canal Rd., Valley View) at the park's north end offers additional historical exhibits about daily life along the river and canal.

Programs & Activities. Throughout the year, the park hosts **special events** including art exhibits, lectures, tastings, classes, and outdoor concerts. Given the diversity of the terrain, **hiking** is popular, and along the way you can sometimes spy wildlife such as raccoons, beavers, river otters, muskrats, coyotes, foxes, and deer. **Bird-watching** is also popular here. Given the park's more than 200 species, the National Audubon Society has designated Cuyahoga an Important Bird Area.

Fishing in the Cuyahoga has regained its popularity. A fishing license is obtainable at drugstores and sporting goods stores, and is required when angling in the river or at Kendall Lake, home to largemouth bass, crappie, and bluegill. You can even try ice fishing in Kendall Lake in winter. From early December through late February, rangers rent snowshoes and cross-country skis for **winter exploring**, and concessionaires provide gear for sledding and snow tubing.

Lodging. Cleveland and Akron have abundant options, like the 189-room **Drury Plaza Hotel Cleveland Downtown** (1380 E. 6th St., 216/357-3100, www.druryhotels.

³

com), occupying the restored 1931 former Department of Education building downtown.

It's relaxing to stay inside the park, though choices are limited. The nine-bedroom **Stanford House** (6093 Stanford Rd., Peninsula, 330/657-2909) has shared baths in all but one guestroom and offers a full kitchen (bring your own groceries) plus prime trail access. Built in 1848, the six-room, landmarked **Inn at Brandywine Falls** (8230 Brandywine Rd., Sagamore Hills, 330/467-1812, www.innatbrandywinefalls.com) overlooks the cascade. Towpath-trail and backcountry-trail users can reserve five primitive **campsites** (330/657-2909 ext. 130) from late May through late October.

1. Brandywine Falls. **2.** Canal Exploration Center. **3.** Biking through the park. **4.** Cuyahoga Valley Scenic Railroad.

⁴

Death Valley National Park

CALIFORNIA/NEVADA

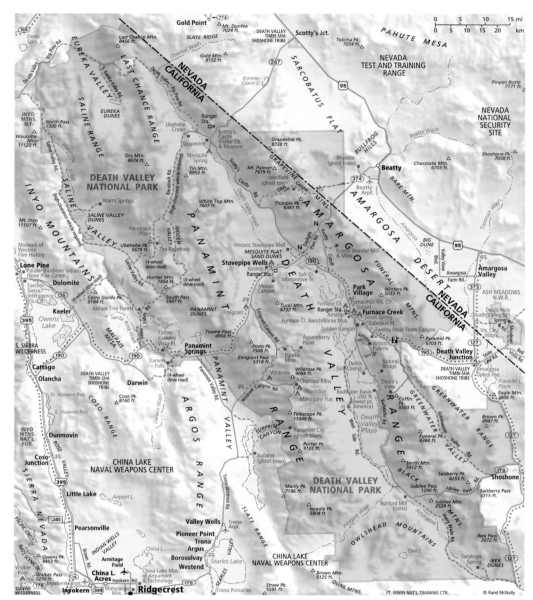

If you've ever marveled at the desolate landscapes in some *Star Wars* movies, you've already experienced Death Valley. To George Lucas, its otherworldly terrain was the perfect stand-in for galaxies far, far away.

But Death Valley is very real. In a way, it's surreal. It has the nation's lowest point (282 feet below sea level), its highest temperatures (a record 134 degrees F in July 1913), and it gets only 2 inches of rain a year.

There's still plenty to see, though. The park has many geological curiosities, and, en route from low desert to canyons and mountains, the climate and vegetation change, providing surprisingly diverse habitats. Still, Death Valley has a hauntingly desolate beauty that must be seen to be believed. Even then, you might not believe it.

Park Basics

Established: February 11, 1933 (national monument); October 31, 1994 (national park).
Area: 5,270 square miles; 3,373,063 acres.
Best For: Astronomy, Geology, Hiking.
Contact: 760/786-3221, www.nps.gov/deva.

Death Valley National Park, CA/NV

1. Coyote. **2.** Mosaic Canyon. **Opposite Page:** Zabriskie Point.

SAFETY IN DEATH VALLEY

Staying safe in the desert environment of America's fifth-largest national park (it's larger than the state of Connecticut), requires planning—whether you're hiking, biking, or just driving through. First and foremost is timing your trip. October through April see more ranger-led programs, but, for outdoor activities, visit November through March, when temperatures are (relatively speaking) coolest. Here are a few more desert safety tips:

- **Don't rely solely on GPS devices and smartphones.** They might not work in remote areas; pack your atlas and road/trail maps for backup.
- **Check on roads and trails at visitors centers.** Conditions and accessibility are subject to change, and this might not be reflected on maps.
- **Check the weather.** If a rain storm's on the way, flash floods could follow.
- **Make sure your vehicle is in good condition** (oil, lights, wipers, tires— including the spare—etc.). Fill the tank at the start of your trip; top it off whenever you see a gas station (it might be the last one for miles).
- **Bring plenty of water:** at least 2 quarts (roughly 68 ounces) for short winter hikes, a gallon or more for longer warm-season hikes. Dehydration is also an issue at higher elevations, so drink plenty of water on mountain outings, too, even if it's cooler.
- **Stay energized:** pack apples and energy bars or other high-protein snacks.
- **Be mindful of sun and heat stroke.** If you get a headache or feel dizzy or nauseous, find shade, and rehydrate with water or energy drinks. If symptoms continue or worsen, seek medical help.

Getting Oriented: Highway 190 (aka CA 190), the main paved route through the park, connects two of its key resort areas. On the western side is **Panamint Springs**, about 240 miles northeast of Los Angeles International Airport and 50 miles southeast of the community of **Lone Pine** (www. lonepinechamber.org). To the east and 55 miles from Panamint Springs is **Furnace Creek**, roughly 117 miles northwest of Las Vegas's McCarren International Airport and home to the park's main **Furnace Creek Visitor Center & Museum**, which is close to many highlights.

Aside from hair-raising drops and switchbacks in the eastern Amargosa and western Panamint ranges, the park's roads are generally flat. It has nearly 800 miles of paved routes, many drawing cyclists. Its hundreds of miles of rougher roads—some of them hard-packed and accessible even without 4WD—primarily draw mountain bikers and off-roaders.

Park Highlights

Drives, Viewpoints & Trails. Must-see sights are in every direction. Using Furnace Creek, site of the main visitors center, as a starting point, travel about 5 miles southeast on Highway 190 to **Zabriskie Point**, where it looks as if the desert has been encased in concrete and painted white, beige, ochre, and gold. This overlook is a popular place to watch both sunrises and sunsets.

In the late 1800s, **20 Mule Team Canyon**, just a half-mile southeast of Zabriskie Point, made history when miners arrived to extract the sodium salt and borax left behind when the waters above it evaporated. You can drive (smaller vehicles only), walk, or bike the unpaved 2.7-mile loop road here.

A drive roughly 25 miles southeast of Furnace Creek along both Highway 190 and the Furnace Creek Wash Road takes you to the turn-off for **Dante's View** (5,475 feet), which offers a commanding look west across the valley to the far distant Panamint Range. It's a great place to watch the sunset.

Plan to spend a day exploring sites along **Badwater Road**, an unpaved, hard-packed route (cars, vans, and small RVs only) that travels south from Furnace Creek. Some 9.5 miles along is **Artists Drive**, a one-way, 9-mile loop road (small vehicles only) lined with multihued volcanic and sedimentary hills, with spectacular views at **Artists Palette**. South another 3.5 miles down Badwater Road is the **Devil's Golf Course**, an expanse of rock salt eroded by wind and rain into jagged formations so treacherous that "only the devil could tee off on this terrain."

About 5 miles farther south is **Badwater Basin**, a 200-square-mile salt flat that reveals how low you can go: 282 feet below sea level. It's an easy 1-mile hike out and back to the edge of the flats. If you're more intrepid, you

can cross (5 miles) to the other side of the flats and back. Just don't undertake either hike when it's hot.

When you feel like heading west, follow Highway 190 for 19 miles from Furnace Creek to the **Mesquite Flat Sand Dunes**, the park's largest dunefield—a vast, empty place that looks like the end of the Earth. If it's not too hot, hike to the top of the highest dune; although the 2-mile round-trip route is considered easy-to-moderate, remember that you're walking in sand and 1 mile of it is uphill.

Continue west past the dunes, and, as you begin the long, slow climb out of the valley, you'll find plenty of scenery at every cliff and turn. Near the park's western border and just past Panamint Springs, the **Father Crowley Vista Point** offers a pullout with a majestic view from 4,000 feet.

Still More Trails. Including those at Badwater Salt Flats, Mesquite Flat Sand Dunes, and 20 Mule Canyon, the park has 21 cross-country, canyon, and ridge routes. They range in difficulty from the easy 1-mile outing to **Natural Bridge** to the moderate 3-mile hike

NOW YOU SEA IT, NOW YOU DON'T

If you've ever seen a lake where the water levels had dropped, then you've probably noticed that the exposed ground looks strangely different than what you expected. That's how it is in Death Valley.

Essentially, during the Pleistocene era (think roughly 170,000 years ago), salty, inland lakes known collectively as Lake Manly, formed in the center of Death Valley, covering about 1,600 square miles at an average depth of 1,000 feet. Over the eons, evaporation reduced the lake to roughly one-third of its size, leaving behind what you see today: unusual geological formations; salt flats and borax deposits; and the fossils of plants, mollusks, reptiles, and fish.

to **Golden Canyon** to the difficult 14-mile **Telescope Peak** trek.

Cyclists can ride on any park route that's open to public traffic, and more miles of roads are just right for mountain biking. One of the easiest routes is the 1-mile path from the visitors center to the Harmony **Borax Works**. There's also the moderately tough **Hole-in-the-Wall Road** (4 to 7 miles on loose gravel) and the rocky 10-mile **Trail Canyon Road**.

Museums & Sites. At the **Furnace Creek Visitor Center**, a small but impressive museum has a 20-minute orientation film and in-depth displays on geology, botany, hydrology, and wildlife. You'll also learn about the Timbisha Shoshone, who are thought to have been here for at least a millennium (some tribal members still live in the area); about how the "Black Forty-Niners" accompanied a party of Death Valley travelers in the 1800s; and about the 65 Japanese American internees who, during WW II, were temporarily relocated to a CCC barracks here after a riot in a California internment camp.

There's also information on the Chinese laborers who built Panamint City, constructed a 160-mile-long road through the salt pinnacles, and toiled at the borax works. To learn still more about the area's mining operations, visit the remnants of the **Harmony Borax Works**, just north of the Furnace Creek Visitor Center, and the privately owned **Borax Museum** (760/786-2345) at the Oasis at Death Valley resort.

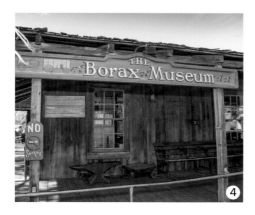

Programs & Activities. Numerous ranger-led guided walks, lectures, backcountry hikes, and other programs are only offered between October and April since temperatures between May and September are just too high.

The **Paleontology Tours** are among the park's most popular offerings—so popular that they fill up quickly via a lottery. What's more, for preservation's sake, *very* few of these tours are offered, and the number of people on each is capped at 15. Check the

3

park website for details; registration periods are finite, so sign up for the lottery as soon as you see announcements. The tour involves a moderately strenuous, 7-mile, day-long hike leading to a dramatic scene: a deep canyon with high cliff walls where you'll see well-preserved fossilized evidence of birds, horses, camels, and mastodon-like creatures.

Death Valley was registered as an International Dark Sky Park in 2013, and viewing the stars here is an awe-inspiring event. Be sure to look into the ranger-hosted **astronomy evenings** to experience the wonder of the Milky Way.

Lodging. The park has nine seasonal **campgrounds** (Recreation.gov) and numerous primitive sites. Privately owned campgrounds in the area include some with full RV hookups.

One of life's mysteries is why there's a four-star resort in the middle of Death Valley. Don't question it—just be glad it's here. In addition to a name change in 2017, the famous Furnace Creek Resort underwent a multimillion dollar refresh and renovation to create the environmentally sensitive, water-neutral **Oasis at Death Valley** (760/786-2345, www.oasisatdeathvalley.com). Here, you'll find historic luxury in the **Inn at Death Valley's** 66 rooms and 11 casitas and a family-oriented vibe at the 224-room **Ranch at Death Valley**. There's also a variety of restaurants and bars (including one that's poolside), a town square with a general store and a saloon, and activities such as golf—on the world's lowest course (at 214 feet below sea level)—and horseback riding.

On Highway 190 in the park, **Stovepipe Wells** (760/786-2387, deathvalleyhotels.com)

has a general store, 83 motel rooms, a restaurant, an RV park, camping, gas, a pool, and a saloon. On the park's western edge along Highway 190, a few miles from the base of the Inyo Mountains, the **Panamint Springs Resort** (775/482-7680, www.panamintsprings.com) is a family-owned motel with RV sites, a restaurant, and bar.

1. Hiking in Cottonwood Canyon. **2.** Badwater Salt Flats. **3.** Entrance to the park. **4.** The Borax Museum.

Denali National Park & Preserve

ALASKA

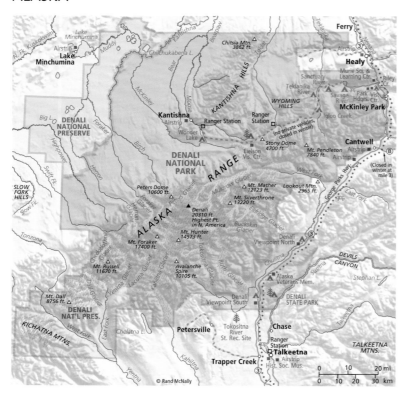

A vast tract of outback in the center of Alaska, Denali National Park surrounds North America's highest point: the summit of the park's namesake mountain, 20,310 feet above sea level.

The minds behind Denali National Park made a bold decision when they chose to ban passenger cars from entry, and it has paid off in an authentic wilderness with an intact ecosystem. No parks in the lower 48 are as untouched by human beings. Although you have to ride a shuttle

bus on the only park road, this lets you truly focus on the passing scenery; also, the bus will stop whenever and wherever you like so you can hike across the tundra.

Sweeping views abound, but it's often easier to see Denali—which translates to "the tall one" and "mountain-big" in Native Alaskan languages—from afar rather than from inside the park. In summer, you're more likely to glimpse a grizzly than the cloud-shrouded summit more than 3 miles above.

Park Basics

Established: February 26, 1917 (as Mt. McKinley National Park); December 2, 1980 (incorporated Denali National Monument and renamed Denali National Park & Preserve).
Area: 9,492 square miles; 6,075,030 acres.
Best For: Climbing; Hiking; Wildlife Watching (caribou, Dall sheep, grizzly bears, moose).
Contact: 907/683-9532, www.nps.gov/dena.
Getting Oriented: Denali is in central Alaska, west of AK 3 (aka George Parks Highway); the prime visiting season runs from early June to mid-September. Major airports near the park are Ted Stevens Anchorage International

Denali National Park & Preserve, AK

(243 miles south of the park entrance) and Fairbanks International (120 miles north).

Denali Visitor Center is just inside the park's one entrance, on the east side of Denali. A model of eco-friendly design, **Eielson Visitor Center** is at Mile 66 on Park Road (66 miles west of the entrance). **Walter Harper Talkeetna Ranger Station** (B St., Talkeetna, 907/733-2231), 152 miles south of the park, is home base for Denali's mountaineering rangers and the check-in point for summit expeditions. Nearby towns with lodging, dining, and other services include **Healy** (www.denalichamber.com), 11 miles north of the park entrance, and **Talkeetna** (www.talkeetnachamber.org), 152 miles south.

Park Highlights

Natural Attractions. It's hard to ignore **Denali** (formerly known as Mt. McKinley), the park's massive centerpiece. While other peaks are higher, the more than 18,000-foot ascent from Denali's surrounding lowlands is greater than Mt. Everest's rise above the Tibetan Plateau. Don't fixate only on the big mountain, though. The park's boundaries encompass numerous other peaks of the Alaska Range, including 17,400-foot **Mt. Foraker,** the sixth-highest peak in North America, and the glaciated, 13,220-foot **Mt. Silverthrone** on the park's east side.

Treeless **tundra** atop perpetually frozen permafrost dominates the park. In areas below 3,000 feet in elevation, a 6-foot thicket of dense brush can cover the tundra; above 3,000 feet, alpine tundra has less vegetation and is easier to traverse on foot. Fed by glaciers and mountain snow, numerous **braided rivers**— including the Toklat, Savage, and Teklanika— are so named for their multiple, ever-changing channels in wide gravel floodplains that crisscross the tundra.

Denali is also a prime **wildlife habitat**. You may see grizzly bears and many hoofed mammals—such as moose, Dall sheep, and caribou—roaming the tundra.

Trails, Drives & Viewpoints. Denali is a
hiker's paradise but has few developed trails; many routes follow the braided rivers. **Stony Creek** (Mile 60, Park Rd.) makes a great access point for exploring the tundra or mountains; the first 3 miles are relatively flat. Near the park entrance, the difficult 5-mile round trip

to the **Mt. Healy Overlook** culminates in sweeping views of the Alaska Range.

While Park Road is closed to private vehicles, the two-lane **Denali Highway** (aka AK 8) runs parallel to the Alaska Range for 135 miles from Paxson to Cantwell, 27 miles south of the park entrance. Only 22 miles of the highway are paved; the rest is gravel. The entire highway, however, stretches along jaw-dropping scenery and offers countless opportunities for wildlife watching, hiking, and boating. The main route to the park from either Anchorage or Fairbanks, the **George Parks Highway** also has plenty of spellbinding views.

Programs & Activities. The park concessionaire operates **shuttle buses** (800/622-7275, www.reservedenali.com) that go as far as Kantishna (92 miles one-way, 13 hours round-trip) and offers some bus tours. You should reserve shuttles and tours; two-thirds of the seats are sold in advance. Ranger-led **Discovery Hikes**, available daily in summer, are for experienced hikers only; sign up in person at the Denali Visitor Center.

Offering a different perspective, the **Alaska Railroad** (800/544-0552, www.alaskarailroad. com) runs between Anchorage and Fairbanks, stopping near the park entrance daily in summer. You can see Denali from above on a "flightseeing" trip with **Denali Air** (907/683-2261, denaliair.com) that departs from a private airstrip near the park entrance. **Denali**

Outdoor Center (907/683-1925, www. denalioutdoorcenter.com) guides rafting trips on the Nenana River, just east of the park.

Lodging. The park has six campgrounds. Tents and RVs are allowed at the 147-site **Riley Creek Campground**, just inside the park entrance and open year-round. **Wonder Lake Campground** (Mile 85, Park Rd.), open only in summer, has 28 tent-only sites. Reservations (800/622-7275, www.reservedenali.com) are highly recommended at all park campgrounds.

A few wilderness lodges operate on privately owned land (inholdings) within the park. At the foot of Denali in the Kantishna Mining District, for instance, **Camp Denali** (Mile 92, Park Rd., 907/683-2290, campdenali.com) is on an inholding. Take your pick of its rustic cabins, or try the cozy rooms in nearby sister property, **North Face Lodge**. Both are accessible only via the park's shuttle bus.

Outside the park, Healy and Talkeetna have a smattering of motels, cabin complexes, and lodges. **EarthSong Lodge** (Mile 4, Stampede Rd., Healy, 907/683-2863, www. earthsonglodge.com), north of the park entrance, offers comfortable log cabins, as well as an on-site coffeehouse and seasonal dogsledding tours.

1. Dall sheep. **2.** Rafting trip on the Nenana River with the Denali Outdoor Center. **3.** Fall color of Denali and Wonder Lake.

Dry Tortugas National Park

FLORIDA

Despite its name, Dry Tortugas National Park is anything but dry. With just a few scattered islands, most of the park lies in the watery Gulf of Mexico.

Less than 1% of the park is above ground, and this quirk of geography makes it a magnet for those who relish the challenge of reaching a park so remote that it lacks water and food service. From Key West in south Florida, Dry Tortugas is a 2.5-hour boat ride or speedier half-hour flight. With 100 square miles of tropical waters, it draws divers and snorkelers, paddlers, anglers, and nature lovers to its coral reefs and bird life.

The park also lures historians because Ft. Jefferson on Garden Key doubled as a federal prison: The infamous

Dr. Samuel Mudd served time here after setting the broken leg of a fleeing John Wilkes Booth. Dry Tortugas takes an extra special effort to visit, but that might make your trip extra special as well.

Park Basics

Established: January 4, 1935 (national monument); October 26, 1992 (national park).
Area: 101 square miles; 64,701 acres.
Best For: Bird-Watching (egrets, terns, warblers); Boating; Diving/Snorkeling; Fishing; Wildlife Watching (crocodiles, sea turtles).
Contact: 305/242-7700, www.nps.gov/drto.
Getting Oriented: Dry Tortugas is pretty much in the middle of nowhere, with no trails, roads, or restaurants. The closest major airport is Miami International, 160 miles northeast of Key West. The park's Garden Key

Dry Tortugas National Park, FL

is 70 miles west of Key West, and reaching Dry Tortugas from Key West requires taking a private boat, boarding the *Yankee Freedom* **ferry** (100 Grinnell St., 305/294-7009, www. drytortugas.com), or flying in with **Key West Seaplane Adventures** (305/293-9300, keywestseaplanecharters.com) based at Key West International Airport.

Make all transportation reservations well in advance. If you want to visit any area of the

44

park other than Garden Key, it's BYOB (Bring Your Own Boat) or arrange a diving excursion.

The **visitors center** at Ft. Jefferson on Garden Key is the park's only development. For overnight stays, consider **Key West**, **Marathon** (50 miles east of Key West), and **Key Largo** (110 miles northeast of Key West), www.fla-keys.com for information; or **Miami** (www.miamiandthebeaches.com).

Park Highlights

Natural Attractions. A few clues reveal you're getting close to Dry Tortugas: a fleet of pleasure boats, a sprinkling of islands, and a massive 19th-century fortress on Garden Key. That's Ft. Jefferson, where you'll begin exploring the beautiful natural world around you. A strong Gulf of Mexico current south of Dry Tortugas brings with it **marine life** that is often much larger than what is found in other regions of the Florida Keys: grouper, tarpon, barracudas, nurse sharks, and brightly hued reef fish. These same waters nourish colorful **coral reefs** that lure divers from around the world. About 30 species of rock-hard, razor-sharp coral live just beneath the surface, including elkhorn and staghorn coral protected under the Endangered Species Act.

Garden Key and other small islands shelter 300 species of **birds**, and the islands' protected beaches provide safe nesting sites for endangered **sea turtles**. Joining sea turtles on the park's list of threatened and endangered species are crocodiles, manatees, and whales.

Museums & Sites. Even after almost 30 years (1846–75) of construction, **Ft. Jefferson** on Garden Key was never finished. Work never stopped because the United States feared an enemy could use this ground to attack ships and control vital shipping lanes. With a mission to defend warships that patrolled the Gulf of Mexico and Straits of Florida, including during the Civil War, Ft. Jefferson was where ships would take on supplies and seek shelter during storms. Abandoned as a base in the mid-1870s, today the largest brick masonry structure in the Western Hemisphere serves as the park's centerpiece and its visitors center. It has a moat, a few beaches, and a primitive campground.

Programs & Activities. Dry Tortugas has few ranger-led activities, although a guide from the *Yankee Freedom* ferry offers a tour of Ft. Jefferson. The moat encircling the fortress is popular for **swimming and snorkeling** to see a mix of marine life and protected artifacts like reef squid, nurse sharks, hogfish, cement barrels, anchor chains, and pilings. At the edge of the swim area, massive coral heads offer sanctuary to brilliantly colorful parrot fish, angelfish, clown fish, triggerfish, and damselfish. Don't touch any coral: A touch can kill it, and fire coral—as well as resident jellyfish, sea urchins, and venomous lionfish—can sting.

Reefs such as Little Africa off Loggerhead Key (3 miles west of Garden Key) are accessible only by private boat and dive charters and feature the park's numerous **wreck sites**. More than a century after going down, the *Avanti* sits near the island's south end in 20 feet of water; it's a popular place to snorkel.

Fishing requires a Florida saltwater fishing license, and park visitors must also pay entrance fees. Private boats from kayaks to fishing boats have to file a boat permit at Garden Key. For fee and permit information, check the park website.

Lodging. The park's first-come, first-served 8-site primitive **campground** (there is also a group campsite and an overflow area) on Garden Key compensates for the spartan experience with magical star-gazing.

Most people stay in lively Key West, where choices range from chain hotels to B&Bs (florida-inns.com). Within walking distance of the commercial district are the independent **Island City House Hotel** (411 William St., 844/308-0031, www.islandcityhouse.com) and **Eden House** (1015 Fleming St., 305/296-6868, edenhouse.com).

1. Campground and visitors center, Ft. Jefferson. **2.** Snorkeling near Dry Tortugas **3.** Ft. Jefferson on Garden Key.

③

Everglades National Park

FLORIDA

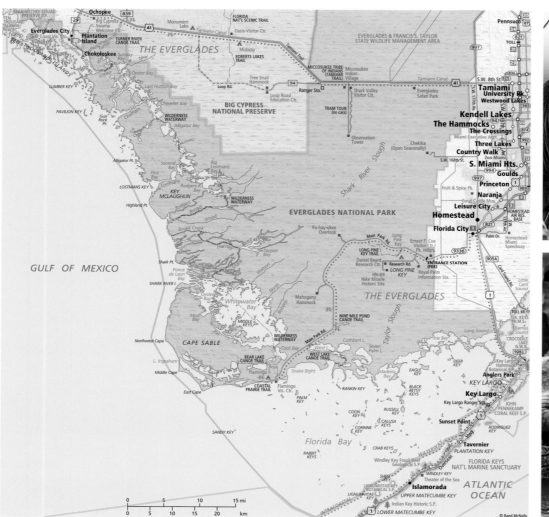

To fully appreciate the beauty in one of the world's natural wonders, you just need to know where to look. Hint: It's all right in front of you.

The Seminoles called it Pa-hay-okee (Grassy Water) and treasured it as a sanctuary. River of Grass was the name environmentalists gave this slow-moving, 60-mile-wide body of water—overflowing from the Kissimmee River floodplain and seeping from Lake Okeechobee to Florida Bay. But some settlers, developers, and industries dismissed it as useless swamp and commenced draining and diverting its waters, reducing it from 6.2 million acres to about 1.5 million.

What has been preserved is still enough to make this the largest

wilderness east of the Mississippi River, and one of the largest national parks in the lower 48. Still, the ecosystem faces constant pressure from South Florida's expanding population and agricultural and industrial interests. Environmentalists and others might yet have their work cut out for them.

Park Basics

Established: May 30, 1934 (established); December 6, 1947 (dedicated).
Area: 2,410 square miles; 1,542,526 acres.
Best For: Bird-Watching (bald eagles, cormorants, hawks, herons, ibis, pelicans, peregrine falcons, osprey, roseate spoonbills); Canoeing; Fishing; Hiking; Kayaking; Wildlife Watching (alligators, iguanas, manatees, panthers, sea turtles).
Contact: 305/242-7700, www.nps.gov/ever.
Getting Oriented: It's important to stop at

Everglades National Park, FL

a visitors center before entering to get your bearings and to pinpoint what you'd like to see and do in this vast park. There are four main centers; choosing which one might depend on where you're coming from in Florida.

1. Great blue heron. **2.** Alligator. **Opposite Page:** Boardwalk path on the Anhinga Trail.

Park headquarters are just 11 miles west of Homestead at the **Ernest F. Coe Visitor Center** (40001 State Rd. 9336) on the eastern side near the main entrance. From here, the nearest major gateway cities, both with international airports, are Miami (39 miles northeast) and Fort Lauderdale (66 miles northeast). For some, the **Shark Valley Visitor Center** (305/221-8776), 39 miles due west of Miami, might be more convenient.

If you're arriving from Florida's west coast, your best bet is the **Gulf Coast Visitor Station** (815 Oyster Ln., 941/695-3311), set up temporarily in Everglades City after the official Gulf Coast Visitor Center was damaged by Hurricane Irma in 2017. The far distant **Flamingo Visitor Center and Marina** (941/695-2945) is tucked deep inside the park on the shores of Florida Bay, 38 miles southwest of Ernest F. Coe.

As important as knowing where to go is knowing when to go. Even locals have trouble with sticky summer humidity (and mosquitoes). It's best to visit between December and April, when there are more ranger programs, the weather is cooler and drier, and the chance of seeing wildlife—including an abundance of birds—is greater.

Park Highlights

Natural Attractions. Only three places on Earth have been declared an International Biosphere Reserve, a UNESCO World Heritage Site, *and* a Wetland of Global Importance. Everglades National Park is one of them.

The Everglades are within the migratory **Great Florida Birding Trail** (floridabirdingtrail.com) and are a prolific breeding ground for tropical wading birds. Approximately 350 bird species, including several threatened and endangered ones, thrive in habitats ranging from mangrove and cypress swamps to pineland and estuarine bays. What will you see? Well, roseate spoonbills, ibis, herons, egrets, cormorants, anhingas, pelicans, bald eagles, osprey, peregrine falcons, and hawks—for a start.

In addition to being attracted to an environment that lends itself to nesting, many birds (raptors especially) come here to feast on the unlimited buffet of fish, crabs, crayfish, mollusks, and shrimp that thrive in waters that are fresh, salty, and estuarine (a blend of freshwater and saltwater). An estimated 48 species of fish live in the Everglades, with the game fish of Florida Bay (snook, redfish, spotted sea trout, tarpon) challenging sport fishermen while playful dolphins delight other visitors. The park is also a hothouse for flowers, with 25 species of wild orchids alone.

Visitors are always looking for alligators, and odds are high that the alligators are looking back. There's no way of knowing exactly how many are hiding in the reeds and waters, but estimates go as high as 200,000. You might also spot other reptiles (snakes, geckos, iguanas, lizards) as well as amphibians (frogs, toads, newts) and mammals (bobcats, minks, opossums, raccoons, deer, rabbits, and bear). In addition, certain types of sea turtles and snails are among the 36 Everglades creatures listed as threatened or protected under the Endangered Species Act.

The two creatures here most closely associated with Florida are the manatees that navigate park canals, rivers, and bays, and the elusive Florida panther, found in the park's hammocks and pinelands. Roughly 200 panthers live in or near the park. Keep a lookout.

Trails, Drives & Viewpoints. There's no better way to explore the Everglades than by car, unless it's by canoe, kayak, airboat, or bicycle. Or foot. Or tram. All are options for experiencing this park's diverse environments.

The **Anhinga Trail/Gumbo Limbo Trail**, located at the Royal Palm Information Center near the main entrance and Ernest F. Coe Visitor Center, gives you an easy glimpse of the Everglades. South of here, old fire roads and logging trails have found new life as the bicycle paths of the **Pineland Trail**. It's a rough ride that requires a sturdy mountain bike, but you're under no pressure to go the

THE SEMINOLES, UNCONQUERED

They knew it was coming. After word got out that the federal government had signed the Indian Removal Act of 1830, Native American tribes in the southeast realized their days were numbered. Although tens of thousands were commanded to leave their homes and join a forced march to Oklahoma, some never took a single step on the infamous Trail of Tears.

Rather than surrender to the U.S. Army at the beginning of the Second Seminole War (aka the Florida War, 1835–42), members of the Seminole and Miccosukee tribes headed deeper and deeper into Florida until they had disappeared into the Everglades. The tall grasses, marshes, and piney woods provided infinite hiding places. The environment (and some ingenuity) also provided them with everything they needed to survive: birds, fish, deer, crops, shelter, and fresh water.

By 1842, the United States government knew it had been outsmarted and outlasted. It gave up on its quest to relocate the Seminoles who, by never surrendering and never signing a peace treaty, had set themselves apart. Of the 566 Native American tribes recognized by the United States government, the Seminoles can claim a unique distinction: *Unconquered*.

①

②

(305/559-2255, gatorpark.com), and **Airboat USA** (305/431-7064, www.airboatusa.com).

Museums & Sites. Each of the park's four visitors centers has information on tours and activities, interpretive exhibits on cultural and natural history, and a gift shop. The largest museum is at **Ernest F. Coe Visitor Center**, where highlights include an introductory film and exhibits on how wet and dry seasons affect park wildlife.

Just west of the Shark Valley Visitor Center along Alligator Alley (aka US 41) you'll find the **Miccosukee Indian Village** (305/480-1924, www.miccosukee.com/indian-village), whose residents make and sell woodcarvings, beaded items, baskets, dolls, and other traditional crafts. A museum has photographs, historic clothing, and tribal art. Alligator-wrestling demonstrations, airboat rides, and a resort casino round out the offerings.

Lodging. Aside from RV and tent camping at the park's **Long Pine Key** and **Flamingo campgrounds** (reservations recommended) and numerous backcountry campsites, the park has no lodging. You do, however, have endless choices in Miami. There are also several options in Homestead, including the historic but basic **Hotel Redland** (5 S. Flagler Ave., 305/246-1904, www.hotelredland.com), and a handful in Everglades City, among them the historic but rustic **Rod & Gun Club** (199 Riverside Dr., 239/695-2101, everglades-rodandgunclub.com).

Near the Shark Valley Visitor Center, the Miccosukees' **Miami Resort** (305/222-4600, www.miccosukee.com/resort) offers modern rooms, upscale dining, and a casino. At **Flamingo Marina** (239/695-2591, www.evergladesnationalparkboattoursflamingo.com) you can rent a houseboat, go exploring, and then spend the night moored at the dock or anchored in a bay or inlet.

1. Airboat tour with Coopertown Airboats.
2. Aerial view.

distance (43 miles). A walk in these woods is equally enjoyable.

A shorter, 15-mile **hiking-and-biking loop** begins and ends at the Shark Valley Visitor Center. Just south of here, you can rise above it all by scaling a 65-foot high **observation tower** for a 360-degree aerial view.

In the vicinity of the Flamingo Visitor Center, several **canoe and kayak trails** (239/695-2591, www.evergladesnationalparkboattoursflamingo.com)—Nine-Mile Pond, Noble Hammock, Hell's Bay, Mud Lake, Bear Lake—can take a few hours or a few days to reveal their environments. These include everything from freshwater marsh to mangrove forest to the shores and open waters of Florida Bay.

From the Gulf Coast Visitor Center, you can put in on the 99-mile **Wilderness Waterway** (239/695-2591, www.evergladesnationalparkboattoursgulfcoast.com), which navigates interconnected inland bays, rivers, ponds, and small keys on what can, but doesn't have to be, an eight-day voyage. The free-form trail channel parallels a section of coastline called **Ten Thousand Islands**, a maze of waterways and mangrove islands in Florida's southwest corner.

Programs & Tours. The park has numerous ranger-led programs including talks and nature walks covering everything from the park's formation to its wildlife to its cypress swamps or other unique environments. Offerings and schedules vary not only by season (with far more of them between December and April) but also by visitor center, so it's wise to call ahead to see what's on.

If you're here on a day trip, the two-hour **Shark Valley Tram Tour** (305/221-8455, www.sharkvalleytramtours.com), departing from the visitors center of the same name, is the best way to get a sense of the park. The wildlife you'll see on the 15-mile loop varies depending on the season (wet or dry) but almost always includes birds, alligators, fish, and turtles. Several stops give you time to take photos; during one, you can exit the tram and scale the observation tower.

For **water excursions**, concession boat captains set sail on daily cruises along the Ten Thousand Islands, Whitewater Bay, and Florida Bay. Perhaps the most exciting way to see the Everglades, though, is aboard an airboat—a propeller-driven craft that skims across the backwaters at a peppy clip. Four authorized **airboat tour** concessionaires can give you a lift: **Coopertown** (305/226-6048, coopertownairboats.com), **Everglades Safari Park** (305/226-6923 or 305/223-3804, www.evergladessafaripark.com), **Gator Park**

Gates of the Arctic National Park & Preserve

ALASKA

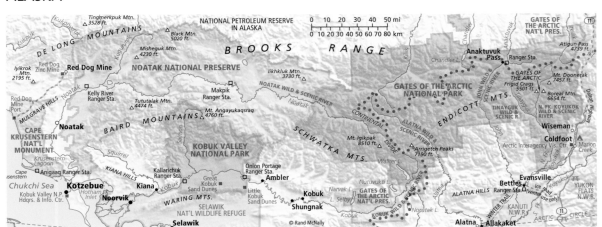

True to its name, Gates of the Arctic is a portal to the far north's unique ecosystem. Only about 11,000 visitors set foot in this vast park annually. On a weeklong adventure, you might not encounter another soul.

Although it's not the nation's largest park (that honor belongs to Wrangell-St. Elias, also in Alaska), Gates of the Arctic comes in a close second, encompassing a wilderness that's larger than the entire state of Maryland! Also true to its name, this park preserves important wildlife habitats, especially that of the large Western Arctic caribou herd.

For the region's indigenous peoples, caribou have long been an important source of not only food but also shelter, warmth, and tools, with hides used to make tents, clothing, and blankets and sinew and rawhide employed in creating snowshoes and fishing nets. Indeed, for many, particularly the inland Nunamiut

Gates of the Arctic
National Park & Preserve, AK

Eskimos, caribou is still an important source of physical, cultural, and spiritual sustenance.

Park Basics

Established: December 1, 1978 (national monument); December 2, 1980 (national park).

Area: 12,982 square miles, 8,308,258 acres.

Best For: Backcountry Camping; Hiking; Wildlife Watching (bears, beavers, caribou, moose, wolves).

Contact: 907/692-5494 (June–Sept.), 907/459-3730 (Oct.–May), www.nps.gov/gaar.

Getting Oriented: Gates of the Arctic is 280 miles north of Fairbanks, home to park headquarters, and about 30 miles east of its sister park, Kobuk Valley. The famous **Dalton Highway** (road trippers earn bragging rights if they've "done the Dalton") runs along Gates of the Arctic's eastern edge. On the highway and just outside the park, the town of **Coldfoot** has a ranger station (907/678-4227) and the **Arctic Interagency Visitor Center** (907/678-5209 summer only), with information on conditions and wildlife in Gates of the Arctic, Kobuk Valley, and other public lands.

You can fly from Fairbanks to either of two backcountry villages. **Bettles**, just south of the park, has a ranger station (907/692-5494 summer only). **Anaktuvuk Pass**, on a caribou migratory path amid the Brooks Range, is home to many Nunamiut Eskimo families and its own ranger station (907/661-3520 summer only). Park-approved **air taxis** (aka bush planes) accommodate 3 to 10 passengers and land on airstrips. The views are worth the often-bumpy ride!

Park Highlights

Natural Attractions. Gates of the Arctic is dominated by the Central Brooks Range, considered one of the continent's most spectacular. It features the granitic **Arrigetch Peaks**, collectively a National Natural Landmark, along with **Mt. Doonerak** (7,457 feet) and **Mt. Igikpak** (8,510 feet).

It's estimated that there are 300,000 **caribou** in the Western Arctic herd, which migrates south of the range in winter and north of it in summer. Although winter brings snow to the mountains, the park's interior remains comparatively dry. Lower-elevation slopes have forests of either black spruce or white spruce, aspen, and birch. Thickets in the valley and at the tree line often make hiking difficult, as does the tundra of moss and lichen in higher elevations.

Six officially designated **Wild and Scenic Rivers** flow through the park: the Alatna, John, Kobuk, North Fork of the Koyukuk, Noatak, and Tinayguk. Many

early adventurers—including explorers, cartographers, geologists, and prospectors—accessed the region along these rivers. Indeed, the pioneer Gordon Bettles, for whom the village south of the park is named, arrived here along the Koyukuk during one of the great northwestern gold-rush stampedes.

Shallow creeks and rivers throughout the region are often marked by **beaver** lodges in ponds created by dams of up to 20 feet high. These structures are sometimes maintained and expanded by generations of industrious, monogamous, family-focused beavers. The watery habitats they create also attract many other creatures, including fish, frogs, mink, moose, waterfowl, and eagles.

Activities. Driving the **Dalton Highway** as it edges Gates of the Arctic's eastern boundary is a great way to experience the spectacular scenery. **Hiking** is another way to do so, but you must be intrepid: There are no roads of any kind into the park. Nor are there any developed trails. Hikers traverse the tundra, which is often an overgrown thicket at lower elevations and fragile moss and lichen in higher spots, or they stick to dry streambeds if the water level is low. Five miles is considered a good target for a day.

Annually, average temperatures range from a low of -22 to a high of 70 degrees Fahrenheit, though the thermometer can defy the averages on any given day and in any given season. Few visit during the short, cold days of winter, despite the spectacular Northern Lights shows. Most people come between June and September, when the days are long: Indeed, in the Land of the Midnight Sun, the weeks between early June and early July feature 24 hours of daylight.

Unless you're a well-seasoned outdoorsperson, it's best to enlist an outfitter for guided trips to this remote park. Fairbanks-based **Arctic Wild** (907/479-8203, arcticwild.com) offers backpacking—including caribou-migration treks—packrafting, canoeing, and custom trips. They also have excursions that combine visits to Gates of the Arctic and Kobuk Valley.

Lodging. There are no in-park lodgings or developed campgrounds—rather just endless opportunities for backcountry camping. In the village of Bettles, where you can board air taxis, **Bettles Lodge** (907/692-5111, bettleslodge.com) has a definitively Alaskan vibe and year-round accommodations. **Coldfoot Camp** (Mile 175, Dalton Hwy., 907/474-3500, www.coldfootcamp.com) has basic rooms, RV hookups, and a gas station.

1. Noatak River, Brooks Range. **2.** Rafters on the Noatak River. **3.** Bush plane and passengers.

Gateway Arch National Park

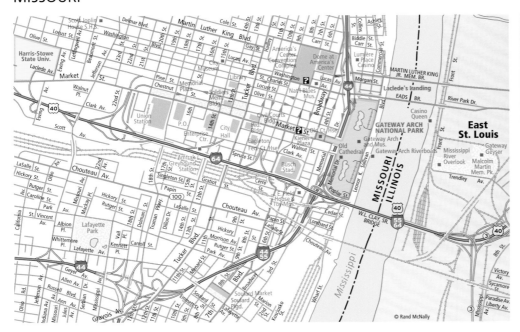

America's newest national park is also its smallest. As the saying goes, though, "Big things come in small packages." And this package contains the country's tallest manmade monument, an iconic structure that memorializes a whole lot of history.

Established in 1935 by President Franklin Roosevelt as the Jefferson National Expansion Memorial, the site honors not only Thomas Jefferson's vision of westward expansion but also the Louisiana Purchase and the Lewis & Clark Expedition. It was just northwest of St. Louis, where the Mississippi and Missouri rivers meet, that the Corps of Discovery began its 1804–06 journey across uncharted territory to the Pacific.

The onset of World War II and other issues delayed the memorial's development. In 1947–48, a design competition was held, and Eero Saarinen's concrete and stainless-steel Arch won out over 172 other entries, including one by his father, Eliel. Rising 630 feet and framing the dome of

Gateway Arch National Park, MO

the Old Courthouse, also part of the park, the Arch was completed in the late 1960s—the perfect Mid-Century metaphor for manifest destiny ideals.

Park Basics

Established: February 22, 2018.
Area: 0.3 square mile; 192 acres (91 federal, 101 nonfederal).
Best For: Cycling, History.
Contact: 314/655-1600 (recorded info), 877/982-1410 (to purchase timed-entry tickets), www.nps.gov/jeff.
Getting Oriented: Gateway Arch is edged by downtown St. Louis on one side and the Mississippi River (across from East St. Louis in Illinois) on the other. It's also ringed by interstates, including I-44 which cuts through the park between downtown and the river. A pedestrian-friendly land bridge crosses I-44, connecting the Old Courthouse with the Arch and its grounds.

North of downtown, I-70 runs to I-44 from the west—including the 15 miles from St. Louis Lambert International Airport—as well as from the east. In the south, I-64, I-44, or I-55 get you to the park. Numerous downtown hotels and public parking lots are within walking distance. **Metro system** (www.metrostlouis. org) buses and trains serve both Missouri and Illinois and include park- or bike-and-ride options. Or buy a full-day fare for the hop-on-hop-off #99 Downtown Trolley (actually, a colorfully painted bus), which includes the park on its list of historical stops.

Park Highlights

Viewpoints. Plenty of national parks feature spectacular views as part of a visit. Here, though, the views are arguably *the* reason to visit. One bank of windows atop the 630-foot **Arch** looks across the Mississippi River and into Illinois. Windows on the other side take in the west as far as the eye can see, which, on a clear day, is roughly 30 miles.

Some people wonder why this very small, very urban site was made a national park. To be fair, the National Park Service has always overseen it, and it does commemorate a pioneering history without which there might be fewer vast, wild spaces farther west for the park service to protect. Timing might also have played a part: A new name and upgraded designation seem a fitting cap to a 5-year, $380 million makeover completed in 2018.

To experience the refurbished glory and classic vistas, purchase timed-entry, **Journey to the Top** tickets for 4-minute tram rides up well in advance through **GatewayArch.com**, the park's concessionaire partner. Although the tram system accommodates up to 6,400 visitors daily, tickets can sell out. Also, arrive at least 30 minutes early to allow time for airport-style security screening. Stay in the observation

③

area as long as you like; trams for the 3-minute ride down depart every 10 minutes or so. Note, though, that there are no restrooms or other facilities at the top; plan accordingly.

If you prefer to stay grounded, you can check out top-side views on live web cams; see the documentary *Monument to the Dream*, covering the Arch's construction and significance; and visit the underground Museum of the Gateway Arch (formerly the Museum of Westward Expansion).

Museums, Programs & Activities. Six refurbished galleries in the **Museum of the Gateway Arch** look back across time using very forward-facing technology. Video and other interactive displays cover the Native American and Creole cultures of early St. Louis; Jefferson's vision for westward expansion; the steamboats, railroads, and other industries that helped to propel expansion; and the building of the Arch itself.

Two historic legal cases are highlighted on the daily, 45-minute, ranger-led tours of the **Old Courthouse**: The landmark Dredd Scott Case, involving emancipation and heard here in 1847 and 1850 (before a U.S. Supreme Court decision in 1857), and the 1870 case of Virginia Minor, a suffragette who sued for the right to vote.

For a leisurely park experience, board a replica 19th-century steamboat for a one-hour **riverboat cruise** (GatewayArch.com) with fantastic views of the Arch from Old Muddy. For a more active approach, look into biking, in-line-skating, or walking/running along the paved, 11-mile **St. Louis Riverfront Trail** (www.traillink.com).

Lodging. Almost two dozen chain hotels—from luxury to budget—are within 2 miles of Gateway Arch. Historical options include **Hilton St. Louis Downtown at the Arch** (400 Olive St., 314/436-0002, www3. hilton.com), in an 1888 Greek Revival that once housed a bank, and the grand, 1894, Romanesque Revival **St. Louis Union Station Hotel** (1820 Market St., 314/231-1234), also run by Hilton. The **Magnolia Hotel St. Louis** (421 N. 8th St., 314/436-9000, magnoliahotels.com/stlouis), which opened in 1924 as the Mayfair Hotel, originated the hospitable tradition of leaving chocolates on the pillow.

Who says you can't camp in the city? Though there are several area campgrounds—some of which allow tents—**St. Louis RV Park** (900 N. Jefferson Ave., 800/878-3330, stlouisrvpark. com) is right in downtown.

1. Old Courthouse. **2.** Downtown St. Louis skyline. **3.** Gateway Arch.

Glacier National Park

MONTANA

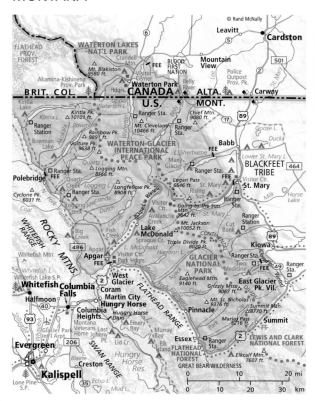

Scoured by glaciers over thousands of years, this mountainous park is a geologic masterpiece with show-stopping scenery at every bend in the road.

Above the captivating waterfalls, mirror-like lakes, and old-growth forests, Glacier's high country is traversed by the spectacular Going-to-the-Sun Road, with a new panorama around each of its hairpin turns. Although drives don't get any more beautiful than this, be sure to hike some of the park's 700 miles of trails. Note, too, that this park is one of the few places in the lower 48 where gray wolves still roam; it's also home to mountain goats, wolverines, and grizzly bears.

While some wildlife has rebounded, the park's glaciers have become endangered. Hotter summers have sped their melt-off, and some scientists fear they could be gone by 2030. More immediate, though, are the affects of 2017 wildfires, including the large Sprague Fire, which burned roughly 17,000 acres near Lake

McDonald. Trails, campgrounds, and even Going-to-the-Sun Road viewpoints were affected; check ahead.

Park Basics

Established: May 11, 1910.
Area: 1,583 square miles; 1,013,324 acres.
Best For: Boating; Cycling; Hiking; Kayaking; Wildlife Watching (elk, grizzly bears, moose, mountain goats).
Contact: 406/888-7800, www.nps.gov/glac.
Getting Oriented: Located between US 2 to the south and the Canadian border in northwestern Montana, the park is typically accessed via Missoula International Airport (134 miles south of West Entrance) or Great Falls International Airport (156 miles southeast of St. Mary Entrance).

The **St. Mary Entrance** is at the east end of Going-to-the-Sun Road, the only route through the park, which ends—after 56 spectacular miles—at the West Entrance and the town of **West Glacier**. This western gateway is closer to the park's prime attractions than the St. Mary Entrance. There are **visitors centers** at St. Mary, on Going-to-the-Sun Road at Logan Pass, and on the west

Glacier National Park, MT

side at Apgar. A free shuttle provides two-way service between Apgar and St. Mary.

You'll find lodging, dining, and other services in **East Glacier Park** (www.eastglacierpark.info), a small village at the Two Medicine Entrance on US 2, 142 miles north of Great Falls. On the park's northwest side, **Polebridge** (glaciermt.com) is a tiny town at the lesser-visited entrance of the same name, accessed via largely unpaved roads north of Columbia Falls. The resort town of **Whitefish** (explorewhitefish.com), 26 miles southwest of the West Entrance, also makes a good base.

Park Highlights

Natural Attractions. The park's namesake glaciers are spectacular, despite being rarer and smaller than they were a century ago.

There are 25 named glaciers in the park (down from about 150 in 1850), including iconic **Jackson Glacier**, which is visible from Going-to-the-Sun Road. Still, the landscape that the glaciers sculpted remains majestic, including mountains like **Heavens Peak** (8,976 feet) and **Mt. Wilbur** (9,308 feet).

The telltale lines of glaciers receding over time mark many peaks, in fact, and the melting ice continues to feed crystalline lakes, including **Lake McDonald**, **Bowman Lake**, and **St. Mary Lake**. Glacier has earned the nickname "The Crown of the Continent" largely because the **Continental Divide** runs through the park. All water that flows west from it ends up in the Pacific Ocean, whereas the east side flows toward either the Gulf of Mexico or Hudson Bay.

Just across the park's northern border—which doubles as the Montana–Alberta line— **Waterton Lakes National Park** (403/859-5133, www.pc.gc.ca) is a Canadian national park with stunning terrain. The two parks form **Waterton-Glacier International Peace Park**, established in 1932.

Trails, Drives & Viewpoints.
The hike to **Hidden Lake Overlook**, an easy, 2.8-mile round-trip, starts at the Logan Pass Visitor Center and meanders into an alpine landscape that's fertile habitat for mountain goats. From a trailhead near Lake McDonald, the moderate, 4.6-mile round-trip to **Avalanche Lake** starts with the wheelchair-accessible 1.4-mile round-trip **Trail of the Cedars** loop before a steeper stretch with views of numerous waterfalls. The strenuous **Highline Trail**—one of the park's most scenic hikes— follows a glaciated wall for 7.6 miles one-way

to Granite Park Chalet, a backcountry hostelry with bunks for overnight stays.

Driving **Going-to-the-Sun Road**, which crosses the Continental Divide, is an experience in itself. Expect to spend at least 3 hours one-way on this 50-mile route, accounting for stops at overlooks with spellbinding scenery.

Programs & Activities.
Rangers lead interpretive programs daily, including guided hikes and campfire talks. The **Native America Speaks** program features lecturers and storytellers from local tribes. Narrated **Red Bus Tours** (855/733-4532, www.glaciernationalparklodges.com) afford the opportunity to keep your eyes on the mountains from the comfort of vintage vehicles known as "jammers."

Glacier Park Boat Company (406/257-2426, glacierparkboats.com) offers narrated tours on Lake McDonald, Two Medicine Lake, and other lakes in the park. **Glacier Guides and Montana Raft Company** (800/521-7238, glacierguides.com), an outfitter based in West Glacier, guides rafting, hiking, backpacking, and fishing trips in the park and vicinity—and also rents rafting gear and bicycles.

The **Glacier Institute** (406/755-1211, www.glacierinstitute.org) has a year-round curriculum of daylong courses covering subjects ranging from photography to the ecology of the grizzly bear.

Lodging.
The numerous lodging options within Glacier range from lodges to campgrounds, and you'll find many additional choices in nearby towns. In the park, consider a pair of Swiss-inspired classics: **Many Glacier Hotel** on Swiftcurrent Lake and **Lake**

McDonald Lodge (855/733-4532, www.glaciernationalparklodges.com for both). The grandest lodge might be **Glacier Park Lodge** (844/868-7474, www.glacierparkcollection.com), just outside the park in East Glacier Park.

Also check out budget-oriented motels and cabin complexes within Glacier's boundaries from the same concessionaires. Outside the park, you'll find a wide variety of motels, cabin resorts, and lodges in the West Glacier area and in Polebridge, as well as ski condos, B&Bs, and hotels in Whitefish. Glacier has 13 campgrounds with more than 1,000 sites. Several of them, including **St. Mary Campground** on the park's east side, accommodate RVs; 4 accept reservations (Recreation.gov).

1. Hiking Grinnell Glacier with Glacier Guides and Montana Raft Company. **2.** Glacier Park Lodge. **3.** St. Mary Lake.

Glacier Bay National Park & Preserve

ALASKA

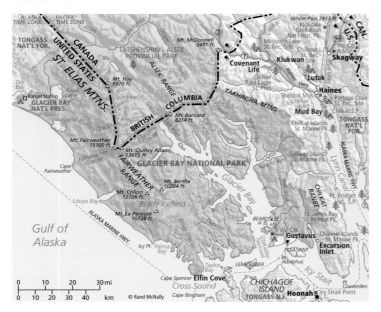

Untouched and unspoiled, the almost 3.3 million-acre Glacier Bay captures Alaska's wild essence and shows why the state's unofficial nickname, the "Last Frontier," remains stunningly apt.

About 200 years ago, much of Glacier Bay was under an ice sheet. Today it encompasses a unique combination of glaciers, rain forests, and the world's largest non-polar icefield, making it an integral part of the 25 million-acre Kluane/Wrangell-St. Elias/Glacier Bay/Tatshenshini-Alsek

UNESCO World Heritage Site. This collective of American and Canadian national parks is in southeast Alaska, northwest British Columbia, and the southwest Yukon Territory. America's sixth-largest national park holds its own among them with magnificent fjords, bays, inlets, mountains, harbors, coves, and, of course, icy-blue glaciers.

It can take some effort to reach the park (only one road leads in) and you might experience this environment for only a brief time (most people see it from the deck of a ship), but when

Glacier Bay National Park & Preserve, AK

you're ready to visit the Last Frontier, Glacier Bay is a great first stop.

Park Basics

Established: February 25, 1925 (national monument); December 2, 1980 (national park and preserve).
Area: 5,128 square miles; 3,281,789 acres.
Best For: Bird-Watching (bald eagles, owls, woodpeckers); Kayaking; Wildlife Watching (bears, moose, sea lions, wolves).
Contact: 907/697-2230, www.nps.gov/glba.
Getting Oriented: You can tour Glacier Bay in several ways. Arriving by ship during an Alaska or Inside Passage cruise is the most popular choice, since captains have mapped out scenic routes. The other option is taking a taxi or driving 10 miles northwest of the small gateway town of **Gustavus** (www.gustavus.com) to the park's "town square," including **Glacier Bay National Park Visitor Center** (907/697-2661) in **Glacier Bay Lodge** (907/697-4000, www.visitglacierbay.com). Lodge guests can take a shuttle between Gustavus and the park. In **Bartlett Cove**, near the lodge, tour boats offer excursions in season.

You (and your car) can reach the park via the **Alaska Marine Highway System ferry** (800/642-0066, www.dot.alaska.gov/amhs), which provides service from Juneau to Gustavus. To reach Juneau, you'll need a cruise ship (most arrive from Seattle, Vancouver, or Anchorage) or a flight into Juneau International Airport (50 miles east of Gustavus). Although it's open year-round, Glacier Bay has one of the shortest seasons of any national park, with most visitors services operating from around Memorial Day to Labor Day.

Park Highlights

Natural Attractions. Since much of Glacier Bay's land is wooded wilderness and much of the rest of the area is water and ice, cruise ships and smaller tour boats that head up-bay are good ways to witness its wildlife and tidewater glaciers. If you're on a cruise,

the night before reaching the park you'll receive a park map; the following morning a ranger comes aboard as the ship sails into the heart of the Fairweather Range. En route, the ranger shares details about the history, wildlife, and glacial formations.

The road into the park from Gustavus is the rare stretch of pavement amid millions of wild acres. You can also make your way into the park aboard the **Glacier Bay Day Tour** (www.visitglacierbay.com), aka the Day Boat. This 150-passenger high-speed catamaran sails from Glacier Bay Lodge on 8.5-hour, 130-mile round-trip tours. Park rangers are aboard to help spot wildlife.

Cruise ship and Day Boat passengers travel to roughly the same areas, but the smaller Day Boat gets closer to the shore, increasing the likelihood of spotting seals and sea lions, otters, mountain goats, moose, wolves, deer, brown bears and grizzly bears, bald eagles, puffins, murres, and maybe even orcas and humpback whales. One peak experience is seeing the Margerie Glacier, a constantly advancing mile-wide river of ice. You'll see this and the Grand Pacific glacier, and perhaps witness a "calving" event as chunks of ice break from the glacier's face.

Trails. The 1.3-mile **Bartlett Loop Trail** near the visitors center and the longer Bartlett River and Bartlett Lake trails in the same area are among the few designated places to walk. You can also stroll the shoreline south of the docks at Bartlett Cove and explore the intertidal zone.

Museum. The **Glacier Bay National Park Visitor Center** has exhibits about natural and cultural history as well as a bookstore, short films, and a hydrophone—a microphone connected to the bay, allowing you to hear sounds from the underwater world.

Programs & Activities. In season, rangers offer daily activities such as guided walks along the beach and interpretive walks through the rain forest on the Bartlett Loop Trail. Daily talks relate to flora, fauna, geology, and cultural heritage, which includes the history of the Native Americans who first settled this region and whose descendants live here today. At the visitors center, nature films shot in the park enhance evening programs.

A popular option is to rent a kayak from **Glacier Bay Sea Kayaks** (907/697-2257, www.glacierbayseakayaks.com) by the visitors center or to work with other outfitters listed on the park website. You can paddle the shoreline of Bartlett Cove en route to Secret Bay and the Beardslee Islands. Some adventurous travelers board the Day Boat with kayak in tow and are dropped off up-bay to paddle before catching a lift back; others camp out and return the following day.

The park also attracts anglers hoping to catch halibut in the bay and trout in the rivers. An Alaskan sportfishing license, available at the visitors center and lodge, is required.

Lodging. The park has a lodge and campground, and nearby Gustavus offers cabins, rental homes, guesthouses, and B&Bs including the **Gustavus Inn** (907/209-6722, www.gustavusinn.com), known for its good cuisine. Inside the park, **Glacier Bay Lodge** (907/697-4000, www.visitglacierbay.com) has a dining room and a porch that affords wilderness views. Campsites are free at the park's **Bartlett Cove Campground**; just notify the lodge or park service.

1. Breaching humpback whale. **2.** Ferry traveling the Alaska Marine Highway through Glacier Bay. **3.** Forested landscape. **4.** Bear in the park.

Grand Canyon National Park

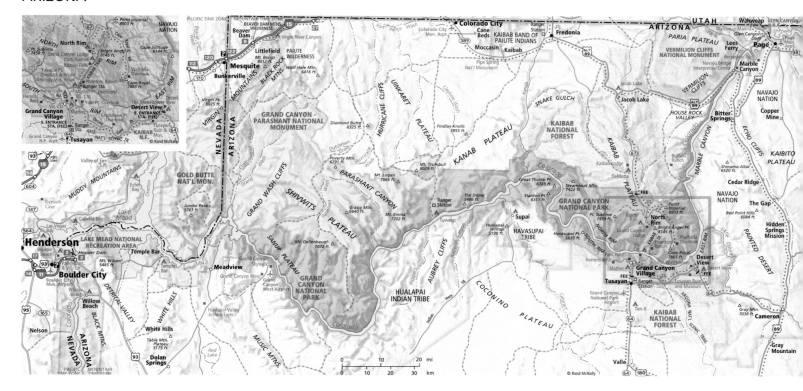

Standing at the edge of one of the Seven Wonders of the Natural World, you take in astounding and unforgettable views. Perhaps equally memorable is watching fellow travelers take in the breathtaking majesty.

Upon seeing the Grand Canyon for the first time, it's common for visitors to cry; some even break down sobbing. For many, this is an unexpectedly spiritual visit, rooted in the canyon's immense beauty and its hallowed place in our culture. The Grand Canyon is part of the American identity.

It's been 6 million years in the making, and nature's work isn't done. Season after season, rain, snow, heat, frost, and wind continue to sculpt the canyon, making it wider, deeper, and longer. As this swath of earth evolves, new generations will visit. And, when they behold the majestic canyon for the first time, some will cry; some will even break down sobbing.

Park Basics

Established: January 11, 1908 (national monument); February 26, 1919 (national park).
Area: 1,877 square miles; 1,201,647 acres.
Best For: Backpacking, Bird-Watching (California condors, eagles, falcons, hawks), Geology, Hiking, History, Whitewater Rafting.
Contact: 928/638-7888, www.nps.gov/grca.
Getting Oriented: The closest major airports are Phoenix Sky Harbor, 230 miles south, and McCarran International in Las Vegas, 270 miles west. (The Grand Canyon National Park Airport serves private and charter aircraft only.)

Most people enter via the **South Rim**, home to great viewpoints, trailheads, and the amenities of historic **Grand Canyon Village**: lodging, restaurants, museums, shuttles to overlooks, and the terminal for the classic **Grand Canyon Railway** (800/843-8724,

Grand Canyon National Park, AZ

www.thetrain.com), with daily round-trip service between Williams, Arizona, and the park.

The South Rim also has the **Grand Canyon Visitor Center**, the main hub for exhibits, souvenirs, seasonal bike rentals, and screenings of a wonderful 20-minute movie about the canyon. Nearby towns—including **Tusayan** (tusayan-az.gov), just outside the south entrance, and **Williams** (experiencewilliams.com), 60 miles south—offer amenities.

The **North Rim** is open only from mid-May through mid-October. There are trailheads, campsites, some services, a visitors center, and access to the once-daily, 4.5-hour **Trans**

1. Trail marker. **Opposite Page:** Colorado River, North Rim.

Canyon Shuttle between the North and South rims. There's also an entrance and scenic overlooks at the **East Rim**.

Park Highlights

Natural Attractions. Obviously, the whole of the Grand Canyon is a natural attraction. But, in addition to seeing it, try to rise early to see some of what lives in and around it. Coyotes, elk, foxes, deer, bobcats, raccoons, and bighorn sheep might be wandering beside a forest or trail before seeking shelter from the afternoon sun.

Earning a generous share of attention from naturalists are the California condors, which were on the brink of extinction in 1992. They were introduced near the park in 1996 and have since adapted to their new home. It takes just a few flaps of their 9-foot wingspans to launch several hours of soaring courtesy of thermals rising from the canyon floor.

Eagles, falcons, and hawks also fly in the park's protected skies. Look into joining fall's HawkWatch conducted by **HawkWatch International** (hawkwatch.org/migration) in partnership with the **Grand Canyon Association**, (www.grandcanyon.org). Between late August and early November, volunteers head to Yaki Point to help count the raptors as they fly south from Canada.

Trails. It takes considerable effort and preparation to hike to the canyon floor (and far more effort to hike back up), but you don't have to go the distance—and probably won't want to. At the South Rim, you're 7,000 feet above sea level, and, unless your body has adapted to the elevation, you'll likely be affected by the thinner air.

The 12-mile round-trip **Bright Angel Trail** starts in the historic village, so it's one of the most popular. It also has water stations (some open seasonally) and several segments that make good targets for shorter out-and-back hikes. This well-defined trail isn't too steep for the first 0.75 mile. Things get steeper after that. But even a short walk below the rim is enough to give you a perspective you can't experience from above.

There's also the 6-mile round-trip **South Kaibab Trail**, which is about 3 miles east of the village and considered one of America's best short hikes. It winds down almost 1 mile to the popular **Ooh-Aah Point** and continues just over 0.50 mile to **Cedar Ridge**, which opens to a stunning view and is a good place to turn around. If it's not too hot (i.e., it's not summer) and you're up for it, it's another 1.5 miles to **Skeleton Point** for a view of the Colorado River. Though maintained, the trail is steep and has little shade (and no water), so wear appropriate clothing; carry plenty of water; and don't forget the fruit, salty snacks, and protein bars.

Drives & Viewpoints. By river course, the Grand Canyon is 277 miles long, which means there's about 554 miles of viewpoints along the South and North rims—even more when adding the park's East Rim. The park service makes reaching spectacular viewpoints easy with low-emission shuttle buses (equipped to carry bikes) that travel to scenic spots west of the historic village—**Hopi Point, Mojave Point, The Abyss**, and **Hermits Rest** among

them—and east to **Yaki Point** and beyond. They follow routes used by carriages at the dawn of the 20th century, with stops that offer different, yet equally awe-inspiring views.

You can bicycle along **Hermit Road**, which runs almost 8 miles from the South Rim visitors center to Hermits Rest and has nine viewpoints. This is especially pleasant between March and November, when private vehicles aren't allowed. Roughly parallel to this road but closer to the canyon rim is the **Hermit Greenway Trail**, 3 miles of which are also good for bicycling.

From the historic village, it's roughly 25 miles along the **Desert View Drive** to the East Rim entrance station. Although shuttles also travel this route and stop at several overlooks, they don't go all the way to the end. To reach farther-flung overlooks like **Moran Point** and **Lipan Point** (considered one of the park's most picturesque), plan to drive.

Museums & Sites. With 10,000 of years of human habitation and more than a century as a vacation destination, the Grand Canyon has plenty of history to share. In the historic village, be sure to visit the **Kolb Studio**. The Kolb brothers were among the first to promote the canyon by selling their photographs across the nation. They even shot a silent film of a Colorado rafting trip, which they narrated for paying viewers in their rim-side studio. The Kolbs are gone, but the film is still shown in this combination museum, overlook, and gift shop.

Next door, the **Lookout Studio** is one of several structures designed by architect Mary Colter in a style now called "National Park Rustic." In the early 1900s, while helping the Fred Harvey Company and Santa Fe Railroad develop canyon amenities, Colter took inspiration from the landscape for her building designs and interior decor. She was later dubbed the "Architect of the Southwest."

DANGER ZONE

Sadly, the most popular book sold in Grand Canyon gift shops is *Over the Edge: Death in Grand Canyon*, which details park mishaps. Each year, in addition to hundreds of rescues, the park deals with more than a dozen deaths due to falls. And yet, it's still common for visitors to stand precipitously on cliffs and retaining walls. Put safety before selfies: Stay behind rails and far from the rim at all times, step back if you feel dizzy, and keep a firm grip on children.

Another Colter gem is the **Hopi House** adjacent to the hotel El Tovar (both built in 1905). Initially, Native American artisans lived and sold pottery from the multistory building. Today it houses a museum, gift shop, and gallery selling contemporary tribal artwork. To see more of Colter's work, head west to **Hermits Rest**, which she designed in 1914 as a rest stop beside the westernmost vista. It has a gift shop and snack bar and sits beside a path to a rim-side picnic area.

East of the historic village is the small **Yavapai Geology Museum**. Although not a Colter design, it's nevertheless impressive for its exhibits on canyon geology—and the view of the canyon itself through a wall of windows. Continuing east will take you to Colter's masterpiece: the **Watchtower**, a focal point of the Desert View overlook. Inspired by Hopi structures and accented with paintings by celebrated Hopi artist Fred Kabotie, there are nearly as many photographs taken of the 70-foot observation station as from it.

En route to or from Desert View, stop at the **Tusayan Museum and Ruin**, which features artifacts found at the site of a Pueblo Indian community. A short walk through the grounds reveals the foundations of homes and kivas (rooms used for religious and political gatherings) built more than 800 years ago. Notably, this is just one of hundreds of park archaeological sites, whose locations are known only to rangers and archaeologists to protect them from artifact hunters.

Programs & Activities. Ranger-led tours are free and cover history, geology, geography, wildlife, and more. In season, Native Americans conduct weekend storytelling sessions and traditional dance performances. In addition, the park-affiliated **Grand Canyon Field Institute** (866/471-4435, grandcanyon.org) offers dozens of classes and more than 200 hikes each year.

Many park tours are conducted by **Xanterra South Rim** (928/638-2631, www. grandcanyonlodges.com); some are offered for a fee and require reservations. En route to the lookout point during the 90-minute **Sunrise/ Sunset Tours**, guides offer natural-history lessons that add to the brilliance of seeing dawn break above the rim or the sky turn blue, orange, red, and pink as the sun sets.

Book well in advance for the **South Rim mule trips**, which head down to the Phantom Ranch for overnight stays on the canyon floor. Even more thrilling is a **Colorado River rafting expedition**: You can float into the canyon's heart and marvel at surreal rock formations for a day, or join a multi-day whitewater-adventure trip.

A helicopter tour is an admittedly indulgent excursion, but the sights are magical, and it provides a lesson in dimension: Even at 100 mph, it takes several minutes to cross the canyon. Choose from **Grand Canyon Helicopters** (702/835-8477, www.grandcanyonhelicopter.com), **Papillon** (702/736-7243, www.papillon. com), or **Maverick** (702/261-0007, www. maverickhelicopters.com). Or take flight across the canyon aboard a wide-windowed aircraft with tours by **Grand Canyon Airlines** (702/835-8484, grandcanyonairlines.com) or **Grand Canyon Scenic Airlines** (702/638-3300, www.scenic.com).

Lodging. There's a range of in-park lodging options, most offered by **Grand Canyon National Park Lodges** (928/638-2631, www.grandcanyonlodges.com). In the historic village, just steps from the rim, the premium choice is the classic 78-room **El Tovar**, with a concierge, room service, fine dining, and an upscale gift shop. Nearby are the motel-style **Thunderbird** and **Kachina** lodges as well as the **Bright Angel** and **Maswik** lodges, both of which have rooms and cabins.

About a mile east of the village are **Yavapai Lodge** and the nearby **Trailer Village RV Park** (contact for both is 877/404-4611, www.visitgrandcanyon.com). Among the park's other campgrounds are the **Mather** (877/444-6777, Recreation.gov) and the **Desert View**, which doesn't accept reservations.

1. Sunrise from Lookout Studio. 2. Guided mule trip. 3. Grand Canyon Railway.

Grand Teton National Park

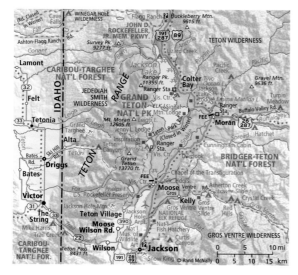

There are spectacular mountain views; then there are the Tetons. It's nearly impossible to take a picture here without framing a panorama of the park's namesake peaks. They are, in a word, mesmerizing.

You can drive through this park in about two hours—enjoying the sights from afar—but the landscape demands that you get up close. Myriad trails take you from merely seeing the majestic peaks to truly experiencing them, as they rise more than 7,000 feet from the valley floor to the 13,770-foot summit of Grand Teton.

On the flat expanse of the valley of Jackson Hole, spreading eastward from the park's namesake peaks, there's plenty of water for anglers and boaters to love, including the Snake River and crystal-clear lakes along the Tetons' eastern flank. Winter brings snowshoers and Nordic skiers to the trails. When spring arrives, it's time for chirping birds, wildflowers, and rushing creeks, alongside some of the prettiest scenery in all of the Rocky Mountains.

Park Basics

Established: February 26, 1929 (expanded September 14, 1950).
Area: 484 square miles; 310,044 acres.
Best For: Backcountry Camping; Climbing; Fishing; Hiking; Wildlife Watching (elk, grizzly bear, moose).
Contact: 307/739-3399, www.nps.gov/grte
Getting Oriented: Grand Teton is in the northwest corner of Wyoming between the slick resort town of **Jackson** (www.jacksonholechamber.com) to the south, and **Yellowstone National Park**, 18 miles north

Grand Teton National Park, WY

of Colter Bay Visitor Center on Jackson Lake. US 26/89/191 and Teton Park Road traverse the park north–south, merging near Jackson Lake on the park's northeast side and Moose at the southern entrance. From Jackson Lake, US 26/287 continues east past the Moran Entrance to the town of Dubois.

The nearest major airports are Utah's Salt Lake City International (290 miles southwest of the Moose Entrance) and Colorado's Denver International (500 miles southeast); the regional Jackson Hole Airport is 5 miles south. The main **Craig Thomas Discovery**

and Visitor Center is in Moose; others are at **Jenny Lake** and **Colter Bay** on Jackson Lake.

Park Highlights

Natural Attractions. Jutting skyward with few foothills, the **Teton Range** is the park's undeniable superstar, with the Cathedral Group of Grand Teton, Middle Teton, Mt. Owen, and Teewinot; and Mt. Moran to the north. Between the peaks, glaciers cut a series of dramatic canyons into the mountains, feeding a series of jewel-like lakes below.

The trout-rich **Snake River** winds across the valley floor of Jackson Hole. The valley itself offers varied habitats for resident wildlife, including bears, bald eagles, bison, and elk.

Trails, Drives & Viewpoints. If you're going to hike just one trail, try the moderate, 7.6-mile **Jenny Lake Loop Trail**; you can cut it in half by taking the shuttle (fee) across the lake. From the West Dock, it's worth the uphill hike to Hidden Falls and Inspiration Point, which adds another 2.4 miles but rewards the extra effort with sweeping views. Diehards can continue on the **Cascade Canyon Trail**, the prime route for mountaineers looking to summit Grand Teton and its sister peaks of the Cathedral Group. On the park's south side, the Laurance S. Rockefeller Preserve offers a network of fairly level trails, such as the 6.3-mile **Phelps Lake Loop Trail**, which culminates with mountain and canyon views from its namesake lake.

Scenic drives and viewpoints abound. The lesser-traveled **Moose-Wilson Road** enters the park 8 miles north of Teton Village and has many hiking and moose-spotting opportunities. For superlative views on the park's north side, drive the 5-mile **Signal Mountain Summit Road** (May–Oct.) and stop at the Jackson Point Overlook. Numerous turnouts along **Teton Park Road**, including Jenny Lake Overlook and Jackson Lake Overlook, showcase spectacular vistas.

Museum/Site. On the park's south side off Teton Park Road, the famed **Chapel of the Transfiguration**, with an altar window framing the Cathedral Group, is in **Menor's Ferry Historic District**, an important Snake River crossing before a new bridge put it out of business in 1927.

Programs & Activities. Free ranger programs include daily, guided hikes and talks from spring through fall, and guided **snowshoe walks** Monday through Saturday in winter. Rivers and lakes provide **boating opportunities** (307/543-2811, www.gtlc.com), including rafting trips on the Snake River and narrated cruises on Jackson Lake.

③

Jenny Lake Boating (307/734-9227, jennylakeboating.com) offers shuttles to the Hidden Falls trailhead and lake cruises.

Based in Jackson, Teton Science Schools' **Wildlife Expeditions** (307/733-1313, www.tetonscience.org) runs safari tours of Grand Teton and Yellowstone. Just south of the park off US 26/89/191, the **National Elk Refuge** (307/733-9212, www.fws.gov) is set aside as a wintering ground for the local herd. Sleigh rides tour the refuge in winter.

Lodging. There are campgrounds and other overnight options within park boundaries, and Jackson and the small nearby towns of Wilson and Kelly provide many choices. **Grand Teton Lodging Company** (307/543-2811, www.gtlc.com) operates the midcentury gem Jackson Lake Lodge, luxury guest ranch Jenny Lake Lodge, and Colter Bay Cabins in the park. Another in-park option is lakefront **Signal Mountain Lodge** (307/543-2831, www.signalmountainlodge.com) on the north end of Teton Park Road.

Of the park's six campgrounds (more than 1,000 sites in all), tents-only **Jenny Lake Campground** is a short walk from the lakeshore. **Colter Bay Village Campground** accommodates tents and RVs (with or without hookups) near Jackson Lake. Both are first-come, first-served, unless you're reserving a group campsite.

Just 13 miles south of the Moose Entrance via US 26/89/191, Jackson provides chain and independent hotels, B&Bs, and luxury resorts. Teton Village, at the base of the slopes at **Jackson Hole Mountain Resort** (307/733-2292, www.jacksonhole.com), has condominiums and ski lodges 9 miles south of the Moose Entrance via Moose-Wilson Road. The 1941 **Wort Hotel** (50 N. Glenwood St., Jackson, 307/733-2190, www.worthotel.com) is a ritzy place to hang your hat. In Teton Village, **The Hostel** (3315 Village Dr., 307/733-3415, www.thehostel.us) offers private rooms that are Jackson Hole's best value.

1. Camping in the park. **2.** Bison. **3.** Canoeing the Snake River at Oxbow Bend. **4.** Jenny Lake Lodge.

④

Great Basin National Park

NEVADA

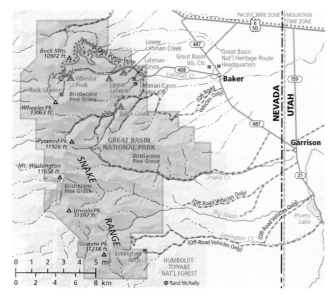

Nevada is far more than Las Vegas, just as New York is far more than New York City. In fact, there could hardly be a more dramatic counterpart to glitzy Las Vegas than the rugged simplicity of Great Basin National Park.

Aside from its striking landscapes of high desert and mountainous subalpine forest, there are few distractions in this 77,000-acre park in east-central Nevada near the Utah border. It's simply nature, left on its own, that appeals to the 145,000 visitors who come here each year.

If you're among them, you'll experience a swath of the American West. You find it when you descend into the intricate network of Lehman Caves, when you see the environment

change as you enter the South Snake Range, and when you look into the evening sky for an astronomical light show far surpassing anything on the Strip. In other words, Great Basin National Park delivers the best of heaven and earth.

Park Basics

Established: January 24, 1922 (national monument); October 27, 1986 (national park).
Area: 120 square miles; 77,180 acres.
Best For: Astronomy; Bird-Watching (bald eagles, hawks, owls, woodpeckers); Geology; Hiking; Wildlife Watching (bobcats, elk, mountain sheep, mule deer).
Contact: 775/234-7331, www.nps.gov/grba.
Getting Oriented: To access Great Basin, find your way to Baker (population 68) in remote east-central Nevada via State Route 487, south of US 6/50. The closest major

Great Basin National Park, NV

airports are Utah's Salt Lake City International (230 miles northeast of Baker) and Nevada's McCarran–Las Vegas International (298 miles south).

The **Great Basin Visitor Center** is just north of Baker; the **Lehman Caves Visitor Center** (SR 488), half a mile beyond the main eastern entrance, is the starting point for cave tours and Wheeler Peak Scenic Drive. There are lodging options in **Baker** and even more in **Ely, Nevada** (www.elynevada.net), 62 miles west of Baker.

Park Highlights

Natural Attractions. The top sights are mostly in the park's northern third, although what you see depends on when you visit. Wheeler Peak Scenic Drive, with its range of ecosystems from high desert to subalpine mountains, can close due to snow; call for road reports. Visible from Lehman Caves Visitor Center is the **Great Basin Desert**, seen just across the valley; west of the visitors center, near Wheeler Peak Scenic Drive, are 13,063-foot **Wheeler Peak**, a **Bristlecone pine grove**, and the **Rock Glacier**. In the far southwest, **Lexington Arch** is one of the West's largest limestone arches, accessible via a dirt road that requires a high-clearance 4WD.

To see **Lehman Caves**, the underground centerpiece of Great Basin, sign up for one of the tours (fees vary) that depart from Lehman Caves Visitor Center and cover 550 million years of history and geology. The limestone cave (a chilly 50 degrees) delivers all the sights you'd expect: stalactites, stalagmites, helictites, flowstone, popcorn, and shield formations. You may also see Townsend's big-eared bat, one of 10 species that live in the cave.

Trails, Drives & Viewpoints. From the Lehman Caves Visitor Center, the narrow, winding, 12-mile-long **Wheeler Peak Scenic Drive** takes you west into the South Snake Range and, ultimately, near Wheeler Peak. You begin at nearly 7,000 feet, and rangers point out that because of the rise in elevation during the 45-minute drive, you'll see the same ecoregions you'd pass in an epic drive north to the Yukon. Sagebrush gives way to piñon and juniper pines at around 8,000 feet, and curl-leaf mountain mahogany appears at 8,500 feet. At 9,000 feet you enter a forest of mixed conifers: white fir, Douglas fir, and ponderosa pine. Eventually you reach a subalpine forest and a splendid view of the mountain.

To savor the outdoors, try some of the park's more than 60 miles of trails. The moderate, 2.8-mile **Bristlecone Trail** leads from the Wheeler Peak Campground to a photogenic 3,000- to 5,000-year-old pine grove; the moderate, 2.7-mile **Alpine Lakes Loop Trail** begins at the Bristlecone parking area and takes in Stella and Teresa lakes.

The return trip along the same road may take longer than 45 minutes if you stop for pictures. Pullouts at scenic overlooks serve the dual purpose of letting others pass while reminding you to stop for wonderful views of Mount Moriah, Lehman Creek, Wheeler Peak, the Snake Valley, and Jeff Davis Peak. One last thing: Put your car in low gear as you descend. It can save your brakes—and perhaps your life.

Programs & Activities. Choose from two ranger-led tours of **Lehman Caves**: The half-mile, one-hour Lodge Room Tour visits the cave's Gothic Palace, Music Room, and Lodge Room; the 90-minute Grand Palace Tour adds the Inscription Room and the Parachute Shield formation (yes, it looks like a parachute). Reservations, which can be made up to six months in advance through Recreation.gov, are strongly recommended.

Thanks to its low humidity, minimal light pollution, and high elevation, Great Basin is a certified International Dark Sky Park. On a clear night, you don't need a telescope to see planets, star clusters, satellites, meteors, and the Andromeda and Milky Way galaxies. Rangers bring out telescopes for **astronomy programs** several nights a week in summer and most Saturdays in spring and fall.

Lodging. The park has campgrounds and tiny Baker has some options, but the greatest variety of lodgings is about an hour west in Ely, where there are chain hotels and a few casinos. Great Basin has 124 sites at 5 first-come/first-served campgrounds in the north sector, basic camping farther south, and backcountry camping for outdoor enthusiasts. Rustic lodgings in Baker include the **Stargazer Inn** (115 S. Baker Ave., 775/234-7323, www.stargazernevada.com) and the **Border Inn** (US 6/50, 775/234-7300, borderinncasino.com).

1. Rock formations inside Lehman Caves.
2. Bristlecone pine landscape. **3.** Wheeler Peak.

Great Sand Dunes National Park & Preserve

COLORADO

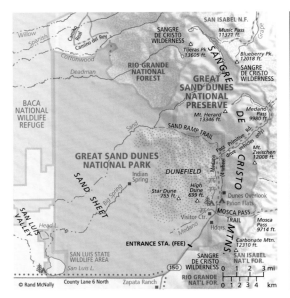

Take three crucial ingredients—wind, water, and time—and just add sand. The result is the unexpected grandeur of the Great Sand Dunes, North America's tallest dunes and a one-of-a-kind geologic spectacle.

The park is tucked into a corner of south-central Colorado's San Luis Valley under the towering peaks of the Sangre de Cristo Mountains. Terrain and weather have provided an equilibrium for the dunes for the past 440,000 years: Storm winds erode the mountains and blow the debris to the valley floor, where prevailing winds and streams push stray sand back into the slowly shifting dunes.

The dunefield is absolutely massive—occupying more than 30 square miles (about 6 miles by 5 miles)—and is visible from afar. Forested peaks to the east and a flat valley floor provide stark, surprising contrasts on all sides of this natural wonder. Somehow it all seems perfectly in place here: The San Luis Valley is known for its many unexpected features, ranging from

Great Sand Dunes National Park & Preserve, CO

unusual manmade attractions to sublime landscapes.

Park Basics

Established: March 17, 1932 (national monument); September 14, 2004 (national park and preserve).
Area: 233 square miles; 148,988 acres.
Best For: Backcountry Camping, Geology, Hiking.
Contact: 719/378-6395, www.nps.gov/grsa.
Getting Oriented: Great Sand Dunes is in southern Colorado, east of US 285 and north of US 160. Most visitors fly into Denver International Airport, 249 miles northeast of the park. Another option, Albuquerque International Sunport in New Mexico, is 239 miles southwest.

The nearest towns are **Alamosa** (www.alamosa.org), 32 miles southwest of the park's one entrance via CO 150 and US 160, and **Crestone** (townofcrestone.org), 54 miles north via CO 150 and 17. The **Great Sand Dunes Visitor Center** is just west of CO 150, near the Dunes Parking Area. Spring and fall are the best times to visit; summers are hot, winters notably cold.

③

Park Highlights

Natural Attractions. Venturing into the vast dunefield is akin to entering another world. From the first ridgeline, you get the full scope of the park's ever-changing heart. A bit farther, **Star Dune** is the park's tallest, measuring 755 feet from the valley floor. **Medano Creek** and other perimeter streams erode the dunes and deposit sand onto the dunefield's east side.

The rugged **Sangre de Cristo Mountains** dominate the park's east side. The name means "Blood of Christ" in Spanish and might have come from the red-tinged alpenglow that illuminates the peaks at dawn and dusk. **Mt. Herard**, at 13,346 feet, marks the highest point inside park boundaries.

Trails, Drives & Viewpoints. The dunes don't have designated trails—the sand shifts and erases footprints in hours—but hiking them is a must. You can easily walk from the parking lot for an up-close look and some playtime in the sand. Most hikers head to 699-foot **High Dune**, the zenith of the first ridge west of the parking area. The round-trip to High Dune requires about 2 hours; the round-trip to **Star Dune** takes about 5 hours. Both are difficult hikes, so be sure to bring water and wear sunscreen.

For hikes beyond the dunefield, **Montville Nature Trail** is an easy, 1-mile trek in a forested area with stellar views of the mountains, dunes, and valley. The **Mosca Pass Trail** ventures up a low mountain pass, a

difficult 7-mile-round-trip trek. Both trailheads are near the visitors center

No paved roads traverse the dunes. The **Medano Pass Primitive Road**, for 4WD vehicles only, heads north from the visitors center and accesses numerous stellar viewpoints, including one by way of the steep, 1-mile round-trip hike on the **Dunes Overlook Trail**.

Museums & Sites. The only alligator farm in the Rockies, **Colorado Gators Reptile Park** (9162 CR 9 N., Mosca, 719/378-2612, www.coloradogators.com) is one of the valley's prime oddities. The **UFO Watchtower** (201–249 CO Hwy. 17, Center, 719/378-2296, www.ufowatchtower.com) stands as a roadside attraction of another kind, featuring kitschy extraterrestrial touches, campsites, and a platform where you can look for flying saucers.

Programs & Activities. Ranger programs (May–Nov.) include evening presentations in an outdoor amphitheater. Talks often cover the geology of the dunes, astronomy, and park wildlife.

Adventurous types go sand sledding, skiing, or boarding on the dunes. Specialized equipment rentals are available at **Kristi Mountain Sports** (3223 Main St., Alamosa, 719/589-9759, www.kristimountainsports.com). Just outside of the park, **Oasis** (7800 CO Hwy. 150 N., Mosca, 719/378-2222, www.greatdunes.com) rents sleds and boards spring through fall.

Lodging. The park has only one campground, but options exist in the nearby communities

and the vast spaces in between them. Alamosa, a city of 10,000 residents, has some chain hotels and independent motels, as does smaller Monte Vista, 40 miles southwest of the park. The small town of Crestone has a few bed-and-breakfasts and spiritual retreat centers with overnight lodging.

Just south of the entrance, **Great Sand Dunes Lodge** (7900 CO Hwy. 150, Mosca, 719/378-2900, www.gsdlodge.com) features private patios with dune views. A cattle and bison ranch about 10 miles south of the entrance, **Zapata Ranch** (5305 CO Hwy. 150, Mosca, 719/378-2356, www.zranch.org) offers activities—including bison tours that take guests and non-guests to see the 2,000-head herd—and lodging in a historical homestead and bunkhouse. **Best Western Movie Manor** (2830 US 160 W., Monte Vista, 719/852-5921, www.bestwesternmoviemanor.com) is a motor lodge built around a drive-in theater; you can see the screen from your room.

Piñon Flats Campground (Recreation.gov), adjacent to the visitors center, is the park's only developed campground. It accepts both tents and RVs but has no hookups. You need a permit (free) for backcountry camping; the most popular backpacking routes are in the mountains on the park's northeast side.

1. Exploring Great Sand Dunes on a Horseback Experience with Zapata Ranch. **2.** Sunset view at the park. **3.** Sandboard with equipment rentals from Kristi Mountain Sports.

Great Smoky Mountains National Park

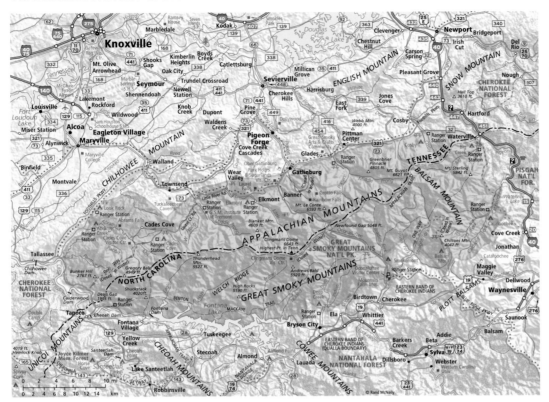

Many are surprised to learn that this national park straddling Tennessee and North Carolina is America's most popular, with almost twice the number of annual visitors as runner-up Grand Canyon.

Its sustained popularity says a lot, given that, nearly a century ago, the landscape here looked like a battleground. With little regard for the environment, logging companies had stripped forested mountains down to their roots, and the resulting mudslides choked rivers with tons of debris.

With the survival of the Great Smoky Mountains at stake, a unique confederation of governments (local, state, and federal) as well as philanthropists (John D. Rockefeller, Jr. chief among them), environmentalists, schoolchildren, and other private citizens united to purchase the land. It was a wise investment. This is now a UNESCO World Heritage Site as well as a national park. Its 11.3 million annual visitors hear the same birdsong, fish

the same rivers, and hike some of the same paths (today, there are 800 miles of trails) as their predecessors did more than a century ago.

Park Basics

Established: May 22, 1926 (authorized); February 20, 1930 (established for protection); June 15, 1934 (for development); September 2, 1940 (dedicated as a national park).
Area: 816 square miles; 522,426 acres.
Best For: Backpacking; Bird-Watching (cuckoos, nuthatches, owls, sparrows, warblers, woodpeckers, wrens); Botany; Fishing; Hiking; Wildlife Watching (black bears, deer, elk, raccoons, turkeys).
Contact: 865/436-1200, www.nps.gov/grsm.
Getting Oriented: In Tennessee, the closest gateway community is **Gatlinburg** (www.gatlinburg.com), near the park's north entrance. Both **Pigeon Forge** (www.mypigeonforge.com) and **Sevierville** (visitsevierville.com) are just a few miles farther north. The most convenient airport is Knoxville's McGhee Tyson, 45 miles northwest of Gatlinburg.

On the North Carolina side, the towns of **Cherokee** (www.cherokeesmokies.com) and **Bryson City** (www.greatsmokies.com) are

Great Smoky Mountains National Park, TN/NC

close to the **Oconaluftee Visitor Center** at the south entrance. Asheville Regional Airport is 56 miles east of Cherokee.

US Highway 441 runs north–south for about 40 miles through the park between Gatlinburg and Cherokee. Highway 73 and Little River Road run along the park's northern edge, connecting Gatlinburg with the community of Townsend. Along the way is the **Sugarlands Visitor Center**, the largest of the park's four, which, in addition to Oconaluftee, include the **Cades Cove Visitor Center** and **Clingmans Dome Visitor Center**.

1. Wildflowers in the park. **2.** Exploring the Trillium Gap Trail in Tennessee. **Opposite Page:** Newfound Gap.

Park Highlights

Natural Attractions. The natural appeal of this park, which is about half the size of Rhode Island, is found in its cool forest trails, ravines, and rivers that sweep through the mountains. Indeed, the beauty of the trees and rocks and rivers is so omnipresent that it all might begin to seem, well . . . ordinary. When you feel that you can't see the forest for the trees, though, take a closer look.

The lower **woodlands** are filled with sweet gum, poplar, dogwood, sycamore, pine, and oak. Higher elevations have forests of spruce, maple, ash, and fir. Ecosystems here also include wetlands and grassy balds. And that haze you see? That's the "smoke" of the Smoky Mountains—hydrocarbons released by all the vegetation lend the air a misty, bluish cast.

And don't forget the **flowers**! This one park is home to more than 1,600 varieties—trout lilies, yellow trillium, flame azaleas, mountain laurels, rhododendrons, and fire pinks among them. In fact, nearly 100 species of wildflowers here can be found only in the southern Appalachian Mountains, leading some to call this "Wildflower National Park."

Fly-fishing for bass and trout (brook, brown, rainbow) is extremely popular in the shallow rivers. On a walk in the woods, you might spot a few of the 120 species of birds or the 30 types of salamanders. One of the country's most unique wildlife experiences, however, takes place here nightly for about a week between late May and early June: the **synchronous firefly display**. A unique mating ritual (flying males flash, stationary females flash back) explains the choreography of this species, one of the park's 19.

Each year, a fortunate few visitors receive passes (distributed via lottery through Recreation.gov) to park at the Sugarland Visitor Center. From here, shuttles transport them to a firefly viewing area near the Elkmont Campground. Lottery registration generally opens in late April; watch the national park site for announcements, and be ready: Recent years have seen some 18,000 registrants apply for roughly 1,800 parking passes. Alternatively, book a stay at the Elkmont Campground, whose guests have access to the show.

RISING FROM THE ASHES

Had things continued unchecked, the Great Smoky Mountains National Park would not exist today. When it was obvious that clear-cutting and logging would destroy this unique land, groups joined together to buy about 800 square miles of forest and mountains. But that was just the beginning.

In 1933, to help Americans work their way out of the Great Depression, President Franklin Roosevelt initiated a series of public works programs, among them the Civilian Conservation Corps (CCC). At the program's peak, in this park alone, as many as 4,000 young men worked at 22 camps to create roads, bridges, cabins, and campgrounds. They built trails, planted trees, stocked rivers with fish, and fought fires. These efforts—very visible by the time President Roosevelt dedicated the park in 1940—perfectly complemented the earlier, less visible efforts to preserve the land.

Drives, Trails, & Viewpoints.

US Highway 441 south follows lazy turns and steep ascents between Gatlinburg and Cherokee, passing pullouts, picnic areas, and photo-worthy viewpoints. A popular first stop is **Chimney Tops Picnic Area** on the west prong of the Little Pigeon River. Nearby is the trailhead for the **Chimney Tops Trail**, a popular 2-mile route that has been rehabilitated after a devastating 2016 fire.

Over the next several miles the road twists still farther upward. Your ears pop, the views improve, and signs note that you've risen in elevation from around 1,450 feet in Gatlinburg to one of the park's highest points (5,048 feet) at one of its most popular viewpoints: the **Newfound Gap** on the Tennessee–North Carolina border. Nearby, the nearly hidden **Charles Bunion Trail** is actually a stretch of the 2,178-mile Appalachian Trail, 70 miles of which follow the state line through the park. Your reward for taking this 8-mile round-trip hike is the chance to rest at a stone outcrop opening to a gorgeous view of interlaced mountains.

South of the gap, a spur road off US Highway 441 travels 7 miles southwest to **Clingmans Dome**, which, at 6,643 feet, provides views that equal or surpass those at Newfound Gap. There's a visitors center here as well as a steep 0.5-mile trail that leads to the summit and an observation tower. Another trail leads nearly 2 miles over hills, across a ridge, and through a forest to **Andrews Bald**, a grassy area where a rancher first let his cattle graze in the 1840s. Beyond the bald, the **Forney Ridge Trail** continues for another 4 miles to the **Springhouse Branch Trail**.

After Clingmans Dome, it's downhill all the way to the park's southern entrance near Cherokee. To see more of North Carolina, consider a side trip to **Cataloochee Valley** via I-40 to US Highway 276 to Cove Creek Road. Although the final 11 miles travels a winding, gravel-covered section with steep drops, the reward is a peaceful mountain valley with historic churches, a school, homes, and outbuildings. There are also opportunities for camping, hiking, and fishing as well as for spotting deer, turkey, and other wildlife.

Other wonderful driving routes surround the park, including the magnificent **Blue Ridge Parkway** (www.blueridgeparkway.org), which traces the park's southern border and has its own majestic, unforgettable views.

Museums & Sites. For more than 20 miles at the park's northern edge, Little River Road scribbles along a twisting waterway. It brings you to Laurel Creek Road and a one-way, 11-mile loop drive that surrounds historic **Cades Cove**. Preserved and silent now, this area was once home to a mountain community where families lived for generations.

When the land was purchased to save it from environmental disaster in the 1930s, the families were relocated. Several of the community's structures reflecting Appalachian pioneer life were preserved, though, including churches, a gristmill, stores, and cabins. In 1977, what's now known as the **Cades Cove Historic District** was placed on the National Register of Historic Places.

In peak season, the route to Cades Cove can be extremely congested, with traffic grinding to a crawl. At other times of the year, though, you might find the road nearly empty. Either way, allow time to get out and explore the open fields, peaceful woods, and historic structures.

The Oconaluftee, Cades Cove, and Clingmans Dome visitors centers all have exhibits, bookstores, and rangers who offer guidance on programs, activities, classes, and tours. The main **Sugarlands Visitor Center** also has an orientation film and museum.

Programs & Activities. Pick up a copy of the *Smokies Guide*, a quarterly newsletter (also available online) loaded with timely insights on park programs and happenings.

Although the National Park Service does an extraordinary job tending to America's 84 million acres of parkland, some parks, like this one, receive additional assistance from nonprofit organizations. Consider taking a guided interpretive hike with **Friends of**

the Smokies (friendsofthesmokies.org) or volunteer with its **Trails Forever program** to help maintain park trails. The **Great Smoky Mountains Association** (www.smokiesinformation.org), which publishes the *Smokies Guide*, offers cultural activities, night walks, guided hikes, and more.

The **Great Smoky Mountains Institute at Tremont** (865/448-6709, gsmit.org) is an environmental education center offering summer/family camps, naturalist workshops, and hikes. The **Smoky Mountain Field School** (865/974-0150, www.smfs.utk.edu), a University of Tennessee educational outreach program, offers workshops, day hikes, and family adventures conducted by those recognized as experts in their fields.

Lodging. The park has 10 developed campgrounds (reserve through Recreation.gov), all with restroom/shower facilities and some suitable for RVs, though there are no hookups. There's also the very basic **Le Conte Lodge** (865/429-5704, www.lecontelodge.com), which is accessible only by following one of the five hiking trails that lead to the top of Mt. Le Conte (6,593 feet).

Gatlinburg, Pigeon Forge, Sevierville, and Cherokee all have a variety of chain hotels and motels. In Gatlinburg, there's also the 41-suite **Lodge at Buckberry Creek** (961 Campbell Lead Rd., 865/430-8030, buckberrylodge.com) which, with its rustic-elegant "parkitecture" style, has the feel of a park lodge. In Bryson City, the wood-and-stone **Fryemont Inn & Suites** (245 Fryemont St., 828/488-2159, www.fryemontinn.com) rests on a mountain shelf overlooking both the town and the park. Built in 1923, history comes standard in the main lodge, which is listed on the National Register of Historic Places; separate contemporary accommodations are available as well.

BLACK BEARS & YOU

It's estimated that within the park's borders there are two black bears per square mile—that's a population of about 1,500 of them living in the largest protected habitat in the east. Despite vintage home movies showing park guests playfully feeding these creatures, remember that you're no match for them. They're wild and big, weighing on average 100 (females) to 250 (males) pounds, though individuals of more than 600 pounds have been documented here. They can see colors and have a keen sense of smell. They can also run up to 30 miles an hour, climb trees, and swim.

Although it's unlikely you'll encounter bears, rangers (and common sense) will tell you there's little benefit in approaching them—and even less in having them approach you. Brush up on the park's bear-safety guidelines before hitting the trail. If you do have an encounter, keep your distance, using binoculars, a telephoto lens, or a spotting scope to get a closer look. (You'll know you're too close if your presence causes a bear to change its behavior.) And, please don't feed them, directly or indirectly by leaving edibles out around campsites: Bears that have regular access to human food and garbage live only 6 to 7 years, as opposed to their natural life span of 12 to 15 years.

1. Thistle and goldenrod in Cades Cove. **2.** Historic Mingus Mill just north of the Oconaluftee Visitor Center. **3.** Black bear in Cades Cove.

Guadalupe Mountains National Park

TEXAS

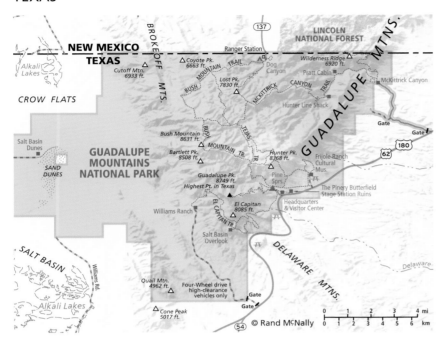

The stark, remote Guadalupe Mountains shoot up from the forbidding West Texas plains. Venture beyond the roadside, though, and you'll find some of the prettiest scenery in the Lone Star State.

About 250 million years ago, a shallow sea covered the arid landscape in the Delaware Basin east of what is now El Paso. The park's namesake mountains began as a reef, but the sea dried up as the climate changed. Geologic uplift thrust them skyward some 60 million years ago. This phenomenon ultimately pushed the mountaintops 3,000 feet above the surrounding Chihuahuan Desert, a transformation that resulted in a dramatic patchwork of dunes, salt flats, wooded ravines, and imposing peaks.

The park annually draws about 200,000 visitors, a fraction of the crowds that descend on big-name parks like Yellowstone and Grand Canyon. It rewards those who explore it with solitude, as well as some surprises: The rugged terrain cradles unexpectedly verdant canyons, islands of life in an often harsh wilderness.

Park Basics

Established: September 30, 1972.
Area: 135 square miles; 86,367 acres.
Best For: Astronomy; Bird-Watching (hummingbirds, peregrine falcons, road runners); Geology; Hiking.
Contact: 915/828-3251, www.nps.gov/gumo.
Getting Oriented: Guadalupe Mountains is in West Texas between US 62/180 and the New Mexico state line. The nearest major airport is El Paso International, 103 miles west of the Pine Springs entrance. Albuquerque International Sunport is 336 miles northeast in New Mexico's largest city.

Pine Springs Visitor Center, just off US 62/180 at the Pine Springs entrance, is the main point of visitor contact. On the north side, **Dog Canyon Ranger Station**, accessed from New Mexico via NM 137, provides backpacking permits and information. The closest towns are **Van Horn, Texas**, 63 miles south of Pine Springs entrance; and, in New Mexico, **Whites City**, 35 miles northeast, and **Carlsbad** (www.carlsbadchamber.com), 56 miles northeast.

Despite the heat, summers are the most popular time to visit; the park cools off between October and April. A good place to visit in tandem with Guadalupe Mountains is **Carlsbad Caverns National Park** (www.nps.gov/cave) in New Mexico, 37 miles northeast of the Pine Springs entrance via US 62/180.

Guadalupe Mountains National Park, TX

Park Highlights

Natural Attractions. The park is centered on the southern stretch of the **Guadalupe Mountains**, the limestone escarpment that dominates the scenery from afar. Rising 8,749 feet above sea level, the summit of **Guadalupe Peak** is the highest point in Texas. Another notable peak is 8,085-foot **El Capitan** (not to be confused with the formation of the same name in Yosemite), the castle-like southern tip of the Guadalupe escarpment. It has been a wayfinding signal for travelers for centuries. Northeast of the peaks, desert ecosystems transition to woodlands in the stunning **Dog and McKittrick canyons**.

About 10 miles east of Dell City on the western fringes of the park, the bright white **gypsum sand dunes** at Salt Basin offer a counterpoint to the mountains and canyons. From the parking lot at the eastern terminus of Williams Road, a short trail gives you an up-close look.

Thanks to the varied ecosystems, about 300 species of birds have been spotted, such as broad-tailed hummingbirds, turkey vultures, and spotted owls. Other park wildlife includes lizards, javelinas, mule deer, and elk.

Trails & Viewpoints. No roads traverse the park, but you can explore more than 80 miles of hiking trails. The difficult **Guadalupe Peak Trail** ascends more than 3,000 feet to the park's high point, aka "The Top of Texas," with one of the park's best views. The trail is a round-trip of 8.5 miles from Pine Springs Campground near the visitors center.

Nicknamed "the most beautiful spot in Texas," **McKittrick Canyon** ranks as one of the park's top hiking destinations, with a trail that rises through woodlands and crosses streams en route to Wallace Pratt Lodge (a moderate, 4.8-mile round trip) and "The Notch" (a difficult, 9.8-mile round-trip). For the trailhead, drive 7 miles northeast from Pine Springs on US 62/180; turn left on McKittrick Road and drive 4 miles. Starting from the visitors center at Pine Springs, the **Pinery Trail** is an easy hike of less than a mile on the former Butterfield Overland Mail stagecoach route. You can still see the ruins of Pinery Station.

Museums & Sites. About 1.5 miles north of the visitors center, the **Frijole Ranch**

Cultural Museum (off US 62/180) explores ranching history with exhibits in a ranch house on the park's east side. Natural springs here create a desert oasis, and you can walk an 0.2-mile paved trail to Manzanita Spring. Sporadically open to visitors, **Pratt Cabin** (also known as Wallace Pratt Lodge) is just off the trail in McKittrick Canyon. It's named for the oil geologist who built it as a getaway in the 1930s before donating his landholdings to the National Park Service in the 1960s.

Programs & Activities. Ranger programs include guided hikes and campfire talks on topics ranging from geology to wildlife several times a week from June to September and sporadically at other times. Star-gazers, take note: This is one of the areas with the least light pollution in Texas, making for amazing views at night.

Lodging. The park has campgrounds but no other accommodations; chains dominate in nearby towns. The nearest places with lodging and other services are Van Horn, Texas, and Whites City, New Mexico. A larger selection of chain motels exists in Carlsbad, New Mexico, near Carlsbad Caverns National Park.

Built in 1930, the restored **Hotel El Capitan** (100 E. Broadway St., Van Horn, 432/283-1220, www.thehotelelcapitan.com) has

Spanish Mission–inspired architecture and 49 comfortable guest rooms.

The park's two campgrounds are 40-site **Pine Springs**, adjacent to the visitors center just off US 62/180, and **Dog Canyon**, a 13-site campground in woodland on the north side. Both are first-come, first-served for tents and RVs. No RV hookups are available.

1. Entering the park. **2.** Gypsum sand dunes at Salt Basin. **3.** El Capitan.

Haleakalā National Park

HAWAII

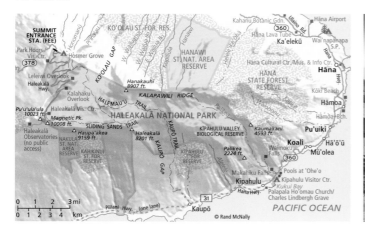

On the 10,023-foot summit of Haleakalā, you can watch the sunrise pierce through fast-moving clouds washing over barren cinder cones—or stare up at thousands of stars in Maui's night sky.

You can also gaze downward at terraced green slopes or across the Pacific to the island of Hawai'i (aka the Big Island). That all these views can be experienced in the same spot is just one of this park's spectacular flights of fancy. Haleakalā is a volcanic wonder of the world that emerged front and center on Maui, one of America's most verdant paradises. And ascending or descending Haleakalā can be just as exciting as the view from the summit itself.

That's not all you can experience here. In another park section, just steps from the ocean at sea level but far from the trappings of the modern world, a different natural aesthetic is on view: a tropical paradise of lush vegetation—including bamboo forests, banyan trees, and palm fronds—all leading up to magnificent waterfalls plunging into dazzling pools.

Haleakalā National Park, HI

Park Basics

Established: August 1, 1916 (part of Hawaii National Park); September 13, 1960 (renamed Haleakalā National Park).
Area: 52 square miles; 33,265 acres.
Best For: Astronomy, Backcountry Camping, Cycling, Geology, Hiking.
Contact: 808/572-4400, www.nps.gov/hale.
Getting Oriented: Haleakalā National Park spreads across eastern **Maui** (www.gohawaii.com) and comprises two districts: Summit (mountainous) and Kīpahulu (coastal). No interior road connects the two districts. The island's main airport, Kahului, is 27 miles (1-hour drive) northwest of the **Summit Entrance** via the Haleakalā Highway (HI 37/377/378). The Park Headquarters Visitor Center is about a mile past the entrance, and the actual summit and Haleakalā Visitor Center are 11 miles farther along the road. From **Kula**, a great park base, it's a 35-minute drive (13 miles) to the Summit Entrance. From the resort areas of **Lahaina** or **Wailea**, the drive to the Summit Entrance takes about 90 minutes.

The **Kīpahulu Entrance** and visitors center, at the park's southeastern tip, are a 50-mile, 3.5-hour drive from the Summit Entrance via HI 378/377/37/31 or a 70-mile, 4.5-hour drive taking HI 378/377/360. The shorter route includes the coastal Pi'ilani Highway; on the longer route, you'll travel the famously scenic, curvaceous Hāna Highway, or "Road to Hāna." The picturesque town of Hāna is 10 miles (45-minute drive) from the Kīpahulu Entrance. Note: All of these roads feature hairpin turns and switchbacks.

Park Highlights

Natural Attractions. Although the air is thin, the panoramas from the **summit of Haleakalā** ("House of the Sun" in Hawaiian) are unforgettable. Lava doesn't actively flow from this volcano, but the vast cinder desert is striking. People routinely obsess over whether to head for the summit at sunrise (reserve at Recreation.gov to enter the park pre-dawn) or at sunset (no reservations required). But it's much more important to just go.

The **Kīpahulu** section is a jungle, featuring waterfalls and rain-forest vegetation. It's very much worth the long drive to get here, though, as you'll experience magnificent coastal views along the way.

Trails, Drives & Viewpoints. Driving up the winding, 12.4-mile **Haleakalā Highway** between the Summit Entrance and the summit is particularly dramatic. Views westward of Maui's swaths of green are replaced by scrub vegetation as you ascend. Even that begins to

fade at the **Leleiwi Overlook** (8,840 feet), where you can see the mountain's bare slopes and cinder cones. Wraparound views of Maui are at **Pu'u'ula'ula** (Red Hill), the 10,023-foot summit of Haleakalā.

At Kīpahulu, the moderate, 4-mile (round trip) **Pīpīwai Trail** to Waimoku Falls is a must. You'll pass a bamboo forest and waterfall-fed pools en route to Waimoku, where the waterfall plunges into another small pool. Kīpahulu also features the **Pools of 'Ohe'o**, which start on one side of Hāna Highway and cascade down to the coast. The pools are actually a series of steps, with each level fed from above by a small waterfall. Note that swimming is currently prohibited, and access to the pools can change due to conditions, including rockslides.

Wilderness hikes are ideal escapes from the crowded summit. From the **Halemau'u Trailhead** (7,990 feet), hike 1.1 miles (moderate) to the Crater Rim for amazing views; then turn back or continue on for longer hikes. At the summit, the **Pā Ka'oao Trail** (less than an 0.5-mile round trip but moderate due to elevation) takes you around the edges of cinder cones at over 10,000 feet.

Programs & Activities. A classic way to experience Haleakalā is to bike down its switchback slopes. Outfitters such as **Haleakala Bike Co**. (808/575-9575, www.bikemaui.com) offer various ways to do this, including picking you up at 3 am to catch the sunrise from the summit and driving you to 6,500 feet so you can bike—or glide, as more braking than hard pedaling is required—the rest of the way down.

The stars from this elevation are clear as a bell. **Maui Stargazing Tours** (808/298-8254,

www.mauistargazing.com) runs group tours—using your own vehicle and the company's equipment—from Kula Lodge to the summit, starting two hours before sunset, and sets out its portable telescope for a stargazing session.

Lodging. Although the park has no lodging except for three wilderness cabins (Recreation.gov) and two backcountry camping options—**Hōlua** and **Palikū** campsites (maximum of 25 people at each)—Maui has many hotels, motels, B&Bs, and rentals.

Choose an upscale suite experience at **Montage Kapalua Bay** (1 Bay Dr., Lahaina, 808/662-6600, www.montagehotels.com) on Maui's luxurious northwest coast or stay at a friendly inn in remote Hāna, such as the oceanfront **Bamboo Inn on Hāna Bay** (4869 Uakea Rd., 808/248-7718, www.bambooinn.com).

To stay as close as possible to the park, consider the **Kula Lodge** (15200 Haleakalā Hwy., 808/878-1535, kulalodge.com) in Kula.

1. Volcanic lava field. **2.** 'Ohe'o Gulch, Kīpahulu. **3.** Pīpīwai Trail. **4.** Oceanfront view at Bamboo Inn on Hāna Bay

Hawai'i Volcanoes National Park

HAWAII

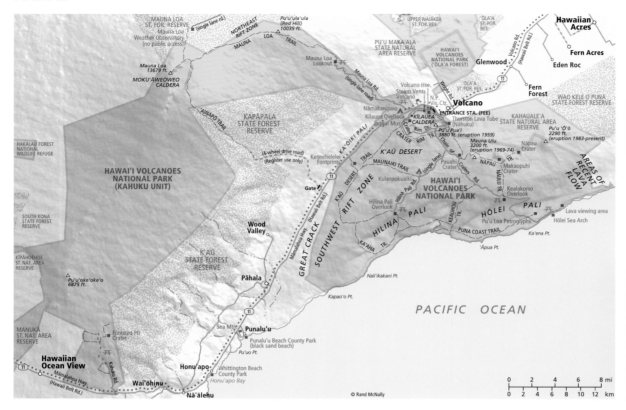

Timing is everything at Hawai'i Volcanoes National Park, where the schedule is dictated by the Kīlauea Volcano. Recently, that schedule changed dramatically when this moderately active volcano became very, very active.

In April and May of 2018, the Earth here began to morph and move in drastic ways: Earthquakes rumbled, fissures opened, craters exploded and collapsed and overflowed. Lava seeped and flowed. Roads and homes were damaged, and the park service closed its main visitors center and many (but not all) areas of the park.

What does this mean for you? Well, it means that a visit here affords you the chance to experience natural history in the making, a rare, real-time opportunity to learn about geological forces. It also means that checking on volcanic conditions—always important prior to a visit here—is now critical to making plans, staying safe, and managing your expectations.

Park Basics

Established: August 1, 1916 (part of Hawaii National Park); September 22, 1961 (renamed Hawaii Volcanoes National Park).
Area: 505 square miles; 323,431 acres.
Best For: Geology, Hiking.
Contact: 808/985-6000, www.nps.gov/havo.
Getting Oriented: Hawai'i Volcanoes National Park sprawls across the southern half of the **Big Island** (www.gohawaii.com), as the island of Hawai'i is informally known. It lies between two main towns, **Kailua-Kona** (West Coast), which is home to Kona International Airport, and Hilo (East Coast), which has both the Hilo International Airport and the **Mokupāpapa Discovery Center** (76 Kamehameha Ave., 808/933-8180, www.papahanaumokuakea.gov/education), one of the places that park rangers set up shop during the eruption.

Highway 11 (HI 11), which runs in and around the park, remained open as a through road (so no stopping for selfies or other beauty shots!) during the eruption. You can follow it southwest from Hilo to the Volcano Art Center in Volcano Village and the park's Kahuku Unit. From Kailua-Kona, follow HI 11 southeast or take the longer northern route through Waimea and Hilo along HI 19 and HI 11. Road and visibility conditions can change, so always check before heading out.

Hawai'i Volcanoes National Park, HI

Park Highlights

Attractions & Activities. Legend holds that Kīlauea's massive caldera (cauldron-like crater) is the home of Pele, the beautiful but capricious goddess of fire and volcanoes. Although she and her volcano have been particularly busy of late, geologists normally label Kīlauea's level of volcanic activity as "moderate." On most (but not all) days prior to the 2018 eruption, you could hike, bike, or drive to or near the summit crater or enjoy volcano flightseeing adventures by small plane or helicopter. As long as there's a high level of volcanic activity at this crater, the area around, below, and above it will be off limits.

③

Check ahead on the status of closed trails and sites such as the original visitors center; the Thomas A. Jagger Museum and Hawaiian Volcano Observatory; the 11-mile Crater Rim Drive, which circumnavigated the cauldron; the 18.8 mile Chain of Craters Road, with all its numbered stops and viewpoints; and the Kīlauea and Kīlauea Iki overlooks.

So, what can you do? First, visit the **Mokupāpapa Discovery Center** (76 Kamehameha Ave., 808/933-8180, www. papahanaumokuakea.gov/education), where rangers can update you on volcanic activity as well as current park offerings and amenities. Operated by the National Oceanic and Atmospheric Administration (NOAA) and situated in a historic downtown Hilo building, the center also has a 3,500-gallon aquarium and interactive exhibits and programs on regional nature, history, culture.

Rangers are also on hand in Volcano Village, just east of the park, at the Niaulani Campus of the **Volcano Art Center** (19-4074 Old Volcano Rd., 808/967-7565, volcanoartcenter. org). In addition to checking on what's

happening with the park and its volcano, you can check out traditional Hawaiian visual and performing arts and crafts—from painting to weaving to hula. The popular **After Dark Near the Park** programs (formerly After Dark in the Park) also take place here.

In the park's **Kahuku Unit**, at Mile Marker 70.5 along HI 11, rangers give talks, conduct guided hikes, and host cultural **'Ike Hana No'eau programs**. Again, though, check on the status of things before heading out. Air-quality and other volcanic conditions might affect hours and programming.

Lodging. Ordinarily, you'd have several in-park lodging options, including the 33-room Volcano House, the Nāmakanipaio and Kulanaokuaiki campgrounds, and backcountry camping sites. All were closed during the 2018 eruption, so check on their current status. You can, however, still stay in Volcano Village. Relax in a rain-forest cabin at **Volcano Village Lodge** (19-4183 Kawailehua Rd., 808/985-9500, www.volcanovillagelodge.com) or enjoy a Hawaiian vibe at **Aloha Happy Place**

farmstead (19-3870 Old Volcano Rd., 808/989-5050, www.alohahappyplace.com).

Hilo and Kailua-Kona have abundant lodging options. The **Inn at Kulaniapia Falls** (100 Kulaniapia Dr., Hilo, 808/935-6789, www. waterfall.net/the-inn) is an eco-friendly but luxurious property with a bamboo garden; rooms, suites, or cottages; and, of course, its very own waterfall. The ultra-contemporary and conveniently located **Hilo Seaside Hotel** (126 Banyan Way, Hilo, 808/935-0821, www.hiloseasidehotel.com) is a slightly more modest option.

At the **Hale Maluhia Country Inn** (76-770 Hualalai Rd., Kailua-Kona, 808/329-1123, www.hawaii-bnb.com), a traditional Hawaiian plantation house south of town, tree frogs sing you to sleep at night, and a lavish breakfast buffet greets you in the morning. A stay at the budget-friendly **Kona Bay Hotel** (75-5739 Ali'i Dr., Kailua-Kona 808/961-5818, unclebilly. com) puts you right in the historic village.

1. Hōlei Sea Arch. **2.** Volcano Village Lodge.
3. Kīlauea Caldera at twilight.

Hot Springs National Park

ARKANSAS

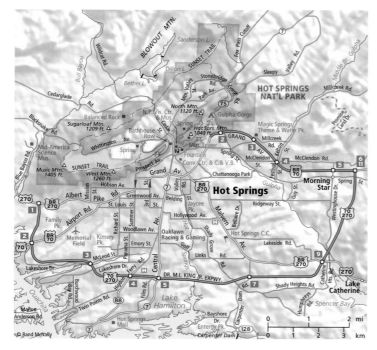

Nothing relieves stress and aching muscles like a long, hot bath. Native Americans knew this well: Even opposing tribes in the Ouachita Mountains agreed that where thermal springs flowed freely, they would visit the "Valley of the Vapors" in peace.

After white settlers claimed this land in central Arkansas, the town of Hot Springs evolved into a Gilded Age resort where tourists arrived to "take the waters" and departed feeling refreshed and rejuvenated by the healing power of naturally heated mineral springs.

Traces of the Gilded Age remain in Hot Springs National Park. On one side of Central Avenue, you're in the county seat. On the other, you're in a National Historic Landmark District, where ornate bathhouses let you relive history. Some of the 1.5 million annual visitors still "take the waters," and depart feeling refreshed and rejuvenated—by the healing power of naturally heated mineral springs.

Park Basics

Established: April 20, 1832 (federal reservation for future recreation); March 4, 1921 (national park).

Area: 8.7 square miles; 5,549 acres.

Best For: Bird-Watching (golden eagles, great horned owls, red-headed woodpeckers, ruby-throated hummingbirds); Hiking; History; Wildlife Watching (coyotes, gray foxes, white-tail deer).

Contact: 501/620-6715, www.nps.gov/hosp.

Getting Oriented: Hot Springs (www. hotsprings.org) is 55 miles west of **Little Rock** (www.littlerock.com) and the Bill and Hillary Clinton National Airport. Take I-30 west to US 70 West and follow signs to the historic district. Near the **Fordyce Bathhouse** (the park visitors center) along Central Avenue's Bathhouse Row, you'll find classic hotels, shops, attractions, and the bathhouses.

Park Highlights

Natural Attractions. Mountains and forests make up most of the park, with **Hot Springs Mountain** (1,040 feet) behind Bathhouse Row the most accessible. A brief drive up Mountain Road leads to the peak, with pullouts along the way. Lookout points above Ouachita Valley offer commanding views, and the 216-foot **Hot Springs Mountain Tower** (501/881-4020, hotspringstower.com) reveals regional

Hot Springs National Park, AR

panoramas. Additional roads and hiking trails lead to the park's other peaks.

The town's 47 **hot springs** flow between 700,000 and 1 million gallons per day, but the springs are primarily diverted into spas and the bathhouses. Some are partially visible, mainly in ever-flowing "jug fountains" on Central Avenue and Reserve Street, where you can fill bottles and jugs (sold nearby). You can see one spring between the park and the Arlington Resort Hotel, with steam rising from the 143-degree waters.

Trails, Drives & Viewpoints. In the late 1800s, activities such as strolls or bike or horse-back rides along mountain trails and carriage roads were considered therapeutic enhancements to soaking in (or drinking) mineral-rich waters. Today, between the Fordyce and Maurice bathhouses, stairs lead to the **Grand Promenade** that runs parallel to Central Avenue. Completed in the 1950s and decorated with multihued bricks, this half-mile

walkway has views of Central Avenue and the historic downtown.

The park's 26 miles of hiking trails provide more natural pursuits. The 23 trails range from the easy, 528-foot **Fountain Trail** to the strenuous 1.5-mile **Mountain Top Trail**. The longest, the 10-mile **Sunset Trail**, follows the spine of the mountains to the park's highest elevations and farthest reaches, passing wildflowers and wildlife along the way; you can walk it in sections.

Museums & Sites. The park's focal point is the eight bathhouses on Central Avenue's **Bathhouse Row**, the first built in 1892 and the most recent in 1923, each replacing far more rustic structures that served an earlier era of guests. At the resort's peak in the late 1940s, more than 1 million visitors annually savored baths in the heated waters, earning Hot Springs its reputation as the "Great American Spa."

At the circa-1912 **Fordyce Bathhouse**, now the visitors center and a must-see, you can learn about the town's quirky history, from the Quapaw Indians to 20th-century gangsters who combined relaxation with bootlegging and gambling. Ranger-led and self-guided tours provide a nostalgic look at the early days of exercise, including a vintage gymnasium with its pulleys and medicine balls and immaculately restored tile baths.

At Central Avenue's restored **Buckstaff Baths** (www.buckstaffbaths.com), you can still enjoy thermal mineral baths, old-fashioned steam cabinets, and Swedish massages. Nearby, the privately operated **Quapaw Baths & Spa** (quapawbaths.com) offers thermal baths, massages, facials, reflexology, and aromatherapy in a restored setting that recalls the Gilded Age.

Not every Central Avenue bathhouse is still a bathhouse. Following World War II, advances in modern medicine made "taking the waters" an anachronism. The park's main gift shop is in the Lamar; the Ozark is an event space that presents works by artists-in-residence; the Superior has been renovated into a microbrewery and restaurant; the Hale and the Maurice await an entrepreneur's vision.

Programs & Activities. In summer, rangers lead walking tours from the Fordyce Bathhouse to the Grand Promenade, and then by Bathhouse Row and back to the Fordyce, discussing the area's unique geology. Other activities include campfire programs at the Gulpha Gorge campground.

Lodging. The **Gulpha Gorge Campground** on the far side of Hot Springs Mountain has 40 full hook-up spaces for RVs. You can also park your vehicle and pitch a tent.

In Hot Springs, the iconic 1924 **Arlington Resort Hotel & Spa** (239 Central Ave., 501/623-7771, www.arlingtonhotel.com) was sold in 2017, with restoration planned. **Prospect Place Bed & Breakfast** (472 Prospect Ave., 501/777-3164, www.472prospectplace.com) provides attractive rooms in a Queen Anne–style home four blocks from Central Avenue.

1. Waterfall in the park. **2.** Bathhouses in the park. **3.** A Hot Springs National Park view.

Isle Royale National Park

MICHIGAN

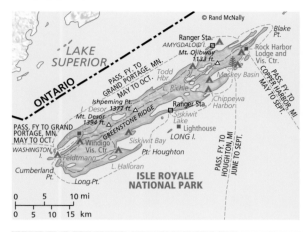

The largest island in North America's largest lake, Isle Royale is a massive slab of volcanic rock jutting out of Lake Superior and home to an isolated wilderness of dense forest, untouched wetlands, and rocky shoreline.

Just 15 miles from mainland shores but a world away, the park is a hiker's and boater's paradise with no roads, no cars, and little development. At 45 miles long and 9 miles across at its widest, the island is ideal for 5- to 7-night backpacking expeditions, among the most popular ways to explore the park.

Remote Isle Royale is the least visited park in the lower 48, attracting only about 20,000 adventurers annually. You won't see many others on the trails: a good thing. A boat is the only way to reach many areas, so it's common to rent one or hail a water taxi to go even farther off the beaten path.

Isle Royale National Park, MI

Park Basics

Established: April 3, 1940.
Area: 893 square miles; 571,790 acres (133,782 acres of land; the rest is water).
Best For: Backcountry Camping; Bird-Watching (bald eagles, loons); Boating; Fishing; Hiking; Wildlife Watching (foxes, moose, wolves).
Contact: 906/482-0984, www.nps.gov/isro.
Getting Oriented: North of Michigan's Upper Peninsula but closer to Minnesota and Canada, Isle Royale is accessible only by seaplane, ferry, or private boat. **Isle Royale Seaplanes** (21125 Royce Rd., 906/483-4991, isleroyaleseaplanes.com) offers flights from Hancock, Michigan, and Grand Marais, Minnesota, to both Windigo and Rock Harbor on Isle Royale. Most travelers fly to Houghton County Memorial Airport in Calumet, Michigan, via O'Hare International Airport in Chicago (411 miles south) or Minneapolis–St. Paul International Airport (378 miles southwest), and then take a ferry or seaplane.

Seasonal ferries operated by the park and its concessionaires depart from **Houghton** (73 miles south of the park, www.keweenaw.info) and **Copper Harbor** (56 miles southeast, www.keweenaw.info) on Michigan's Upper Peninsula, as well as from **Grand Portage, Minnesota** (22 miles west, www.visitcookcounty.com). Depending on the destination, a one-way ferry trip takes 90 minutes to 6 hours, versus a 35-minute one-way flight.

Ferries arrive at docks on either end of Isle Royale: **Rock Harbor**, near the eastern end, is the most developed area and has lodging, dining, and a visitors center. On the western side, **Windigo** also has a visitors center as well as a store, cabins, and a campground. A third park visitors center is in the mainland town of **Houghton**. Park facilities are typically open June through September; it's best to visit near the end of summer, after a light freeze takes care of the notorious mosquitoes.

Park Highlights

Natural Attractions. The park is an archipelago that includes Isle Royale and about 400 smaller islands. **Greenstone Ridge** runs northeast–southwest through the heart of Isle Royale. Named for chlorastrolite, the green semiprecious stone that's often visible on its surface, the ridge tops 1,000 feet in places. At 1,394 feet, **Mt. Desor** is the island's high point.

The Palisades, the rocky outcroppings and cliffs at the island's far eastern tip, just beyond Rock Harbor, culminate in **Scoville Point**—land's end—surrounded on three sides by Lake Superior. About 10 miles west of Rock Harbor, **Moskey Basin** is a popular scenic area; rocks on this idyllic harbor are speckled with multihued lichen. Isle Royale has several sizable lakes; in the biggest, **Siskiwit Lake**, you can glimpse **Ryan Island**: the largest island in the largest lake on the largest island in the largest lake in North America.

Resident **wildlife** includes beavers, foxes, turtles, and frogs—and a cyclical predator-prey relationship between its moose and gray (timber) wolves. The populations are uniquely related—after a moose population boom, wolves increase in number and then cull the moose. If moose numbers decline too much, wolf extinction could occur.

Trails & Viewpoints. The park has 165 miles of trails. Most backpackers plan a multiday hike of 6–8 miles a day. The moderate **Greenstone Ridge Trail** runs northeast–southwest for 42 miles across nearly the island's entire length, and trails on **Feldtmann Ridge** and **Minong Ridge** offer options on the southwest and north sides, respectively.

From Rock Harbor, the moderate, 4.2-mile hike to **Scoville Point** and back has lake panoramas. In the Windigo area, the **Windigo Nature Trail** is an easy, 1.2-mile loop; the moderate, 9.4-mile **Huginnin Cove Loop** traverses wetlands on the way to views of Canada. Climb the stairs at the **Ojibway Fire Tower**, a 3.5-mile round-trip trek from Daisy Farm Campground, for stellar views.

Museum. Across the harbor from Daisy Farm Campground, **Rock Harbor Lighthouse**, built in 1855, features exhibits on the island's maritime history. You can access it only by boat and 0.25-mile hike.

Programs & Activities. Rangers give lectures and lead hikes at Windigo, Daisy Farm, and Rock Harbor; they also conduct presentations aboard the ferry from Houghton. **Rock Harbor Lodge** (906/337-4993, www.rockharborlodge.com) offers canoe, kayak, and boat rentals as well as sightseeing tours, water taxis, and fishing charters.

Lodging. The park's one hotel is the 1950s-era, lakefront **Rock Harbor Lodge** (906/337-4993, www.rockharborlodge.com) on the east side; the concessionaire also has 20 slick cottages in the woods near Rock Harbor and a pair of spartan camper cabins at Windigo. On the Michigan mainland, the **Franklin Square Inn** (820 Shelden Ave., Houghton, 906/487-1700, houghtonlodging.com) is a full-service hotel with a downtown location on the Keweenaw Waterway. Copper Harbor in Michigan and Grand Portage, Minnesota, also offer a variety of overnight accommodations.

Isle Royale's 36 **campgrounds** have tent sites, a water source, and outhouses; many on the shoreline have shelters and picnic tables. Campsites are first-come, first-served for groups of 6 or fewer. Reservations are required for groups of 7 to 10 people; groups larger than 10 must split into smaller groups.

3

1. Scenic overview. **2.** Rocky shoreline. **3.** Kayaking in the park.

Joshua Tree National Park

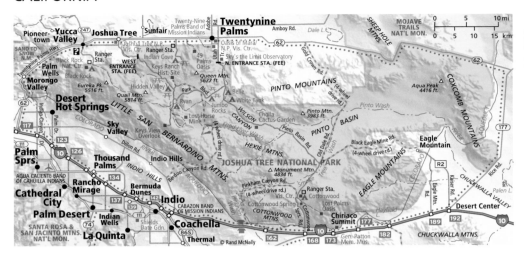

Trees that aren't trees. Boulders that look like skulls, spires, and arches. A vast, dry plateau hiding an oasis. Snowcapped mountain views from a hot desert plain. Welcome to weird, wild, and wonderful Joshua Tree National Park.

You'll know that you're in a unique natural landscape once you've gotten your first glimpse of the Dr. Seuss–like Joshua tree—actually, a type of flowering yucca plant with spiky, bushy orbs of bayonet-shaped leaves and a hairy, spiny bark.

The park's desert eco-system might seem totally devoid of any life. But the longer you spend in this Southern California park, the more you'll begin to notice: hundreds of species of birds; bighorn sheep; cacti with flowers in every color of the rainbow; piñon pine and cottonwood trees; and, of course, your fellow humans, jumping from boulder to boulder, gazing up at the night sky, and generally being awed by this desert masterpiece.

Joshua Tree National Park, CA

Park Basics

Established: August 10, 1936 (national monument); October 31, 1994 (national park).
Area: 1,235 square miles; 790,636 acres.
Best For: Astronomy, Climbing, Hiking, Horseback Riding, Mountain Biking.
Contact: 760/367-5500, www.nps.gov/jotr.
Getting Oriented: Joshua Tree's West Entrance Station and **Joshua Tree Visitor Center** are 148 miles east of Los Angeles International Airport via I-10 and Twentynine Palms Highway (CA 62). Smaller airports serving the area include Palm Springs International, 42 miles west. The park has two other entrances: the North Entrance Station and **Oasis of Mara Visitor Center**, a few miles south of the town of Twentynine Palms, and the South Entrance and **Cottonwood Visitor Center**, near Cottonwood Spring, 26 miles east of Indio on I-10.

Palm Springs (www.visitpalmsprings.com) can be a convenient base, but there are plenty of services along CA 62 north of the park in the towns of **Yucca Valley** (www.yucca-valley.org), **Joshua Tree** (www.joshuatreechamber.org), and **Twentynine Palms** (www.ci.twentynine-palms.ca.us). The desert here is extremely hot June through September; try to visit October through May.

Park Highlights

Natural Attractions. Joshua Tree's striking scenery is due in no small part to the fact that it stretches between parts of two famous deserts: the higher-in-elevation Mojave to the north, and the lower-in-elevation Colorado to the south. In the north, fields of both clumped and lone Joshua trees are everywhere but are especially striking in the park's northwestern section, while bizarre boulder formations dot the northeastern section.

The southern section, in and around Cottonwood Visitor Center, occasionally closes due to flash floods and other natural phenomena (as well as road construction). It's worth the time to explore some excellent trails through the cottonwoods. This is also a premier birding spot; more than 250 species have been recorded in the park.

Trails, Drives & Viewpoints. The 25-mile drive along scenic **Park Boulevard**, which connects the two northern park entrances, can be done in 40 minutes without stopping. Don't do that, since you'd miss, well, virtually everything, including the curvaceous **Arch Rock** (an easy 0.5-mile loop walk); the pockmarked mounds of **Skull Rock** (a moderate 1.5-mile loop trail); **Barker Dam** (an easy 1.3-mile loop where you might see

bighorn sheep); and the sublime **Oasis of Mara**, an 0.5-mile stroll behind the visitors center of the same name.

Sunset is a no-brainer: **Keys View** (Keys View Rd., 20 minutes off Park Blvd.), an overlook at 5,100 feet, gives you a view westward across Coachella Valley—particularly stunning when the sun dips behind the snow-covered San Jacinto Mountains. Bring your camera, tripod, and binoculars: It's worth the trouble, especially to capture iconic Joshua trees in the foreground of those burnished desert sunsets.

Museum. Head down to **Keys Ranch**, built by ranchers and homesteaders Bill and Frances Keys. They raised five children, planted an orchard, built several structures, and lived on-site for 60 years until 1969. Ranch tours, the only way to see this spectacular piece of desert history, require tickets that you purchase at the Oasis of Mara Visitor Center on the morning of the tour.

Programs & Activities. Joshua Tree's ranger-led programs mesh perfectly with what the park is all about. They include the **Joshua Tree Rocks!** geology walk (1 mile, near Skull Rock), an **oasis walk** (easy 0.5-mile stroll from the Oasis of Mara Visitor Center), the **I Speak for the Trees** walk (easy 0.4-mile walk along the Cap Rock Nature Trail), and the more strenuous, steep 3-mile hike to **Mastodon Peak**. Check the park's calendar for changes and additions.

(3)

After sunset, you can appreciate the spectacular, star-filled skies that have made Joshua Tree a designated International Dark Sky Park. The **Night Sky Festival**, usually held in early November, features free talks and solar viewing by day and astronomy programs by night. The park's geology makes it a favorite destination for rock climbing; **Joshua Tree Rock Climbing School** (760/366-4745, www.joshuatreerockclimbing.com) offers courses for all levels. Joshua Tree's backcountry roads and trails are also perfect for mountain biking and horseback riding.

Lodging. The park's 9 campgrounds are so popular that spots are hard to come by. Make reservations at **Black Rock** (99 sites) and **Indian Cove** (101 sites) through Recreation.gov; other sites are first-come, first-served.

There are no lodges within Joshua Tree, but the classic "California Desert Motel" trope is alive and well, especially along the 25-mile stretch of CA 62 between Yucca Valley and Twentynine Palms. Relax by the pool at the funky **Joshua Tree Inn** (61259 Twentynine Palms Hwy., Joshua Tree, 760/366-1188, www.joshuatreeinn.com). Another option is to stay in a quaint adobe or wood cabin at the **29 Palms Inn** (73950 Inn Ave., Twentynine Palms, 760/367-3505, www.29palmsinn.com); do dine at its excellent restaurant. You can also head south to the hip, mid-century-modern oasis of Palm Springs for more posh lodgings.

1. Climbing. **2.** Joshua tree landscape. **3.** Camping in the park. **4.** Joshua Tree Inn.

(4)

Katmai National Park & Preserve

ALASKA

This Southwest Alaska wilderness is truly a land of fire and ice, with both glaciers and volcanoes. It's also the land of the bear, not the automobile: getting here involves travel by plane, boat, or boot.

The violent 1912 eruption of Katmai's Novarupta Volcano—part of the Aleutian Range and within the Earth's notoriously active Ring of Fire—transformed the landscape here radically. It also resulted in Katmai being established as a national monument in 1918. The 20th century's largest eruption released 30 *times* the magma that Washington State's Mt. St. Helens did in 1980. Over a century later, the impact is still visible in craters, lava domes, and other active features in the aptly named Valley of Ten Thousand Smokes.

But perhaps Katmai's biggest draw is watching bears feast on the salmon that spawn in its waters. The Alaska Peninsula is thought to have fewer human inhabitants than it does brown

Katmai National Park, AK

bears (aka grizzly bears), and this park protects an estimated 2,200 of them.

Park Basics

Established: September 24, 1918 (national monument); December 2, 1980 (national park and preserve).
Area: 6,395 square miles; 4,093,067 acres.
Best For: Backcountry Camping; Bird-Watching (bald eagles, waterfowl, puffins); Fishing; Hiking; Kayaking; Wildlife Watching (bears, moose, wolves).
Contact: 907/246-3305, www.nps.gov/katm.
Getting Oriented: Katmai is on the Alaska Peninsula and—like Lake Clark, its sister park to the north—along Cook Inlet southwest of Anchorage (Katmai by 290 miles, Lake Clark by 120). Air taxis from Ted Stevens Anchorage International Airport fly to gateway towns for transfers to various in-park destinations.

King Salmon, 5 miles west of Katmai, has a two-runway airport and a visitors center.
Brooks Camp, 30 miles east of King Salmon by air, is the park's developed and most popular area, with a visitors center (early June–mid-Sept.) and a campground. King Salmon lodges offer outdoor excursions and packages and are great travel resources. So is the main park concessionaire, **Katmailand** (907/243-5448, www.katmailand.com), which oversees in-park amenities.

Park Highlights

Natural Attractions & Activities. To the west, Katmai features large lakes created by dams that were themselves formed long ago by moraines (sediment and rock deposited by glaciers). In the east, the forest along Cook Inlet features entirely different trees—hemlock, spruce, and cedar among them—than Alaska's inland forests.

In between these two regions, it's all about volcanoes. The 6,715-foot **Mt. Katmai**, about 6 miles from Novarupta, partially collapsed after the latter's big bang, leaving a crater lake on the summit. The unearthly landscape of the **Valley of Ten Thousand Smokes** is filled with ash, also from Novarupta's 1912 eruption, and named for the countless vents releasing steam from the still-smoldering landscape.

Katmai has less than 5 miles of maintained trails but is a popular **hiking** destination nonetheless. One of the options from Brooks Camp is the **Brooks Falls Trail**, an easy 2.4-mile round-trip hike featuring a waterfall that blocks salmon runs, making this a great bear-viewing area. Many experienced hikers follow unmaintained routes, traversing riverbanks or tundra. Backcountry campers should consider the moderate, 23-mile one-way **Valley of Ten Thousand Smokes hike**.

Brown bears (aka grizzly bears) and fisherfolk alike are drawn to the park's waterways, laden not only with sockeye and other salmon but also rainbow trout, Arctic char, and other varieties. The **Brooks River** is a great place for both bear-watching, with safely elevated viewing stations at Brooks Camp, and fishing.

Sites & Programs. Katmai is open year-round, but peak season is early June through mid-September, when Brooks Camp amenities are open. The **Brooks Camp Cultural Site Exhibit**, a short walk from the visitors center, features a replica of a prehistoric house excavated in the 1960s. In summer, rangers here offer a guided site tour daily as well as other programs, walks, and talks. For the latest offerings, check the park's official newspaper, *The Novarupta*.

If you're not an experienced outdoorsperson, it's best to explore the park on a guided trip with a lodge or outfitter. The park's main concessionaire, **Katmailand** (907/243-5448, www.katmailand.com), offers **fishing trips** as well as narrated **Valley of Ten Thousand Smokes bus trips**, with either round trip or one-way options, in case you want to get in some hiking. It also operates the three **bear-viewing** platforms at Brooks Camp, so you can safely get a look at these charismatic beasts. Several lodges in King Salmon also offer guided trips.

Lodging. Katmai has one developed **campground** open May to September at Brooks Camp (Recreation.gov); first-come, first-served **camping huts** at the Valley of Ten Thousand Smokes; and endless backcountry-camping opportunities. The in-park **Brooks Lodge** (907/243-5448, www.katmailand. com), operational since 1950 and originally developed as a fishing camp, offers basic, bunk-bed cabins in a wooded area above the Brooks River.

Katmailand also manages two small, fishing-oriented lodges: **Grosvenor Lodge**, with 3 cabins for 6 guests, and **Kulik Lodge**, with 10 cabins on the river of the same name. Demand for in-park lodging outstrips supply; reservations are awarded via an annual lottery.

King Salmon is home to several private lodges. These include **Alaska's Gold Creek Lodge** (907/246-4653, www.alaskasgoldcreeklodge. com), which features log cabins, and **King Salmon Lodge** (907/246-8643, www. kingsalmonlodge.com), which has guest rooms and cabins. If you prefer to base yourself along the coast, look into the **Katmai Wilderness Lodge** (907/486-8767, www. katmai-wilderness.com), which is across Cook Inlet from Kodiak Island. All of these properties offer guided fishing, bear-watching, and other expeditions and packages.

1. Brown bear and gulls in the water. **2.** Aerial view from sea plane. **3.** Valley of Ten Thousand Smokes. **4.** Hallo Bay.

Kenai Fjords National Park

ALASKA

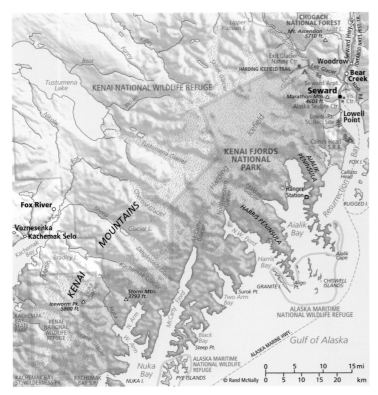

(1)

Visiting Kenai Fjords National Park can spark mixed emotions. The majestic sight of more than three dozen glaciers flowing from the Harding Icefield inspire awe— but also concern about the effects of the changing climate on those shrinking glaciers.

You can consider the issues of climate change at home, but while you're visiting the park, turn your attention to the grandeur of this world of land and sea. A forest road and hiking trails lead to Exit Glacier, one of the park's most popular destinations.

Kayaks, paddleboards, and tour boats help you explore waterways that often bring Kenai Fjords' wildlife into view. Orcas and humpback whales populate the waters; on land you might observe moose and bears. Meanwhile, adaptable seals are at home on shore and in the sea.

Mountains, ocean, and ice converge at Kenai Fjords, one of the state's most accessible national parks. It's a trio that presents Alaska at its natural best.

Park Basics

Established: December 1, 1978 (national monument); December 2, 1980 (national park).
Area: 1,047 square miles; 669,984 acres.
Best For: Bird-Watching (bald eagles, herons, owls, puffins); Hiking; Kayaking; Wildlife Watching (black and brown bears, humpback whales, moose, orcas, sea lions).
Contact: 907/422-0500, nps.gov/kefj.
Getting Oriented: Kenai Fjords is on the Kenai Peninsula in south-central Alaska. The closest major airport is Ted Stevens Anchorage International, 126 miles north of the park entrance. Drive south from Anchorage along Seward Highway (AK 1/9), a National Scenic Byway, to **Seward** (www.seward.com) at the

Kenai Fjords National Park, AK

park's northeastern tip. Another way to see the park is to join a day or multiday summer cruise to Resurrection Bay and Seward.

The park's **visitors center** (1212 4th Ave., Seward), near the harbor and outside the park, has an introductory film. It's 11 miles from the center to **Exit Glacier Nature Center**. **Exit Glacier Shuttle** (907/224-9225, www. exitglaciershuttle.com) transports people without cars into the park via Exit Glacier Road, the only paved road. Seward has hotels and plenty of amenities if you're spending a number of days in the area.

Park Highlights

Natural Attractions. The park's more than 1,000 square miles are roughly divided among the accessible **Exit Glacier** area; the

(2)

backcountry's steeply pitched, glacially formed, coastal fjords; and the challenging wilderness of the **Harding Icefield**, which covers 700 square miles of the Kenai Mountains in glacial snow and ice. Created more than 23,000 years ago, the icefield is thousands of feet thick and spreads to 38 glaciers in the park, the most visible being Exit Glacier. This mountain of blue ice is a monumental vision, albeit one that is fast receding due to climate change.

To help you visit the park's fjords and coastline, **Major Marine Tours** (907/274-7300, majormarine.com) and **Kenai Fjords Tours** (888/478-3346, kenaifjords.com) offer half- and full-day cruises. Park rangers board the vessels of Major Marine to provide commentary about the park, its landscape, and the marine life (sea otters, sea lions, orcas, whales, dolphins), wildlife (wolves, moose, coyotes, bears), and birdlife (191 species including bald eagles, falcons, puffins, murres). On other vessels, the captains narrate.

Trails & Viewpoints. Exit Glacier Road leads to the park's nature center, which is the trailhead for three hikes. **Glacier View Trail**, a mile-long loop, begins and ends at the nature center. The 2.4-mile (round-trip) **Edge of the Glacier Trail**, considered moderately strenuous because of the elevation gain, leads to the edge of Exit Glacier. The most demanding—a strenuous 8-mile, 8-hour round-trip on the **Harding Icefield Trail**—goes above the tree line to reveal views of Exit Glacier, followed by higher elevations and views of the Harding Icefield itself. Since bears enjoy the berries that grow along the longest trail, don't walk alone.

Ask rangers about bear safety measures and trail conditions.

Programs & Activities. Several times a day in summer, rangers lead 90-minute walks from the nature center to Exit Glacier, stopping at Glacier View Lookout and then following the trail to the Edge of the Glacier. Rangers also present a 20-minute midday talk at the Exit Glacier pavilion. Although it's doubtful you'll visit Exit Glacier in winter (Nov.–May, when snow causes road closures), you could reach it via snowmobile, dogsled, cross-country skis, or snowshoes.

On Sundays in summer, youngsters can participate in interactive, hour-long **Junior Ranger Walks** that depart from the visitors center to explore the rocky beach and fjord ecosystem of Resurrection Bay. Participants earn a Junior Fjord Ranger patch.

Kayaking and paddleboarding are popular on Bear Glacier Lagoon, about 12 miles southwest of Seward, where giant icebergs have calved from the park's largest glacier. Transportation services such as **Miller's Landing** (907/331-3113, www.millerslandingak.com) or **Seward Water Taxi** (907/362-4101, www.sewardwatertaxi.com) can take you there, and outfitters can supply gear. Paddling conditions are also good on Aialik Bay or Northwestern Lagoon, both reachable by water taxi but at a steep price due to the distance. Much of the park's 400 miles of rugged coastline are subject to the Gulf of Alaska's wind and waves, so download a kayaking map from the Kenai Fjords website, and check with rangers about destinations before setting out.

Lodging. Kenai Fjords has only limited options, but Seward offers a wide range of accommodations. The park has a single 12-site, tent-only **campground** (no reservations) near the Exit Glacier Nature Center and three public-use **cabins** (Recreation.gov), two in coastal areas and one near the edge of the Harding Icefield. Many guests simply camp on beaches by the fjords, adhering to the strict pack-in, pack-out policy.

Among options in Seward are hotels such as **Harbor 360 Hotel** (1412 4th Ave., 907/865-6224, harbor360hotel.com), B&Bs like **Bear Lake Lodgings** (33820 Bear Lake Rd., 907/224-2288, www.bearlakelodgings.com), and cabins including **Seavey's Ididaride Abode Well Cabins** (12672 Old Exit Glacier Rd., 907/224-8607, ididaride.com).

1. Hiking the Harding Icefield Trail. **2.** Sea lion.
3. Breaching humpback whale. **4.** Exit Glacier.

Kobuk Valley National Park

ALASKA

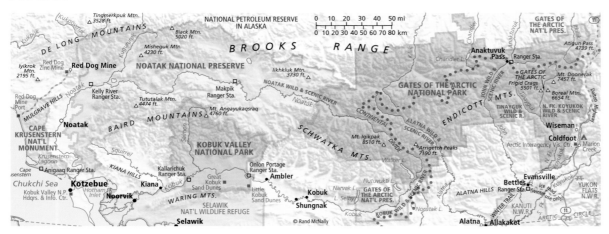

Kobuk Valley is a remnant of the last Ice Age—pristine, ancient, remote. No trails or roads enter or traverse it, and only about 15,000 people visit annually. How do they get here? By bush plane, of course!

The Kobuk River, renowned for its fishing, winds through the park for about 60 miles. Along its southern bank is an unexpected spectacle: 25 square miles of lofty dunes, vestiges of rocks ground to sand by retreating glaciers some 28,000 years ago. It's the largest and most accessible of the park's three dune fields, where summer temperatures climb as high as 100 degrees Fahrenheit.

Don't let the desert-like conditions fool you. This is still the Arctic, where winter has seen a record low of -50 degrees. In spring, plentiful insects attract migratory birds from as far away as Antarctica. In spring and fall, the Western Arctic caribou herd migrates through the valley to and from its Brooks Range breeding grounds.

Park Basics

Established: December 1, 1978 (national monument); December 2, 1980 (national park).
Area: 2,735 square miles, 1,750,716 acres.
Best For: Backcountry camping; Boating; Fishing; Hiking; Wildlife Watching (bears, caribou, wolves).
Contact: 907/442-3890, www.nps.gov/kova.
Getting Oriented: Kobuk Valley is 75 miles

Kobuk Valley National Park, AK

inland from the Chukchi Sea and about 30 miles west of its enormous sister park, Gates of the Arctic. Although adventurers on multiweek backpacking trips do trek or boat in, most visitors arrive aboard 3- to 10-passenger, park-sanctioned air taxis (aka bush planes). These typically fly from **Anchorage** to the village of **Kotzebue** (80 miles southwest of the park) or from **Fairbanks** to **Bettles** (roughly 200 miles east near Gates of the Arctic) before continuing into the park. Flights can be bumpy, but the views are fantastic!

Kobuk Valley's headquarters is at the **Northwest Arctic Heritage Center** in Kotzebue, with seasonal ranger stations along the Kobuk River at **Kallarichuk** (on the park's west side) and **Onion Portage** (on the park's east side). The **Arctic Interagency Visitor Center** (907/678-5209 summer only) in Coldfoot, southeast of Gates of the Arctic on the famous Dalton Highway, is a good source of information for both parks and surrounding public lands.

Park Highlights

Natural Attractions. The park's broad wetland valley, full of glacial silt, is a transition zone between boreal forest and arctic tundra. The eponymous Kobuk River, an officially designated Wild and Scenic River, runs 61 miles through the park. It and other waterways and lakes are filled with a variety of fish, including Arctic char, lake trout, northern pike, and sheefish as well as Chinook, king, pink, humpback, sockeye, and red salmon.

The unexpected star attraction, though, is the **Great Kobuk Sand Dunes**. At 25 square miles, it's the Arctic's largest active dune field and one of three in the park. It's also fairly accessible along the Kobuk River, though some air-taxi services also fly in, landing right on the sand. This remnant of retreating Ice Age glaciers features dunes up to 100 feet high and looks like something you'd find in the Mojave Desert—or even on Mars. Indeed, scientists affiliated with NASA have considered studying this dune field, which is thought to be a good facsimile for Martian landscapes.

Originally the dune field was much larger. But, over the millennia and in a process that continues today, plants took hold, slowly transforming the terrain from one of desert-like sands to one of grasses, shrubs, lichen, and trees. The area in and around the dunes attracts abundant wildlife, everything from porcupines and foxes to wolves and black or grizzly bears. The Western Arctic caribou herd also traverses the dune field on its biannual migrations.

Activities. Park headquarters at the **Northwest Arctic Heritage Center** in Kotzebue offers a changing roster of ranger-led talks, workshops, and outings. Beyond this, though, Kobuk Valley is a place for intrepid hikers, paddlers, and those who enjoy fishing. There are no developed trails or roads of any kind to or within the park. Backpackers traverse rugged terrain that includes overgrown thicket, sand dunes, and fragile tundra. It's slow going, with 5 miles considered a good target distance for a day. Indeed, many visitors prefer floating in and along the Kobuk River.

(3)

Although a low of -50 degrees and a high of 100 (in the dune fields!) have been recorded, average monthly temperatures range from -8 to 80 degrees. Peak season is June to September, with 24 hours of daylight in June and July. Despite spectacular Northern Lights shows, very few visitors come in winter. For logistical and safety reasons, a visit here at any time requires planning and preparation. Look into hiring an outfitter for a guided trip.

Fairbanks-based **Arctic Wild** (907/479-8203, arcticwild.com) offers backpacking, boating, and custom trips. Some of their popular outings feature canoeing, fly fishing, camping in the dune fields, and Kobuk Valley/Gates of the Arctic combination trips. They also offer caribou-migration excursions.

Lodging. Backcountry camping is your only in-park lodging option. In the village of

Bettles, where you can board air taxis to either Kobuk Valley or Gates of the Arctic, **Bettles Lodge** (907/692-5111, bettleslodge.com) has a definitively Alaskan vibe and year-round accommodations.

In Kotzebue, the sleek, contemporary **Nullaġvik Hotel** (907/442-3331, www.nullagvikhotel.com) is a good place to bunk down before or after a Kobuk Valley adventure. It can help you arrange both outdoor and cultural activities. West of Kobuk Valley, **Kobuk River Lodge** (907/445-5235, kobukriverlodge.com) offers lodging and outdoor packages that feature fishing, hiking, and boating trips.

1. Caribou. **2.** Kobuk River. **3.** Great Kobuk Sand Dunes.

Lake Clark National Park & Preserve

ALASKA

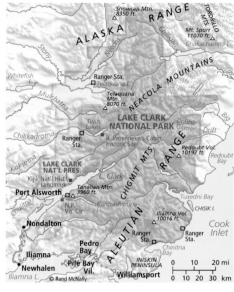

The landscape of Lake Clark is an artful, backcountry jumble of coastal salt marshes, boreal forest, mountains and volcanoes, alpine tundra, and freshwater waterways and lakes, including the park's long, lanky namesake.

Each of these southwestern Alaska ecosystems attracts unique wildlife ranging from caribou, moose, and Dall sheep to waterfowl, seabirds, and song birds to predatory raptors, bears, and wolves. Salmon are the stars of the show, though. Lake Clark was

established to preserve their habitats, and, each July and August, hundreds of thousands of them spawn here.

Protecting this wild land is a much older tradition, however. Indigenous peoples first settled here at the end of the last Ice Age, roughly 14,000 years ago. Their descendants continue to be the model stewards of a wild place where everything in nature has a spirit and where fishing, hunting, and gathering are conducted respectfully and with great reverence.

Lake Clark National Park, AK

Park Basics

Established: December 1, 1978 (national monument); December 2, 1980 (national park and preserve).
Area: 6,297 square miles; 4,030,006 acres.
Best For: Backcountry Camping; Bird-Watching (bald eagles, waterfowl, puffins); Fishing; Hiking; Kayaking; Wildlife Watching (bears, moose, wolves).
Contact: 907/781-2218, www.nps.gov/lacl.
Getting Oriented: Lake Clark and Katmai, its sister park to the south, are both along Cook Inlet's northwestern shore to the southwest of Anchorage (Lake Clark by 120 miles, Katmai by 290). There aren't any roads to or within either park. Air taxis from Ted Stevens Anchorage International Airport fly to gateway towns for transfers—often by floatplane—to other destinations.

In Lake Clark's southwestern quadrant, inland and along the southern shore of its namesake lake, **Port Alsworth** is home to the park's visitors center (open late May–mid-Sept.), two airstrips, and several lodges. Many visitors fly from here north to **Twin Lakes**, site of Dick Proenneke's cabin.

Chinitna Bay, on Cook Inlet, also has a seasonal ranger station and is accessible via air taxis, which land on the beach, or by boat from Homer on the Kenai Peninsula and 50 miles west across Cook Inlet's sometimes rough waters. North of the bay, **Silver Salmon Creek**, which has a seasonal ranger station, and **Crescent Lake** are known for their fishing and bear viewing.

Park Highlights

Natural Attractions & Activities. Lake Clark is open year-round, but most visitors come between June and October when the weather is warmer, and more amenities are open. If you're not an experienced outdoorsperson, book a **guided trip** with a local air-taxi service, lodge, or outfitter; the park website lists more than 80 licensed concessionaires.

Lake Clark itself—about 40 miles long and 5 miles wide—is surrounded by snowcapped peaks. To its north are the Neacola Mountains; to its south are the Chigmit Mountains, which feature the park's twin volcanoes. **Mt. Iliamna** (10,016 feet) hasn't erupted in recorded history but regularly vents steam and sulfur. **Mt. Redoubt**, the Aleutian Range's highest peak at 10,197 feet, last erupted in 2009.

The only maintained hiking routes are the **Tanalian Trails**, which include a moderate 5-mile round-trip trek from Port Alsworth to Kontrashibuna Lake and a more difficult 8.2-mile round trip up and down 3,960-foot Tanalian Mountain. Many hikers traverse riverbanks or tundra on unmaintained backcountry routes, including the **Telaquana Trail**, an ancient route used by indigenous peoples. Check with the park for up-to-date advice on routes and safety.

Each July and August, an estimated 375,000 **sockeye salmon** swim up the Newhalen River to spawn in freshwater creeks, rivers, and lakes. Other varieties of salmon are abundant here, too, as are Arctic char, lake trout, rainbow trout, and northern pike—to name a few. Peak **fishing** season is May through October, and you'll need a state fishing license. Crescent Lake and Silver Salmon Creek are among the top spots.

Where there's salmon, there's bear. Prime **bear-viewing** season is June through September, particularly around Crescent Lake, Silver Salmon Creek, and Chinitna Bay. In this park, the *Ursus arctos* (brown or grizzly bear), outnumbers the smaller *Ursus americanus* (black bear). Both congregate along the coast, where salt marshes teem with life and food is abundant; brown bear populations thrive inland as well.

Brush up on bear safety before heading out. Better yet, check the park website for a list of outfitters that organize day or overnight bear- and other wildlife-watching trips. Dall sheep, moose, caribou, wolves, and a wide variety of birds are among the other creatures you might encounter here.

Sites & Programs. The **Port Alsworth Visitor Center** has cultural and natural history displays, trip-planning guidance, and seasonal Junior Ranger Programs. On the south shore of Upper Twin Lakes is **Proenneke's Cabin** (late May–late Sept.), a popular air-taxi day trip from Port Alsworth. Adventurer, outdoorsman, documentarian, and master craftsman, Richard L. Proenneke not only built the structure, often using his own creative contraptions, but also lived in it alone from the late 1960s to the early 1990s.

Lodging. Port Alsworth has just one developed campground, operated by **Tulchina Adventures** (907/782-4720, www.tulcinhaadventures.com), so backcountry camping is the focus here. Several private lodges offer accommodations (mostly in cabins) as well as guided camping, fishing, bear-viewing, or other park tours.

Lodges in the western reaches include **The Farm Lodge** (907/781-2208, www.thefarmlodge.com) in Port Alsworth and **Windsong Wilderness Retreat** (907/260-5410, www.windsongwildernessretreat.com) on Twin Lakes. For eastern stays, look into **Redoubt Mountain Lodge** (907/733-3034, www.redoubtlodge.com) on Crescent Lake near the Redoubt Volcano, and **Bear Mountain Lodge** (907/252-1450, www.akbearmountainlodge.com) on Chinitna Bay.

1. Puffins on a lichen-covered cliff. **2.** Bears clamming along the coastline. **3.** Kayaking across Twin Lake.

③

Lassen Volcanic National Park

CALIFORNIA

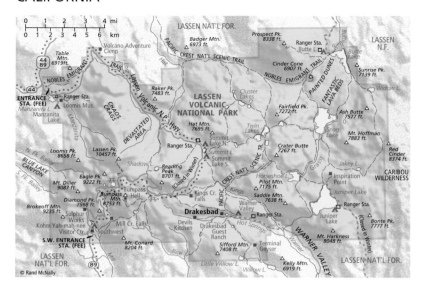

Just when you think you've seen all of California's diverse landscapes—the majesty of the Sierra Nevada, the stark solace of the desert, the endlessly picturesque coast—you discover the rough-hewn beauty of Lassen Volcanic National Park.

It's a paradox within nature how the destruction of beauty can eventually create a new yet equally memorable aesthetic. At Lassen, volcanic forces have reshaped the landscape. Mounds of broken lava rock rise from the earth a few hundred feet from mature stands of Jeffrey pine, while underground activity creates heated pools and smoking cauldrons.

And yet, you can spend the day at Lassen paddling in a canoe on a bucolic lake surrounded by clear blue sky, your thoughts focused on whether to drop your fishing line in the water or pull out your smartphone and take

Lassen Volcanic National Park, CA

a photo to remind yourself that your time here was more than just a dream.

Park Basics

Established: May 6, 1907 (national monument); August 9, 1916 (national park).
Area: 166 square miles; 106,589 acres.
Best For: Boating, Fishing, Geology, Hiking, Snowshoeing.
Contact: 530/595-4480, www.nps.gov/lavo.
Getting Oriented: Located 250 miles northeast of San Francisco International Airport in Northern California, Lassen is the last (southerly) section of the Cascade Range, which extends from southern British Columbia down through Washington, Oregon, and Northern California. Heading north from San Francisco, mostly via I-5 and CA 36, takes you to the main **Kohm Yah-mah-nee Visitor Center** in the park's southwest corner. You can also enter Lassen from the northwest near Loomis Museum (on Manzanita Lake) or the northeast near Butte Lake.

Small nearby towns such as **Chester** (www.lakealmanorarea.com), **Mineral**, **Shingletown**, and **Susanville** have food, gas, and lodging, but **Redding** (www.cityofredding.org), 47 miles west of the Manzanita Lake entrance on CA 44, is the region's hub for all types of action, including its microbrewery scene.

Park Highlights

Natural Attractions. Lassen is fascinating from a visual as well as a geological standpoint. It contains all four types of volcanoes found on Earth: cinder cone, composite, plug dome, and shield. In one place, you can stand on a lakeside surrounded by achingly green mountain peaks, and in another spot, be staring into a blacker-than-black mound of lava rocks devoid of vegetation. You can gaze at a steaming pool heated by deep geothermal activity or walk past moss-covered rocks en route to a cascading waterfall.

Everything starts with the mountain peaks, including majestic **Lassen Peak**, rising from the Cascade Range at 10,457 feet. This dormant volcano, which last erupted in 1917, is the remnant of the even larger Mt. Tehama (now called **Brokeoff Mountain**, another of the park's famous peaks). Views of Lassen from **Lake Helen** shouldn't be missed, but also allot time for **Kings Creek Falls**, the steaming fumaroles (steam vents) in **Bumpass Hell**, and the blackened, rocky mounds of the **Fantastic Lava Beds**.

Trails, Drives & Viewpoints. The scenic **Lassen Volcanic National Park Highway** (CA 89) wends its way between the park's southwest and northwest entrances

(30 miles one-way; 45 minutes without stops). Picnic at Summit Lake North, gaze on volcanic destruction, spot fumaroles and bubbling mud pots at the Sulphur Works, and pull out your camera for the **Lassen Peak Viewpoint** at the road's highest point—slightly more than 8,500 feet. If you're exploring the region, check out roads that are part of the **Volcanic Legacy Scenic Byway** (www.volcaniclegacybyway.org).

Two hikes are unforgettable: through the **Bumpass Hell** hydrothermal area (3 miles round-trip; easy walking but at 8,000 feet), with its steaming vents and pools; and the **Cinder Cone Trail** (4 miles round-trip, moderate to difficult, accessible via Butte Lake entrance), where lone green Jeffrey pines grow among ashen hills and otherwise barren lava beds.

Museums & Sites. Take in excellent geology exhibits at the **Kohm Yah-mah-nee Visitor Center** (open all year), but also stop at the quaint **Loomis Museum** (open late May–Oct.) on Manzanita Lake. The museum has original photos and seismic equipment used by park benefactor and documentarian B.F. Loomis; his 1926 *Pictorial History of Lassen Volcano* is for sale in the bookstore.

Programs & Activities. Ranger-led talks and walks take place all year, though most are during summer months. The park also hosts the annual **Dark Sky Festival** in August, showcasing Lassen's spectacular night sky. In winter, ranger-led **Snowshoe Walks** are a great way to explore the winter wonderland of snow-covered mountains and ponderosa pines.

Lassen has several scenic lakes with stunning views of surrounding peaks, and **boating** is popular on Manzanita, Butte, Juniper, and Summit lakes. Kayak, canoe, and paddleboard

③

rentals are available at the Manzanita Lake Camper Store through the **California Parks Company** (530/335-7557, lassenrecreation.com); motor boating isn't allowed. **Fishing** is big in this part of California, and fly fishermen descend every summer to ply their rods on lakes and rivers; it's catch and release only, though.

Lodging. Lassen has some great options for staying within the park—in summer. The rustic wooden **Drakesbad Guest Ranch** (866/999-0914, drakesbad.com; closed Oct.–May), accessible from the park's Warner Valley entrance, is classic national park lodging, with a lodge, bungalows, and cabins—plus a hydrothermal-fed pool. The 20 **Manzanita Lake Camping Cabins** (530/335-7557, Recreation.gov) have views of Lassen Peak and make a perfect base for fishing or boating. Lassen also has more than 400 individual and group **campsites** (Recreation.gov) across 8 campgrounds.

Accommodations abound outside the park, with motels, campgrounds, cabins, and rentals in Mineral, Shingletown, Susanville, and Chester, including **Bidwell House Bed & Breakfast** (1 Main St., Chester, 530/258-3338 www.bidwellhouse.com) in a 1901 house. Enjoy a night in Redding, the region's liveliest town, at the renovated-yet-classic **Thunderbird Lodge** (1350 Pine St., 530/243-5422, www.thunderbirdlodgeredding.com), with an outdoor pool.

1. Volcanic crater. **2.** Geothermal pool at Bumpass Hell. **3.** Lassen Peak and Manzanita Lake. **4.** Kings Creek.

④

Mammoth Cave National Park

KENTUCKY

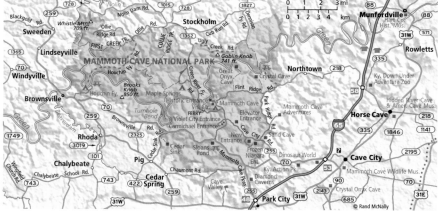

On the surface, it might look as if Mammoth Cave National Park doesn't have much to offer, but it's what is below the surface that attracts 586,000 visitors a year.

That's where there are more than 400 surveyed miles of intricately beautiful caves, chambers, and passageways, along with an underground river populated by eyeless cave shrimp. Even in the 19th century, Mammoth was viewed as one of America's natural wonders. Recognized internationally, the cave attracted notable visitors, and its reputation would grow with the cave itself.

In 1972, the already super-sized labyrinth more than doubled in length when spelunkers discovered that it connected to a neighboring network. With this, the national park was a shoo-in to be named a World Heritage Site (1981) and an International Biosphere Reserve (1990). It also established Mammoth as the world's longest cave system. The runner-up? Sistema Sac Actun. But it's only half as long. And it's underwater. And it's in Mexico. You need only travel as far as south-central Kentucky to visit Mammoth Cave.

Park Basics

Established: July 1, 1941.
Area: 82.5 square miles; 52,830 acres.
Best For: Cycling, Geology, Hiking, Horseback Riding, Spelunking.
Contact: 270/758-2180, www.nps.gov/maca.
Getting Oriented: Louisville International Airport is 85 miles north of the park entrance, and Tennessee's Nashville International is 95 miles south. From Louisville, take I-65 south to Exit 53 in Cave City; from Nashville, take I-65 north to Exit 48 in Park City. Mammoth Cave is 28 miles northeast of Bowling Green via I-65.

In the park's main visitors area, a pedestrian bridge connects the **visitors center** to the Lodge at Mammoth Cave, with the main

Mammoth Cave National Park, KY

entrance to the cave located down the hill. Nearby towns with lodging include **Cave City** (cavecity.com), **Park City**, and **Bowling Green** (www.visitbgky.com).

Park Highlights

Cave Tours. You need to take a tour to see the cave; sign up in advance if possible since tours sell out quickly, especially in summer. For a full list of options, check the park's website. If you arrive without a reservation, stop at the visitors center. Tours last from 75 minutes to 6 hours; prices vary accordingly.

Some tours enter at the Historic Entrance (aka Natural Entrance) by the visitors center; others require a 10-minute bus ride to the New Entrance. Among the easiest and most popular is the 75-minute **Frozen Niagara Tour** highlighting stalactites, stalagmites, flowstones, and Frozen Niagara itself, a formation that looks like a freeze-dried waterfall.

Going deeper into the cave, the moderate, 2-hour **Domes and Dripstones Tour** descends nearly 300 steps to dazzling domes, pits, and dripstone formations before returning to sights seen on the Frozen Niagara Tour. The moderate, 2-hour **Historic Tour** uses the Historic Entrance and leads to places familiar to visitors in the 1800s, including the Rotunda, Broadway, and Fat Man's Misery. Designed for people who use a walker or wheelchair, the 2-hour **Mammoth Cave Accessible Tour** visits unique gypsum formations, historical cave writing, and the Snowball Room, where gypsum nodules cover the ceiling.

Trails & Viewpoints. More than 80 miles of trails for humans and horses (you must bring your own horse, though) fan out across the park, with the easiest and most accessible being the 7 miles of trails that surround the visitors center. On these you can see the Green River, walk along ridges that provide lovely views of Doyle Valley, and trek beside huge depressions caused by sinkholes. The easy, 0.75-mile **Heritage Trail** passes the Old Guides Cemetery, where you can see the grave of cave explorer Stephen Bishop, a mixed-race slave who, in the mid-19th century, navigated uncharted passages to create detailed cave maps.

A popular 9-mile path adjacent to an old railroad bed, the **Mammoth Cave Railroad Bike and Hike Trail** runs from the visitors center to Park City and accommodates bicyclists, pedestrians, joggers, and dogs on a leash. Hybrid bikes can handle the hard-packed gravel.

Programs & Activities. Outside the cave, rangers host free **"surface" talks and presentations** that vary by season. In summer, **evening presentations** are held nightly in the Amphitheater (less often in other seasons), highlighting topics related to Mammoth Cave. There are short **Porch Talks** about the park's cultural heritage; a 45-minute **Heritage Walk** explaining Mammoth Cave Estate and the Old Guides Cemetery; and a 45-minute **Sloans Pond Crossing Walk**. Mammoth Cave is along the Mississippi Flyway, and rangers host two-hour **birding excursions**.

Specialty cave tours supplement regularly scheduled tours and explore the cave in different ways. The strenuous, 4-mile **Violet City Lantern Tour** visits the cave Tom Sawyer–style; you carry a flickering lantern. A handful of "wild" tours, including the very strenuous, 5-mile **Wild Cave Tour**, are for those who can handle tight spaces and don't mind getting dirty. This one finds you donning gloves, knee pads, and a helmet as you walk, kneel, crouch, and crawl your way through the cave.

Lodging. The park has a hotel and campgrounds, and nearby Park City has a few hotels. Cave City has more options, mostly chains; the widest selection is a half hour away in Bowling Green. The most convenient option is the **Lodge at Mammoth Cave** (171 Hotel Rd., 844/760-2283, mammothcavelodge.com) by the visitors center; it offers rooms, cottages, and cabins. The park also has three **campgrounds** (Recreation.gov): Mammoth Cave, near the visitors center, 105 sites; Maple Springs Group Campground, 6 miles north of the visitors center; and 12 riverside sites at Houchin Ferry. Backcountry camping sites require permits from the visitors center.

Outside the park, Park City offers the **Park Mammoth Resort** (22850 Louisville Rd., 270/749-4101), or you can sleep in a concrete tepee in Cave City's quirky **Wigwam Village Inn #2** (601 N. Dixie Hwy., 270/773-3381, wigwamvillage.com).

1. Cave interior, Frozen Niagara section. **2.** Autumn at Mammoth Cave National Park. **3.** A group tour of the cave's Frozen Niagara section. **4.** Cave entrance.

Mesa Verde National Park

COLORADO

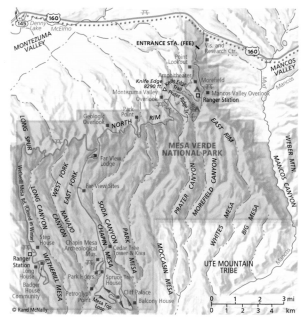

The first national park with an aim of preserving the manmade more than the natural, Mesa Verde features a number of well-preserved cliff dwellings that transport you back a millennium.

The Ancestral Puebloan people, also known as the Anasazi, called the region home for hundreds of years before abruptly abandoning their communal, agrarian settlements around AD 1300. Their multistory sandstone-and-adobe cliff dwellings—among the world's largest—showcase some serious architectural flair and engineering ingenuity. Atop the mesa are pueblos (multi-structure communities) and kivas (below-ground ceremonial rooms). The site was strategic: The 2,000-foot cliffs on Mesa Verde's north side kept would-be invaders at bay.

These southwestern Colorado settlements were mostly lost to history for more than 500 years after the Ancestral Puebloans abruptly left, likely due to drought, famine, and conflict. Ranchers Charlie Mason and Richard Wetherill rediscovered the dwellings along the cliffsides of this flat-topped mountain in 1888. Today many structures are open to visitors, offering you a tantalizing glimpse of Ancestral Puebloan life.

Mesa Verde National Park, CO

Park Basics

Established: June 29, 1906.
Area: 82 square miles; 52,485 acres.
Best For: Archaeology; Bird-Watching (golden eagles, hummingbirds, turkey vultures); Hiking.
Contact: 970/529-4465, www.nps.gov/meve.
Getting Oriented: Mesa Verde is just south

of US 160 between **Cortez** (13 miles west of park entrance; www.cityofcortez.com) and **Durango** (35 miles east; www.durango.org) in southwestern Colorado. The small town of **Mancos** (www.mancosvalley.com) is 7 miles east of the entrance. The main gateway airports are Colorado's Denver International (395 miles northeast of the park) and New Mexico's Albuquerque International Sunport (250 miles southeast).

The park's one entrance is on its northern boundary, and the **Mesa Verde Visitor and Research Center**, just southeast of the entrance, is the primary point of visitor contact. It's best to visit in late spring or early fall; the park tends to be most crowded when schools are on summer break.

Park Highlights

Natural Attractions. Spanish for "green table," Mesa Verde itself is the park's defining physical feature, marked by sheer cliffs, narrow crevasses, and stunning valley and mountain panoramas. Topping out at an elevation of about 8,500 feet, it's technically a cuesta, not a mesa, as it slopes gently to the south, a characteristic that allowed for the alcoves sheltering the dwellings.

The geology and ecology made it ideal for the Ancestral Puebloans, who used the year-round springs here as sources of water and gathered and hunted a variety of native plants and animals. Black bear, mule deer, and Rocky Mountain elk are still found in the park.

Trails, Drives & Viewpoints. About a mile south of the visitors center, the **Far View Sites Complex**, once a densely populated village, is accessible via an easy, 0.75-mile trail. **Point Lookout Trail** starts near Morefield Campground and offers sweeping views of the Montezuma Valley on a moderate, 2.3-mile loop. From a trailhead on Chapin Mesa 20 miles south of the entrance, **Petroglyph Point Trail** provides a moderate hike that's 2.8 miles round-trip; yes, you do see petroglyphs.

The park's most popular scenic drive, the 6-mile **Mesa Top Loop Tour** features 10 stops with overlooks of cliff dwellings or short walks to other structures on the mesa. Expect to spend about 2 hours on the loop, depending on how many stops you make. The 12-mile **Wetherill Mesa Road** forks off the main park road near Far View Lodge and continues on a steep, winding route to lesser-visited attractions on the park's west side. Allow at least 1.5 hours for this drive.

Museums & Sites. Archaeological sites are the centerpiece of Mesa Verde. Many are accessible on ticketed tours with modest fees, though you can explore a few on your own. Rangers guide ticketed tours of 151-room **Cliff Palace**, one of the largest cliff dwellings on Earth, and imposing **Balcony House** daily from early April to late October. Both require you to climb ladders and pass through narrow spaces. You must purchase tickets in person up to two days in advance at the Mesa Verde Visitor and Research Center, Morefield Ranger Station, Chapin Mesa Archaeological Museum, or the Colorado Welcome Center (in Cortez).

Another ticketed tour explores **Long House**, the park's second-largest cliff dwelling, on Wetherill Mesa in Mesa Verde's southwest corner. Nearby **Step House** is open to self-guided tours in summer. Both tours involve moderate hikes of about 2 miles round-trip.

About 20 miles south of the park entrance, **Chapin Mesa Archaeological Museum** displays dioramas and artifacts that depict Ancestral Puebloan life. Free tours of **Spruce Tree House** start at the museum; they're guided by rangers in winter and self-guided spring through fall.

Programs & Activities. In summer, nightly free **ranger talks** take place in the amphitheater at Morefield Campground. Numerous **special guided tours** (Recreation. gov) of ruins in and around Mesa Verde are available; many require a hike.

Lodging. The park has one hotel and one campground, and Durango, Cortez, and Mancos offer a wide range of accommodations. The 150-room **Far View Lodge** (970/564-4300; www.visitmesaverde. com; closed mid-Oct.–mid-Apr.) in the park, 14 miles south of the entrance, is named for panoramas that span hundreds of miles. Four miles south of the park entrance and open to tents and RVs, Mesa Verde's **Morefield Campground** (970/564-4300, www. visitmesaverde.com) has 267 sites and rarely fills to capacity. Reservations are accepted; RV hookups are available.

The same family owns **Rochester Hotel** and **Leland House** (726 E. 2nd Ave., 970/385-1920, www.rochesterhotel.com), across from each other in Durango's delightful historic core. Set on 200 acres southwest of Durango, **Blue Lake Ranch** (16919 Hwy. 140, 970/385-4537, www.bluelakeranch.com) is Colorado's oldest B&B and one of its best. In McElmo Canyon near Cortez, **Canyon of the Ancients Guest Ranch** (7950 County Rd. G, 970/565-4288, canyonoftheancients.com) has distinctive cabins on a working farm and ranch.

1. Spruce Tree House. **2.** Cliff Palace ruins.
3. Petroglyphs along Petroglyph Point Trail. **4.** Scenic view of Cliff Palace dwellings.

Mount Rainier National Park

WASHINGTON

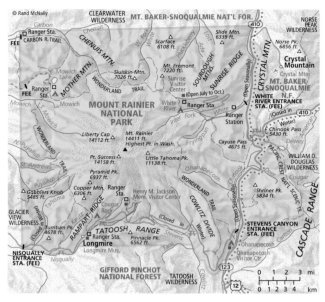

A solitary, snowcapped sight, Mt. Rainier is sometimes visible for hundreds of miles. The tallest peak in Washington State, the volcano is one of the world's true mountaineering meccas.

In 1792, Captain George Vancouver named the highest peak in the Cascade Range for Rear Admiral Peter Rainier, though the latter never actually saw his namesake mountain. The native people called it Tahoma, which means "that frozen water" in the Whulshootseed language, because of its many glaciers and ice patches.

The first recorded ascent of Mt. Rainier took place in 1870, and the peak has

since emerged as one of the pinnacles of the climbing world. About 10,000 people attempt an ascent every year; dozens have perished trying to reach the summit. The mountain acts like a massive catcher's mitt for storms rolling off the Pacific Ocean, making its summit one of the snowiest spots on Earth. In the winter of 1971–72, the annual snowfall set a world record that still stands: 1,122 inches, or 94 feet.

Park Basics

Established: March 2, 1899.
Area: 369 square miles; 236,381 acres.
Best For: Climbing; Geology; Hiking;

Mount Rainier National Park, WA

Wildlife Watching (black bears, elk, marmots, mountain goats).
Contact: 360/569-2211, www.nps.gov/mora.
Getting Oriented: Mount Rainier National Park is 83 miles southeast of Seattle in western Washington; Seattle-Tacoma International Airport is 74 miles northwest of the **Nisqually Entrance** via State Routes

706, 7, 161, and 167. Most visitors arrive via this entrance, open year-round and located near Ashford on the park's southwest side. Four other entrances are open in summer only: **White River** in the park's northeastern corner, **Carbon River** in the northwest, **Stevens Canyon** on the southeast side, and **Mowich Lake** on the west.

The **Henry M. Jackson Memorial Visitor Center** near Paradise Meadows is the primary visitors center; others are at the Longmire Museum, Ohanapecosh, and Sunrise. Towns with lodging include **Ashford** (www.mt-rainier.com), 3 miles west of Nisqually Entrance; **Greenwater**, 5 miles northeast of Carbon River; and **Packwood** (destinationpackwood.com), 15 miles southwest of Stevens Canyon.

Park Highlights

Natural Attractions. In addition to being a volcano, **Mt. Rainier** (14,411 feet) is the most glaciated mountain in the lower 48. Although it's active, the volcano hasn't erupted in 150 years, and geologists don't expect it to anytime soon. The park has 27 named glaciers and many more unnamed ones. At about 4 square miles, Emmons is the largest glacier in the lower 48, and Carbon is the lowest, with a low point of 3,600 feet above sea level.

Melting ice and snow feed several major waterways, including the Cowlitz, Nisqually, and Puyallup rivers. The Carbon River area in the park's northwest corner is Mt. Rainier's rainiest area and resembles a temperate rain forest. You can access it via State Route 165 near the Carbon River Entrance, but no vehicles are allowed past the park boundary here.

Resident wildlife includes cougars, black bears, elk, and deer, as well as marmots and mountain goats in higher elevations. About 180 species of birds nest in the park, endangered northern spotted owls among them.

Trails, Drives & Viewpoints. At Ohanapecosh in the southeastern corner, the **Grove of the Patriarchs Trail** is an easy, 1.3-mile loop through impressive old-growth Douglas firs and red cedars. The moderate 5.8-mile round-trip on the **Comet Falls Trail** takes you to the 320-foot waterfall of the same name, the second-tallest falls in the park. The trailhead is near Cougar Rock Campground on Paradise Road.

The subalpine meadow called **Paradise** is the starting point for most summit hikes. From here, it's a notably difficult 9,000 feet and 6.5 miles to the top; mountaineering skills and being in good physical condition are prerequisites. The strenuous, 93-mile **Wonderland Trail** circumnavigates the entire mountain and often requires two weeks, but you don't have to tackle the whole thing at once.

For a truly **scenic drive**, enter via State Route 706 to the Nisqually Entrance, and head clear across the park to Ohanapecosh (or vice versa). Expect to spend a minimum of 2 to 3 hours on this 42-mile (one-way) route. The **Sunrise** area on the mountain's northeastern flanks has sublime morning views. The difficult **Sunrise Rim Trail** takes you to a pair of impressive overlooks of Emmons Glacier on a 5.2-mile loop.

Museum. The **Longmire Museum** is in a 1916 structure built by James Longmire, who operated a hot-springs resort here in the park's early days. A short, self-guided walking tour showcases the surrounding Longmire Historic District and a replica cabin.

Programs & Activities. The park offers free **ranger programs** at Longmire, Ohanapecosh, Paradise, and Sunrise that include daily guided hikes and walks as well as evening programs at campgrounds.

Due to the unpredictable weather, it's best to climb the mountain with experts. **RMI Expeditions** (30027 SR 706 E., Ashford, 360/569-2227, www.rmiguides.com) offers guided summit climbs and educational seminars for climbers of all skill levels.

Lodging. The park has a number of lodging and dining options, and the Ashford area is home to numerous cabin complexes, B&Bs, and motels; there's also lodging in Greenwater and Packwood. **Rainier Guest Services** (360/569-2275, mtrainierguestservices.com) operates two historic in-park hotels that fill well in advance: **National Park Inn** (47009 Paradise Rd. E.) at Longmire and **Paradise Inn** (52807 Paradise Rd. E.) at Paradise Meadows. Parts of the Paradise Inn are being renovated, but the main inn and its restaurants remain open.

Just west of the park, **Stormking Spa & Cabins at Mt. Rainier** (37311 SR 706 E., Ashford, 360/569-2964, stormkingspa.com) offers cabin-like yurts and romantic ambience. The architecturally distinctive **Deep Forest Cabins** (33823 SR 706 E., Ashford, 360/569-2054, www.deepforestcabins.com) nestle cozily in 20 acres of forest.

The park has more than 500 sites at 5 developed campgrounds. **Cougar Rock Campground** (Recreation.gov) accepts both tents and RVs, but there are no hookups for the latter; reservations are available May through September.

1. Climbers descending the trail to Paradise on Mt. Rainier, with the Tatoosh Range in the background.
2. Deer in the park. 3. Paradise, Mt. Rainier.

National Park of American Samoa

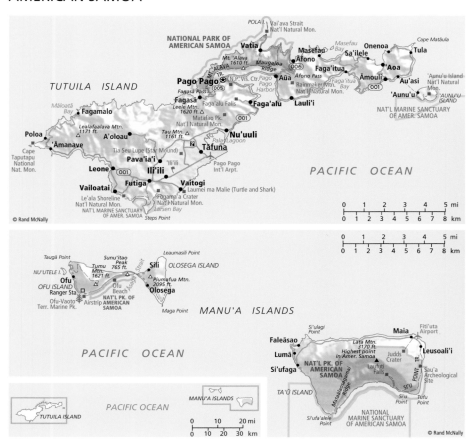

If you've dreamed of traveling to distant, beautiful places, the National Park of American Samoa can fulfill that wish, thanks to a sublime tropical location that is, for most Americans, very nearly at the end of the Earth.

Spread across three islands in the South Pacific—Tutuila, Ofu, and Ta'ū—this is the only U.S. national park located south of the equator, and it's so remote that only three mammals are native to the islands. Created to protect wildlife, safeguard coral reefs, and sustain tropical rain forests, the park also serves to celebrate *fa'asamoa*, the unique customs, beliefs, and traditions of the 3,000-year-old Samoan culture.

Here you'll see volcanic islands with jagged peaks and sheer cliffs, beaches fringed with coconut trees and tropical flowers, and Technicolor reefs populated by blue starfish and green sea turtles. There are national parks

far larger and more visited than this, but the National Park of American Samoa is in a class by itself.

Park Basics

Established: October 31, 1988.
Area: 21 square miles; 13,500 acres (9,500 land acres; 4,000 acres of reefs and ocean).
Best For: Bird-Watching (Samoan starling, spotless crake, Tahiti petrel, wattled honeyeaters, white-collared kingfisher); Diving/Snorkeling; Hiking; Wildlife Watching (bats, dolphins, geckos, sea turtles, whales).
Contact: 684/633-7082, www.nps.gov/npsa.
Getting Oriented: National Park of American Samoa (NPAS) is in the middle of the South Pacific in the territory of American Samoa, 2,600 miles southwest of Hawaii. Coming by air, you'll land on the main island of Tutuila at Pago Pago International Airport. If you arrive on a cruise, you'll dock at Pago Pago Harbor where a ranger will meet you for a tour arranged through the ship's shore excursions. Otherwise, guides at the dock can drive you into the park.

National Park of American Samoa, American Samoa

The park's **visitors center** is in **Pago Pago** (www.americansamoa.gov), the largest town with lodging, amenities, and other services. It's roughly a mile from the harbor and 10 miles from the airport. Many guests take *aiga* buses to the center. From there, it's about 12 miles to the park entrance, so a vehicle is necessary. Reaching park lands in Ta'ū involves a 45-minute flight from Tutuila to Fiti'uta (Maia) village or waiting for the ferry that departs Tutuila each Wednesday. A short flight or boat ride is also required to reach Ofu. Small boats ferry passengers between Ta'ū and Ofu.

Park Highlights

Natural Attractions. Roughly two-thirds of NPAS preserves the **rain forest** and its biodiverse universe, while one-third protects the ocean and coral reefs. Tutuila's mixed-species rain forest is considered the most pristine in the 16 American territories. The park is home to approximately 350 species of flowering plants and a variety of domestic and migrating birds, but its most famous residents are three species of protected bats—two large fruit bats and a smaller insect-eating bat. They're the park's only native mammals and are crucial in pollinating plants.

Colorful **coral reefs** that border Tutuila and neighboring Ofu and Ta'ū are the other prominent natural feature. More than 250 coral species provide shelter and sustenance to nearly a thousand species of fish. Sadly, climate change and carbon dioxide concentrations are threatening the corals' existence. Although the park service doesn't offer reef tours, local vendors can arrange excursions.

Trails & Viewpoints. The visitors center carries maps of trails that include the moderate, 1.7-mile **World War II Heritage Trail** leading to gun emplacements that protected the island from Japanese invasion. The moderate, 0.5-mile **Lower Sauma Ridge Trail** passes an archaeological site called a "star mound" that might have been used in the chiefs-only sport of catching pigeons. The strenuous, 7-mile **Mt. 'Alava Adventure Trail**

follows ridgelines and requires hiking up and down 56 "ladders" and 783 steps en route to the Mt. 'Alava Summit and to Vatia village.

Museums & Sites. The **visitors center** features interactive exhibits about sea life, forest birds, and fruit bats, as well as Samoan culture and handicrafts and tools. Videos show how Samoans create headdresses, weave baskets, and perform tribal dances.

Archaeological sites in and near the park are a testament to 3,000 years of human settlement. That said, accessing most of them is unlikely without prior permission from the family or villagers. If there's a site you are curious about—a grave or structure or a prehistoric village—rangers are your best source of information. If there's no ranger or villager to ask, steer clear.

Programs & Activities. Aside from a **rain forest tour**, there are relatively few ranger-led activities. Rangers meet cruise passengers and set off on the tour from 9:30 am to 1 pm. You visit a shop where weaving demonstrations and the sale of handmade souvenirs showcase Samoan culture, and then head into the park to learn about the rain

forest and the large fruit bats that live here. Interaction with villagers happens primarily when you're exploring the town and visiting shops, restaurants, and historic sites.

Snorkeling, diving, and beach activities are popular, and rangers can recommend beaches in nearby villages and direct you to concessionaires that can reach the reefs. Only Ofu has beaches within park borders, but getting to the island is a challenge, and renting snorkeling and scuba gear is equally iffy.

Lodging. There's no lodging inside the park. Of the 29,000 park visitors who arrive at Pago Pago each year, the majority step ashore from cruise ships. If you stay over, each island—Tutuila, Ofu, and Ta'ū—offers lodging of varying levels, mostly basic. Pago Pago has a handful of hotels including the relatively upscale **Tradewinds Hotel** (Ottoville Rd., 684/699-1000, www.tradewinds.as); the **Sadie Thompson Inn** (3222 Main Hwy., 684/633-5900, sadieshotels.com); and the beachfront **Sadie's by the Sea** (Utulei Beach, 684/633-5900, sadieshotels.com).

1. Tutuila Island. **2.** Beach and palms on Tutuila Island.

North Cascades National Park

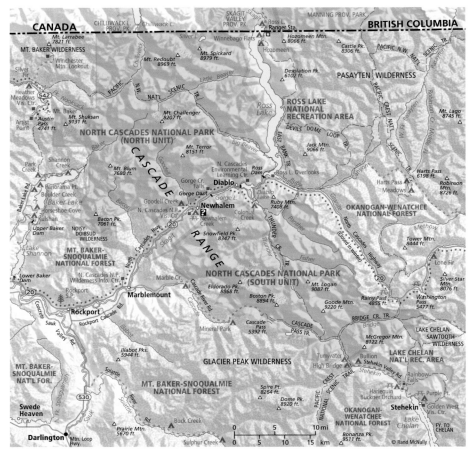

Nicknamed "the American Alps," this park is a Pacific Northwest jewel. Bookended by lakes, it contains villages and resorts accessible only by foot or boat.

The largest wilderness in Washington State is a rugged and remote area with majestic mountain scenery and alpine valleys scoured by glaciers over the millennia. It's not all technically a national park: The North Cascades Park Complex spans two national park units (North and South) as well as the Ross Lake and Lake Chelan national recreation areas, which are popular among boaters of all kinds. More than 90% of the complex is designated as wilderness area.

Despite all of the public land and recreational opportunities, North Cascades remains well off the beaten path, and its remote reaches require multiday backpacking trips to experience. The park sees only a fraction of the visitors who make it to Washington's two other national parks, Olympic and Mount Rainier, and the solitude makes the views that much more stunning.

Park Basics

Established: October 2, 1968.
Area: 789 square miles; 504,781 acres.
Best For: Cross-Country Skiing, Hiking, Kayaking, Snowshoeing.
Contact: 360/854-7200, www.nps.gov/noca.
Getting Oriented: North Cascades National Park is 104 miles northeast of Seattle via I-5 and State Route 20. The latter runs through the park complex and is typically closed November–April. Most out-of-state visitors arrive by way of Seattle-Tacoma International Airport, 119 miles southwest.

Ross Lake is on the northeast side of the complex, and Lake Chelan and Stehekin are on its southeastern side. Stehekin is accessible only by trail, boat, or seaplane. **Lady of the Lake ferries** (509/682-4584, ladyofthelake. com) to Stehekin leave from a dock 1 mile south of the town of Chelan. Similarly, Ross Lake is often navigated by water taxi.

The park has two visitors centers: the main **North Cascades Visitor Center** (Milepost 120, SR 20, Newhalem) and **Golden West Visitor Center** (near Stehekin Landing). Nearby towns with amenities include **Marblemount**, 3 miles southwest of the park's western border, and **Winthrop** (www.winthropwashington.com), 58 miles east of Ross Lake and 41 miles south of the Canadian border.

North Cascades National Park, WA

Park Highlights

Natural Attractions. Its rugged topography, marked by precipitous changes in verticality, defines North Cascades. Its many rocky spires, intertwined with waterfalls and dotted with more than 300 glaciers (a third of the total in the lower 48), rise more than 8,000 feet from the surrounding valleys. At 9,220 feet, **Goode Mountain** is the high point.

Ross Lake, a manmade reservoir on the Skagit River, lies behind a 540-foot-tall dam completed in the 1940s. Glacier-fed Diablo Lake is just south of Ross Lake. Narrow, 50-mile-long **Lake Chelan** is the state's largest; a dam raised the lake's surface by 21 feet in 1927.

Trails, Drives & Viewpoints. Pyramid Lake Trail is a moderate, 4.2-mile round-trip to the mountain lake of the same name. Most trails in the park complex are **multiday backpacking routes**, including Cascade Pass and Sahale Arm trails from the end of Cascade River Road to Stehekin (a difficult, 23-mile hike) and Park Creek Pass from Ross Lake to Stehekin (a difficult, 27.6-mile hike). You can hike part of the routes, though.

In the park's North Unit, **Big Beaver Trail** and **Hannegan Trail** take hikers to some of the most pristine areas but require a water taxi on Ross Lake or a 13-mile drive on Forest Service Road 32 from Glacier to get to the trailhead. Most of these routes in the North Unit are composed of multiple trails and are between 40 and 50 miles in length.

One of the West's most scenic drives, **State Route 20** (aka North Cascades Highway) cuts through the heart of the park; the overlook at **Washington Pass** is a highlight.

Museums & Sites. Measuring 540 and 389 feet high respectively, the **Ross and Diablo dams** on the Skagit River are impressive feats of civic engineering. Operated by Seattle City Light, **Skagit Tours** (360/854-2589, www.seattle.gov) offers guided tours of the Gorge Powerhouse at Newhalem.

Programs & Activities. Free ranger programs include guided walks and talks at various locations in summer. The **North Cascades Institute** (360/854-2599, ncascades.org) offers science and art classes.

Skagit Tours (360/854-2589, www.seattle.gov) provides boat tours on Diablo Lake and dishes out chicken dinners at the Gorge Inn. Extend your Diablo experience at **Base Camp** (360/854-2599, ncascades.org/basecamp), an overnight learning experience on the lakeshore that includes outdoor activities. **Lady of the Lake ferries** (509/682-4584, ladyofthelake. com) offers cruises on Lake Chelan, and **North Cascades Lodge at Stehekin** (509/682-4494, lodgeatstehekin.com) has bus tours.

Lodging. Other than several campgrounds, the park's few lodging options aren't accessible by road, but the gateways of Winthrop and Marblemount have overnight accommodations. Reachable by foot or boat, **Ross Lake Resort** (206/386-4437,

www.rosslakeresort.com) in the park has 12 lakefront cabins and two bunkhouses open July to October. It also rents kayaks, canoes, and motorboats and offers water taxis.

In the village of Stehekin on Lake Chelan, the park's **North Cascades Lodge at Stehekin** (#1 Stehekin Landing, 509/682-4494, lodgeatstehekin.com) rents stylish lodge rooms, cabins, and vacation houses as well as kayaks and canoes. Nearby **Stehekin Valley Ranch** (509/682-4677, stehekinvalleyranch. com) provides basic, comfortable tent cabins and ranch cabins. Both are accessible by Lady of the Lake ferries or hiking the Chelan Lakeshore, Cascade Pass, or Sahale Arm trails.

Just west of the park complex, the historic **Buffalo Run Inn & Restaurant** (60117 SR 20, Marblemount, 360/873-2103, www. buffaloruninn.com) is a hybrid hostel and B&B. North of Winthrop, **Mazama Country Inn** (15 Country Rd., Mazama, 509/996-2681, www.mazamacountryinn.com) has lodge rooms, cabins, and a restaurant; it's amid a vast network of cross-country ski trails.

Open May to September, the park's 111-site **Newhalem Creek Campground** (Recreation. gov) accepts tents and RVs. North Cascades is also a backpacking destination; permits are required.

1. Cedar Hollow Falls along the Ross Dam Trail.
2. Climbing in winter. **3.** View from the Bridge Creek Trail.

Olympic National Park

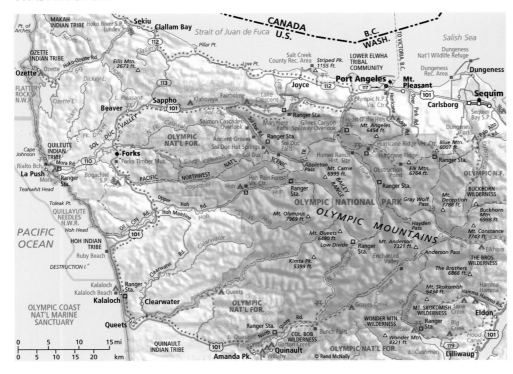

Olympic National Park, WA

Across Puget Sound from Seattle on the Olympic Peninsula, this park is a mist-shrouded, primeval place with lush rain forests, wild coastlines, imposing mountains, and ancient glaciers.

It's a magnificent wilderness, one that's ringed by the Olympic National Forest and home to some of the biggest trees—fir, red cedar, and spruce among them—in the nation as well as some of the wettest spots on the planet. The Hoh Rain Forest alone gets an average of 12 feet

of precipitation annually. And this strikingly verdant area is just one of the peninsula's distinct ecosystems.

Here, you'll also find rain shadows east of the mountains that get about 10% of the annual moisture of the western forests, rushing rivers, crystalline lakes, and long stretches of perfectly desolate Pacific coast dotted with picture-perfect beaches. Simply put, this park is one of most diverse places in North America.

Park Basics

Established: March 2, 1909 (as Mount Olympus National Monument); June 29, 1938 (as Olympic National Park).
Area: 1,441 square miles; 922,650 acres.
Best For: Backcountry Camping, Botany, Canoeing, Hiking.
Contact: 360/565-3130, www.nps.gov/olym.
Getting Oriented: Olympic's winters are exceptionally wet, so it's best to visit between late spring and fall. The primary air gateway is Seattle-Tacoma International Airport, 15 miles south of Seattle. From the airport, it takes roughly three or four hours (south via Tacoma and Olympia) to reach the park along I-5 and US 101. To the north, it's best to take a **Washington State Ferry** (www.wsdot.

wa.gov/ferries) auto/passenger vessel across Puget Sound.

Though no roads traverse the park's rugged center, several entrances and/or ranger stations are along or just off US 101, which circumnavigates much of the park. The main **Olympic National Park Visitor Center** is open year-round and is just outside the northern gateway community of **Port Angeles** (www.portangeles.org) on US 101. The other northern-edge visitors center is at **Hurricane Ridge** (open in summer only), just off US 101 along the Hurricane Ridge Parkway.

From Port Angeles, the northern stretch of US 101 also passes Lake Crescent en route

1. Hiking in the park. **2.** Sea star on Rialto Beach. **Opposite Page:** Ruby Beach.

Many tree specimens here are the largest of their species in the United States, including a 226-foot Pacific silver fir, a 237-foot Western red cedar, and a 281-foot Sitka spruce with a circumference of more than 55 feet. Amidst these old-growth forests, the wildlife population includes cougars, elk, black bears, beaver, deer, salmon, spotted owls, and banana slugs.

Trails, Drives & Viewpoints. At Hurricane Ridge, **High Ridge Trail** is an easy, 0.3-mile loop that connects with the 0.2-mile trail to Sunrise Point, offering incredible views of the Pacific Ocean below and the snow-capped Olympic Mountains above. Starting near the Storm King Ranger Station at Lake Crescent, the moderate, 1.8-mile round trip on the **Marymere Falls Trail** takes you through

to the northwestern gateway town of **Forks** (forkswa.com). The turnoff to the Hoh Rain Forest, which also has a seasonal visitors center as well as a trailhead for a Mt. Olympus hike, is 12 miles south.

Park Highlights

Natural Attractions. The park is centered on the Olympic Mountains, heavily forested peaks that are about 20 miles west of the Pacific Ocean. The 7,969-foot **Mt. Olympus**, the range's tallest and most prominent peak, is also notably steep, rising nearly 7,000 feet in less than 6 miles.

The storms that roll off the Pacific deluge the **Hoh Rain Forest** at Mt. Olympus' western foot with 140 to 170 inches of precipitation a year. It and several other temperate rain forests—including **Bogachiel, Queets, Quinault,** and **Dosewallips**—are North America's best examples of this biome. On hikes here, plan to get wet, and dress accordingly. In addition to the damp climate, you might have to cross creeks. What's more, the prodigious moisture feeds a number of rivers, including the **Elwha**, the **Queets**, and the **Sol Duc**. The park is also home to several notable lakes, with **Lake Ozette** and **Lake Crescent** being the largest.

With 70 miles of undeveloped coastline on its western fringe, Olympic National Park is rife with fog-drenched, driftwood-laden beaches that are ideal for hiking, camping, and exploring tide pools full of sea stars, sea anemones, and hermit crabs. Some of the easiest to access are **Kalaloch** and **Ruby beaches**, off US 101 in the park's southwestern corner. To the north, **Rialto Beach** presents a stunning landscape, fronted by the forested Mora area. In spring and fall, the coast is also an excellent place for whale-watching.

OFF THE BEATEN PATH: OZETTE

Ozette, in the park's far western corner and accessed via Hoko–Ozette Road off WA 112, is one of the lesser-visited areas, yet it has a lot to offer. The native Makah people lived and hunted marine mammals off the coast here for about 2,000 years. In the 1960s, teams of archaeologists uncovered 300-year-old longhouses that shed light on the complex hunter-gatherer culture that thrived here for millennia.

Homesteaded by ranchers in the 1890s, the area is named for **Lake Ozette**, the largest unaltered natural lake in Washington State. Measuring roughly 8 miles by 3 miles, it's a popular area for kayaking and canoeing, with three boat ramps and several boat-in campsites on its shores and islands. At 331 feet below the surface, its deepest point is more than 300 feet below sea level.

Most of the ranchers left when Ozette was designated part of the Olympic National Forest in 1897, and the area became part of the national park in the 1970s and '80s. It now encompasses the lake and more than 20 miles of rugged and untouched coast that abuts the **Olympic Coast National Marine Sanctuary** (360/457-6622, olympiccoast. noaa.gov), a conservation area that's the size of Delaware and Rhode Island combined.

Behind the ranger station are the trailheads for three treks that become boardwalks through prairies and forests en route to the beach. Many hikers combine the 3.1-mile trail to Cape Alava, one of the westernmost (and most electrifying) places to see a sunset in the continental U.S., and the 2.8-mile route to Sandpoint with 3.1 miles on the alternately rocky and sandy coastline for a moderate 9-mile hike known as the **Ozette Loop** (or **Ozette Triangle**).

A campground adjacent to Lake Ozette has 15 tent sites. Just outside the park boundary, the **Lost Resort** (20860 Hoko–Ozette Rd., Clallam Bay, 360/963-2899, www.lostresort.net) offers camping and basic cabins, a deli that serves breakfast and lunch, and a bar that stocks more than 99 bottles (or, rather, brands) of beer!

an old-growth forest to a 90-foot waterfall. From the Sol Duc Ranger Station, the **Sol Duc Falls Trail** offers a graded, level path that's 1.6 miles round trip through a forest of massive hemlock and Douglas fir trees to its namesake waterfall.

In the Hoh Rain Forest, the **Hall of Mosses** is an easy, 0.8-mile loop trail through a forest carpeted in every imaginable shade of green. The **Hoh River Valley Trail** is popular with both day hikers and backpackers. From the trailhead, it's a difficult 17-mile hike to the top of Mt. Olympus, but a shorter, mostly level hike on the first few miles offers a great introduction to the rain forest. For a moderately difficult 10-mile day hike, trek to **Five Mile Island** and back for gorgeous mountain and river views and to possibly see some of the park's resident elk. Both of these trails start at the Hoh Campground, 19 miles east of US 101 on the peninsula's southwestern side.

The 17-mile drive south on **Hurricane Ridge Parkway** from Port Angeles offers a number of stellar roadside viewpoints. The **Salmon Cascades Overlook** in the Sol Duc Valley is the best place to see salmon spawn in early fall. Several Pacific Ocean overlooks are along US 101 near Kalaloch on the park's far southwestern side.

Museums & Sites. Humans have inhabited the Olympic Peninsula for more than 10,000 years, and the roughly **650 archaeological sites** in park boundaries include petroglyphs on coastal rocks in the northwestern Ozette area. In the Elwha River valley in the north, the

③

Humes Ranch is a historic cabin (circa 1900) along a short hiking loop. Note, though, that this valley is undergoing ecological restoration after a dam removal was completed in 2014; the ecosystem should return to its natural state in 15 to 20 years.

Programs & Activities. Ranger programs include campfire talks and guided hikes at numerous locations in the summer and guided snowshoeing expeditions on Hurricane Ridge in the winter. The park also offers a free **phone-based audio tour** (360/406-5056).

Hurricane Ridge Ski and Snowboard Area (848/667-7669, hurricaneridge.com) is a small downhill-skiing area that operates on winter weekends; lessons are available. The park's lakes and rivers are popular for **kayaking and canoeing**. Rentals are available at Lake Crescent Lodge, Log Cabin Resort, and Lake Quinault Lodge (see Lodging, below).

Lodging. The gateways of Port Angeles and Forks offer numerous lodging and dining options, and the park itself has four lodges as well. About 20 miles west of Port Angeles, **Lake Crescent Lodge** (416 Lake Crescent Rd., 888/896-3818, www.olympicnationalparks. com) is a classic national park lodge on the southern shore of its namesake lake. On the lake's north shore, **Log Cabin Resort** (3183 E. Beach Rd., 360/928-3325, www. olympicnationalparks.com) offers one-room cabins and a campground—the only one in the park with RV hookups.

Sol Duc Hot Springs Resort (12076 Sol Duc Hot Springs Rd., 360/327-3583, www. olympicnationalparks.com) is built around naturally heated pools on the Sol Duc River. It has cabins, a campground, and a "river suite." The cedar-sided **Kalaloch Lodge** (157151 US 101, 866/662-9928, www.thekalalochlodge. com), above a rugged beach on the park's far southwest side, offers a diverse selection of rooms and cabins.

④

About 20 miles east of Lake Crescent, the **Olympic Lodge** (140 Del Guzzi Dr., Port Angeles, 360/452-2993, www.olympiclodge. com) is a slick, full-service hotel with a "breakfast bistro" and an outdoor pool. Just south of the park, off US 101, **Lake Quinault Lodge** (345 S. Shore Rd., Quinault, 360/288-2900, www.olympicnationalparks.com) is another historic hostelry that makes a good base (check ahead about ongoing road work, though).

Set on 10 secluded acres, **Manitou Lodge Bed & Breakfast** (813 Kilmer Rd., Forks, 360/374-6295, manitoulodge.com) is just minutes from Rialto Beach. Featuring a definitive Northwest vibe, the eclectically decorated guest rooms and cottages are complemented by a luxury campsite and a pair of basic cabins.

Most of the park's **17 campgrounds** accept both tents and RVs, but only **Sol Duc** and **Kalaloch** accept reservations. With 105 sites between Port Angeles and Hurricane Ridge, **Heart O' the Hills Campground** is one of the park's largest, surrounded by old-growth forest and offering easy access to trails.

1. Lake Crescent. **2.** Hall of Mosses Trail in the Hoh Rain Forest. **3.** Waterfall in the Sol Duc Valley. **4.** Lake Crescent Lodge.

Petrified Forest National Park

ARIZONA

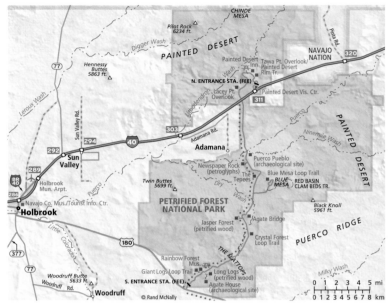

From far away, it looks as if someone scattered logs in the desert and then chainsawed 'em up. Get closer, and you realize that those logs are actually half-ton slabs of multicolored rock, transformed millions of years ago by geologic forces.

And what a desert! Perhaps the most colorful one you'll ever see, the Painted Desert in Petrified Forest National Park stretches for miles, straddlling one of America's longest interstates (I-40) and featuring cinnamon- and vermillion-beribboned mounds of rock as far as the eye can see.

Native Americans were also inspired by this landscape; the remains of both Basketmaker and Ancestral Puebloan culture dot the landscape, ready to be explored. Also in this area are intriguing 200-million-year-old fossilized clam beds from the Triassic Period. Geology, archaeology, paleontology—it's all on display in this stunning eastern pocket of the Grand Canyon State.

Park Basics

Established: December 8, 1906 (national monument); December 9, 1962 (national park).
Area: 346 square miles; 221,416 acres.
Best For: Archaeology, Geology, Hiking, Horseback Riding, Paleontology.

Petrified Forest National Park, AZ

Contact: 928/524-6228, www.nps.gov/pefo.
Getting Oriented: Interstate 40 bisects Petrified Forest in eastern Arizona. Phoenix Sky Harbor International Airport (southwest of the park) and New Mexico's Albuquerque International Sunport (east on I-40) are each about 200 miles away. The town of **Holbrook** (www.ci.holbrook.az.us), 26 miles west of the park, makes a good base for eating,

sleeping, and filling up the gas tank. The park's main, **North Entrance** is on I-40, along with the nearby **Painted Desert Visitor Center**; the **South Entrance** is off US 180 between Holbrook and **St. Johns** (www.sjaz. us). The park is on the southern border of the expansive, semi-autonomous **Navajo Nation** (www.discovernavajo.com), also well worth exploring.

Park Highlights

Natural Attractions. Among the park's greatest natural attractions are the multihued blocks and slabs of **petrified wood**, created by a process in which minerals replace organic material. Easily rivaling them, however, are the spectacular views across the **Painted Desert**, a series of multicolored badlands. This terrain, with rocky slopes and soils that have been eroded by water, wind, and time, stretches north from I-40 into Navajo Nation.

The park's **Red Basin Clam Beds** are another stunning example of badlands. This area, added to the park in 2007, features freshwater-clam fossil beds and petrified wood. You can access the striated, multicolored badlands in this section of the park only by hiking trail, but it's worth the effort.

Trails, Drives & Viewpoints. The 28-mile **park road** winds between the North and South entrances. Its fascinating sites and viewpoints include the **Tiponi Point**, **Tawa Point**, and **Katchina Point** overlooks, all north of I-40 and all looking out over the Painted Desert's rust-colored mounds.

Hiking one of the several relatively short trails is an absolute must. These include **Crystal Forest** loop trail (0.75 mile, easy), which has you walking among giant sections of petrified wood logs; the easy 1-mile loop to **Blue Mesa**; and the **Painted Desert Rim Trail** (1-mile round-trip, easy) that winds along the mesa's rim. Off-the-beaten-path options include the easy 2.5-mile round-trip **Jasper Forest Road** hike, which claims some of the park's biggest samples of petrified wood, and the **Red Basin Clam Beds Trail** (6 miles round-trip, moderate but GPS unit strongly recommended), highlighting the park's colored sandstone formations and giant fossil beds.

Museums & Sites. South of I-40 near the park road, the **Puerco Pueblo** features remains of a 100-room dwelling from around AD 1300. Definitely stop by the Pueblo Revival–style **Painted Desert Inn**, a former shop, restaurant, and inn dating from the 1920s that's on the park road. At this museum and information center, you can learn about the history of Route 66, which runs through the park, as well as admire murals painted

in 1948 by Hopi artist Fred Kabotie. The **Rainbow Forest Museum**, near the South Entrance, has some excellent paleontology exhibits as well as a bookstore. Behind the museum, a short trail leads to the park's biggest log, the aptly named **Old Faithful**.

Programs & Activities. The *Timeless Impressions* orientation film that's shown continuously at both the Painted Desert Visitor Center and the Rainbow Forest Museum gives a great overview of the park's geologic, paleontological, archaeological, and historical attractions. Rangers supplement this with **guided hikes** relating to all these features. The park also has an **artist-in-residence program**; artists give lectures and workshops, including a photographic series. Kids can enjoy finding the various **geocache** and **EarthCache** (highlighting special geosciences features) sites throughout the park.

Horseback riding is allowed within the park's Wilderness Area, but you must bring your own horse. There are no established trails, but there's trailer parking and a series of switchbacks that descend into the Painted Desert.

Lodging. The only way to stay within the park is to **backcountry camp**; otherwise, head west to Holbrook for standard accommodations. Backcountry camping requires a free permit (obtained in person), and park restrictions specify how close you can pitch a tent to certain areas and how far you must hike before pitching a tent (at least 1 mile from each parking lot).

Dozens of chain hotels line I-40 near Holbrook, but skip them and shack up in one of two Route 66–era motels: The **Globetrotter Lodge** (902 W. Hopi Dr., 928/297-0158, hotelsholbrookaz.com) has 10 individually decorated rooms, and the kitschy **Wigwam Motel** (811 W. Hopi Dr., 928/524-3048, www.sleepinawigwam.com) has 15 tepee-shaped rooms that are a throwback to sites built to attract drivers. Holbrook also is home to a **KOA Campground** (102 Hermosa Dr., 928/524-6689, www.koa.com) with a pool, RV hookups, cabins, and tent-camping sites.

1. Blue Mesa. **2.** Petrified logs. **3.** Painted Desert.

Pinnacles National Park

CALIFORNIA

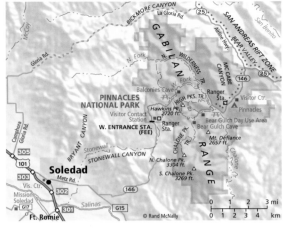

Amid Salinas Valley ranchland and farmland, a group of giant volcanic rocks rise seemingly out of nowhere, enticing intrepid hikers, spelunkers, birders, and rock climbers.

The place? Pinnacles National Park, an hour inland from the beautiful California coast and a few hours from the City by the Bay, San Francisco. Once in this relatively small park, you'll be treated to the sight of soaring raptors drifting on invisible winds high overhead before you descend into pitch-black talus caves, openings (formed by seismic activity) between boulders on mountainsides.

When you emerge from the caves, the Pinnacles themselves—remains of an ancient volcano whose other half is 200 miles farther south along the San Andreas Fault—stand out in front of the blue California sky, ready to be hiked through, climbed on, or just plain admired from wherever you happen to be standing.

Pinnacles National Park, CA

Park Basics

Established: January 16, 1908 (national monument); January 10, 2013 (national park).
Area: 42 square miles; 26,686 acres.
Best For: Astronomy; Bird-Watching (condors, hawks, vultures); Climbing; Hiking.
Contact: 831/389-4486, www.nps.gov/pinn.
Getting Oriented: The park's **East Entrance**, open 24 hours a day, is about 120 miles south of San Francisco International Airport via I-280, Highway 101, and CA 25. The **West Entrance** (less friendly to RVs due to curving roads) is open during the day. Both entrances have visitors centers; however, it's a 21-mile, 1-hour drive between them as they aren't connected inside the park.

Hollister (hollister.ca.gov), 30 miles north of the East Entrance, and **King City** (www. kingcity.com), 24 miles south of the West Entrance, are good bases. Another option is historic **Salinas** (www.cityofsalinas.org), 37 miles north of the West Entrance and the birthplace of writer John Steinbeck.

③

Park Highlights

Natural Attractions. Where to start—caves or rocks? Part of the same ancient volcano that split apart millions of years ago, both are equally enticing. The rocky **High Peaks** of the Pinnacles have slanted striations from upthrusts of volcanic activity. Green, yellow, and orange lichen cling to the spires, providing surprising bursts of color as you're hiking or climbing.

Other views here are dark—very dark. Bring a flashlight or a headlamp (use your smartphone in a pinch) to navigate the **talus caves**. Some are pitch black and might require bending, crawling, and climbing to get through them. All the while, you can gaze up at giant boulders that have tightly wedged themselves between slits in the pinnacles.

Trails, Drives & Viewpoints. If you want stunning views without leaving your car, Pinnacles isn't for you. CA 146 traverses

④

both sides of the park, and although it doesn't connect inside of it, both western and eastern spurs end in trailheads. On the east side, the signature hike is an utterly rewarding **6-mile loop trail**, an unnamed combination of multiple trails, recommended by rangers and viewable on park maps. It starts at the Bear Gulch Day Use Area, passes through the Bear Gulch Cave to Bear Gulch Reservoir (1.2 miles one-way, moderate), and continues on the Rim Trail (0.4 mile one-way, easy) to the first section of the High Peaks Trail to Scout Peak (1.5 miles). From here, glance west to catch the sun lighting up the peaks. To complete the loop, continue on the "Steep and Narrow" section of the **High Peaks Trail** (1.3 miles one-way, strenuous), featuring stairs cut into rock, and then descend via the **Condor Gulch Trail** (1.7 miles, moderate).

On the western side, you can also reach the High Peaks from the **Juniper Canyon Trail** (1.8 miles, strenuous) to connect at the Scout Peak overlook along the High Peaks Trail. The signature route here, though, is the **Balconies Hike**, first along the easy, 0.6-mile one-way Balconies Trail, and then on a moderate, 0.8-mile one-way hike up the Balconies Cliffs Trail. Finally, descend through the dark, narrow, and exciting Balconies Cave Trail (0.4 mile one-way, strenuous). Connect back to the Balconies Trail for a total hike of 2.4 miles.

Programs & Activities. Because Pinnacles is far enough from the Bay Area's metropolis to have dark skies, **stargazing programs** and **night hikes** with park rangers are popular. If you're into **bird-watching**, be on the lookout

for the elusive California condor, which has been reintroduced into this area. (It's more likely that what's circling overhead is a turkey vulture or a common raven, though.)

Rock Climbing is a popular activity, with climbers scaling sheer vertical cliffs such as the Tourist Trap and the Discovery Wall. Conditions change frequently, so climbing areas can open and close. Outfitters such as **Adventure Out** (www.adventureout.com, 800/509-3954) can help beginners get harnessed up, meeting you inside the park with gear.

Lodging. The only in-park lodging is at **Pinnacles Campground** (Recreation.gov) along the road a few miles from the East Entrance. It has a store and 14 group, 37 RV, and 82 tent sites (some set back from the road). Backcountry camping isn't allowed.

If you want a bed, head to one of the towns that form a sort of triangle around the park. In Hollister, cozy up in the Victorian **Joshua Inn Bed & Breakfast** (712 West St., 831/265-7829, www.joshuainn.com). King City's **Fireside Inn** (640 Broadway St., 831/386-1010, www.firesideinnca.com) is a handy downtown motel. In Salinas, the **Country Inn Motel** (126 John St., 831/757-8383) is a few blocks from Main Street's period theaters and the **Monterey Coast Brewing Company** (165 Main St., 831/758-2337, www.montereycoastbrewing.com).

1. Tunnel Rock High Peaks Trail. **2.** Rock climbing in the park. **3.** Balconies Cave Trail. **4.** Condor.

Redwood National & State Parks

Just inland from a hundreds-of-miles-long stretch of magnificent coast are forests with trees so high, so green, and so old that it's hard to believe you're still on planet Earth.

The star attraction? *Sequoia sempervirens*, or the towering coast redwood. Peppering the seaboard from Monterey, California, northward into Oregon are some groves that have been standing for a thousand years. You can get awesome views of the redwoods along several beautiful roads here. Even better, though, is getting out of your car and walking among them. You'll feel their age, and their majesty, deep in your bones.

The four parks that comprise Redwood National & State Parks (RNSP) are jointly administered by the National Park Service and California State Parks: Redwood National Park, Prairie Creek Redwoods State Park, Del Norte Coast Redwoods State Park, and Jedediah Smith Redwoods

Redwood National & State Parks, CA

State Park. Together they preserve thousands of acres—of what was formerly *hundreds* of thousands of acres—of coastal redwood stands.

Park Basics

Established: October 2, 1968 (national park); state parks established 1923–29.
Area: 217 square miles; 139,000 acres.
Best For: Backcountry Camping; Cycling; Hiking; Kayaking; Wildlife Watching (black-tailed deer, Roosevelt elk, sea lions).
Contact: 707/465-7335, www.nps.gov/redw.
Getting Oriented: Redwood National Park, the southernmost park in the RNSP system, is 320 miles north of San Francisco International Airport via US 101; northernmost Jedediah Smith Redwoods State Park is 330 miles south of Oregon's Portland International Airport via I-5.

It's 51 miles on US 101 between Redwood's **Thomas H. Kuchel Visitor Center** and Smith's **Hiouchi Visitor Center**; you pass Prairie Creek Redwoods State Park and Del Norte Coast Redwoods State Park along the way. **Arcata** (www.cityofarcata.org), about 30 miles south of RNSP, is a great base from which to explore if you're coming up from San Francisco; **Crescent City** (www.crescentcity.org) is just outside Jedediah Smith, closest to the Oregon border.

Park Highlights

Natural Attractions. The giant, straight-as-an-arrow coastal redwood is one of nature's most stunning creations. If one was simply plunked down somewhere in a town park, it's conceivable that, at anywhere from 250 to 300 feet tall (or more), it would be the tallest thing for miles around. Its massive bulk is equally impressive, as redwoods can be 20 to 30 feet in diameter; now you know why one tree can provide enough wood to build a small hotel.

The deep green undergrowth at the base of the redwoods—including the ever-present sword fern—provides a great visual counterpoint to the medium-to-dark mahogany tones of redwood trunks. The parks either abut or are just inland from Humboldt and Del Norte counties' magnificent coastline, where secluded coves, windswept beaches, and craggy headlands are more likely to be accessible by hiking trail than by motorized vehicle.

Trails, Drives & Viewpoints. Heading north from Arcata (or south from Crescent City) on **US 101**, you'll eventually run through all four parks with their stunning vistas, tree-lined side roads, and innumerable hiking and biking trails. Drive the 17-mile (one-way) **Bald Hills Road** in Redwood National for an elevated glimpse of the park; the **Newton B. Drury Scenic Parkway** (10 miles one-way) in Prairie Creek for a possible sighting of Roosevelt elk; the **Enderts Beach Road** (2.25

miles one-way) in Del Norte Coast for a great view at Crescent Beach Overlook; and the **Howland Hill Road** (10 miles one-way) for the old-growth redwoods in Jedediah Smith.

Hiking through the redwoods, especially en route to a secluded riverbank or beachhead, is your best answer to the traffic on US 101. Start with the classic **Tall Trees Trail** through Redwood National's true giants (4 miles round-trip, moderate), and move on to the **Fern Canyon Loop Trail** (0.7 miles round-trip, easy) in Prairie Creek for some fern photo-ops. The **Damnation Creek Trail** (2.2 miles one-way, strenuous) in Del Norte starts with redwoods and winds down through Sitka spruce before it ends at a small, rocky beach. The **Stout Memorial Grove Trail** (0.5-mile loop, easy) in Jedediah Smith gets you close to that park's tallest old-growth trees.

Programs & Activities. You can join park rangers on a variety of activities, including a daily one-hour **Forest Walk** at the Simpson-

Reed Discovery Trailhead in Redwood National. Cyclists should note that on Saturdays, the Newton B. Drury Scenic Parkway is closed to vehicular traffic. RNSP has other great biking options, including a 6-mile (one-way, moderate) stretch of the **Coastal Trail** and the **Davison Trail** (3 miles round-trip, easy).

Perhaps the coolest activity with a ranger is the two-hour, summer-only **Smith River Kayak Tour**, beginning and ending at the Jedediah Smith Day Use Area. On this trip, you wend your way through the forest along the chilly Smith River on Class I/Class II rapids.

Lodging. Camping—in a campground or in the backcountry—is the only option at RNSP, but camping among the redwoods, alongside a creek, and overlooking a Pacific beach are all seminal experiences. The four campgrounds (**Jedediah Smith** and **Mill Creek** in Del Norte Coast, and **Elk Prairie** and **Gold Bluffs Beach** in Prairie Creek) can be booked through www.reservecalifornia.com; they have a total of 332 sites. For backcountry camping, spread out over eight locations, check the park's website for permit and other information.

If a cozy California coastal town is more your thing, we understand. You can find many options, such as Crescent City's **Curly Redwood Lodge** (701 US 101 S, 707/464-2137, www.curlyredwoodlodge.com), built from one redwood tree in the 1950s, and Arcata's inviting **Lady Anne Bed & Breakfast** (902 14th St., 707/822-2797, www.ladyanneinn.com). Others include the **Requa Inn** (451 Requa Rd., 707/482-1425, www.requainn.com) in Klamath ("where the river meets the ocean") and the **Trinidad Bay Bed & Breakfast** (560 Edwards St., 707/677-0840, www.trinidadbaybnb.com) overlooking the bay in Trinidad.

1. Towering coastal redwoods. **2.** The view from Bald Hills Road. **3.** Roosevelt elk.

Rocky Mountain National Park

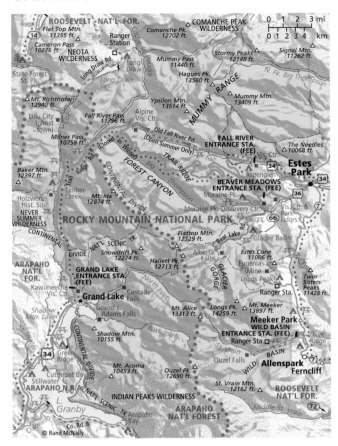

Its majesty crown studded by peaks soaring above the timberline, this park is marked by a treeless ecosystem that is home to some of Earth's hardiest living things.

The wide swath of alpine tundra is largely dormant for half of the year as snow falls, winds howl, and temperatures plunge. But that's just in the high country. Below, verdant meadows hold shimmering lakes, and rivers and streams transport snowmelt down the mountains, where forests define the landscape of this hiker's dream.

In summer you can traverse the vast expanse of stunning scenery—home to elk, black bears, and mountain lions—on Trail Ridge Road, which tops out at 12,183 feet, making it the highest paved road in any U.S. national park. Then, when winter again hits the Rockies, the park's interior shuts down as an annual average of about 20 feet of snow blankets the higher elevations. The entrances remain open for the skiers, snowshoers, and sightseers who come for the hushed silence and solitude.

Park Basics

Established: January 26, 1915.
Area: 415 square miles; 265,795 acres.
Best For: Backcountry Camping; Geology; Hiking; Wildlife Watching (bighorn sheep, elk, moose).
Contact: 970/586-1206, www.nps.gov/romo.

Rocky Mountain National Park, CO

Getting Oriented: Rocky Mountain is in north-central Colorado, 40 miles northwest of Boulder via US 36 and 35 miles west of Loveland via US 34. Denver International Airport is 78 miles southeast of the Beaver Meadows Entrance. The main gateway towns include **Estes Park** (www.visitestespark.com), 3 miles east of the Beaver Meadows Entrance and 4 miles southeast of the Fall River Entrance, and **Grand Lake** (grandlakechamber.com), 2 miles south of the Grand Lake Entrance in the southwestern corner.

The park's Trail Ridge Road runs 48 miles between Estes Park and Grand Lake, and is closed from late October to June. There are visitors centers at the **Beaver Meadows** and **Fall River** entrances on the park's east side,

and **Moraine Park Discovery Center** is 2 miles southwest of Beaver Meadows. **Alpine Visitor Center**, near Trail Ridge Road's high point, is 22 miles west of Beaver Meadows; **Kawuneeche Visitor Center** is at the Grand Lake Entrance.

Park Highlights

Natural Attractions. The star attractions are the park's namesake **Rocky Mountains**. Their formation began about 70 million years ago, when geologic uplift began pushing ancient rocks about a mile skyward. Of the park's 124 named peaks, 20 have summits higher than 13,000 feet. At 14,259 feet, **Longs Peak** is the tallest, and a draw for climbers from all over the world.

Subalpine forests and meadows dominate the mountains' lower flanks. Pine beetles, insects the size of a grain of rice that kill trees by feasting inside the bark, have ravaged many of the forests. Above 11,000 feet, woods and meadows give way to alpine tundra, which makes up more than a third of the park's land area. Windswept and devoid of trees, this fragile ecosystem typically sees at least a little snowfall every month of the year.

Trails, Drives & Viewpoints. Rocky Mountain has more than 300 miles of trails. The easy, 0.6-mile loop around **Bear Lake** is a good scenic introduction to the east side. From the **Glacier Gorge trailhead** nearby, it's a moderate 0.6 miles to Alberta Falls and a moderate 2.8 miles to Mills Lake.

In the Wild Basin Unit, the **Ouzel Falls Trail** offers a moderate, 5.4-mile round-trip to a waterfall named for the bird also known as the American dipper. Just north of Grand Lake, the **North Inlet Trail** is a moderate, 6.8-mile round-trip to Cascade Falls by way of a wide mountain valley; more experienced hikers can continue to a pair of lakes and Flattop Mountain.

Twisting, turning, and gaining more than 3,000 feet along its 48 miles, **Trail Ridge Road** ranks among the highest and most scenic roads in the United States. Numerous endless-view overlooks merit a stop, including Far View Curve and Rainbow Curve. **Old Fall River Road**, the park's original automobile route, is a curving one-way, 11-mile drive that connects with Trail Ridge Road; it has been called "a motor nature trail."

Museums & Sites. On Rocky Mountain's west side, **Holzwarth Historic Site** was homesteaded in 1917 and later became a dude ranch. It's open to the public for guided tours. The area also has a mining legacy: Reachable by a 2.8-mile hike from the Longs Peak Trailhead on the park's east side, **Eugenia Mine** was abandoned in 1919 but has intriguing ruins. The remains of **Lulu City**, a mining boomtown that went bust in the 1880s, are 3.7 miles from the Colorado River Trailhead near Grand Lake.

Programs & Activities. In summer, ranger-led activities include guided hikes, talks on ecology and geology, and stargazing programs. Guided snowshoe walks are available in winter. Horseback riding is a staple, and the park has two stables: **Glacier Creek** (970/586-3244, www.sombrero.com) and **Moraine Park** (970/586-2327, www.sombrero.com).

Climbers flock to Longs Peak and other mountains. The **Colorado Mountain School** (341 Moraine Ave., Estes Park, 720/387-8944, coloradomountainschool.com) offers guided mountaineering and climbing expeditions.

Lodging. The park's 5 campgrounds have more than 550 sites in all; the largest, 247-site **Moraine Park** (Recreation.gov) on the east side, accepts tents and RVs. A fee-based permit is required for backcountry camping.

The gateways of Estes Park, Grand Lake, and Allenspark provide a variety of accommodations. **The Stanley Hotel** (333 Wonderview Ave., 970/577-4000, www.stanleyhotel.com) is the grande dame of Estes Park. Opened in 1909, the hostelry inspired Stephen King to write *The Shining*. **YMCA of the Rockies** (2515 Tunnel Rd., Estes Park, 970/586-3344, ymcarockies.org) offers recreational activities and accommodations from lodge rooms to spacious homes. Historic **Grand Lake Lodge** (15500 US 34, Grand Lake, 970/627-3967, grandlakelodge.com) has comfortable cabins and "Colorado's favorite front porch."

1. Alberta Falls. **2.** Hiking in the park. **3.** A Rocky Mountain National Park vista.

Saguaro National Park

ARIZONA

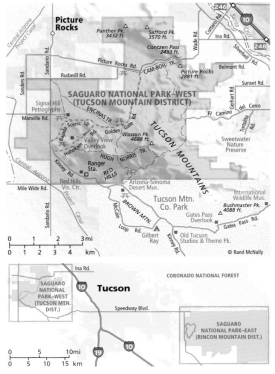

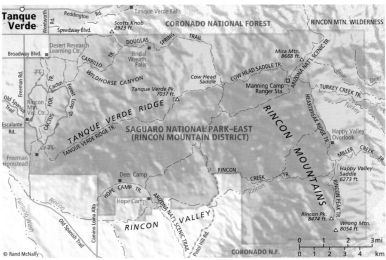

Saguaro National Park, AZ

At first glance, with the powerful Arizona sun beating down on the landscape, it seems unlikely that anything is even alive, let alone moving. But, if you look more closely—and remain patient and still—the Sonoran Desert seemingly springs to life.

Spotted, striped, and horned lizards scuttle about in the vegetation while woodpeckers poke holes in the trunks of 8-foot-high saguaro cacti and Mexican jays wheel about overhead.

As you keep walking, bright flowers on top of giant, rounded cacti reveal themselves to your desert-acclimated eyes before the sun sinks below the mountains ringing the park.

This is both the fun and the challenge of visiting Saguaro National Park, which brackets the bustling city of Tucson. It's easy to drive through and take a gander from the car at the desert landscape. Once you're on a trail hiking through the desert or up the mountains of its roadless

backcountry, though, the park's many layers are yours to experience.

Park Basics

Established: March 1, 1933 (national monument); October 4, 1994 (national park).
Area: 143 square miles; 91,442 acres.
Best For: Astronomy, Backcountry Camping, Cycling, Hiking, Horseback Riding.
Contact: 520/733-5153 (East), 520/733-5158 (West); www.nps.gov/sagu.
Getting Oriented: Saguaro has two districts, east and west, each a few miles from the outskirts of **Tucson** (www.visittucson.org), Arizona's second-largest city. Tucson International Airport has plenty of flights and is at the junction of I-10 and I-19 in southern Arizona, making Saguaro very easy to reach. Its large east section is serviced by the **Rincon Mountain Visitor Center** (3693 Old Spanish Trail, 20 miles from downtown); the significantly smaller west section has the **Red Hills Visitor Center** (2700 N. Kinney Rd., 15 miles from downtown). Both are open daily and are great places to fill your water bottles and discuss hiking options with rangers.

Park Highlights

Natural Attractions. Cactus, cactus everywhere! You'll be amazed by the shapes and sizes of the park's 25 species—and by the sometimes stunning colors of the flowers that many of them sport. The towering saguaro (suh-*wah*-row), for which the park is named, is shaped the way every comic book and animation artist has drawn cacti since time immemorial.

The ground-hugging barrel cactus can feature iridescent yellow, orange, red, or pink flowers at certain times of year. Saguaro's many prickly pear cacti have flowers, too. The tree-like cholla sprouts needles from every one of its contorted branches and is the most dangerous-looking cactus of all. Overlooking this flora is the park's high-elevation, roadless wilderness area in the east section, with ponderosa pine–covered 8,668-foot Mica Mountain lording over it.

Trails, Drives & Viewpoints. Both sections feature a loop road for driving or biking; the east section's 8-mile **Cactus Forest Loop Road** and the west section's 6-mile unpaved **Bajada Loop Drive** provide a great introduction to the desert vistas, studded as they are with the park's eponymous cacti. The mountains surrounding the park serve as a scenic backdrop. If you want to ascend a peak, make the 27-mile drive up 9,157-foot **Mt. Lemmon** (starting where E. Catalina Hwy. turns into Mt. Lemmon Hwy.), just north of Saguaro's east section in the Coronado National Forest; the vistas are spectacular.

Park trails let you get up close and personal with the crazy shapes of the cacti, listen to birds whoosh overhead, and see lizards scampering underfoot. The east section's easy **Mica View Trail** is a great 2-mile loop through the desert; prick up your ears for the park's woodpeckers. In the west section, the 0.4-mile (one-way) **Valley View Trail** is another easy walk through the desert landscape.

Museum. Just outside the park's west section, the **Arizona-Sonora Desert Museum** (2021 N. Kinney Rd, Tucson, 520/883-2702, www.desertmuseum.org) combines a zoo, aquarium, botanical garden, and interpretive center. The museum has walking paths, an art gallery, and live demonstrations as well as a hummingbird aviary and hands-on tide pool.

Programs & Activities. Saguaro's constant stream of ranger talks throughout the year focuses on the park's wildlife (such as the pig-like javelina and the park's most popular denizen, the lizard) and cacti. You can also join guided sunrise, sunset, and moonlight walks, as well as Star Parties celebrating the night sky.

Since the park is hot and water is heavy, long hiking trails in Saguaro can be a challenge. **Biking** is a great way to experience the two loop roads (the west section road is unpaved), as it's easier to carry additional liquids. Better yet, let a horse do the heavy lifting: **Houston's Horseback Riding** (12801 E. Speedway Blvd., Tucson, 520/298-7450, www.tucsonhorsebackriding.com) is just outside Saguaro's east section.

Lodging. If you want to overnight in Saguaro, you must be a dedicated backpacker. Six backcountry camps in the east section, including **Manning Camp** (at 8,000 feet), have a total of 21 sites; obtain permits in person, by mail, or by fax up to two months in advance. To get to any of the camps, you have to hike at least 4 miles (one-way), and only Manning has water.

To keep to the rural aesthetic while staying in Tuscon, try the **Tanque Verde Ranch** (14301 E. Speedway Blvd., 520/296-6275, www.tanqueverderanch.com), a working dude ranch with plenty of amenities just outside the east section. In town, you can stay at the historic **Hotel Congress** (311 E. Congress St., 520/622-8848, hotelcongress.com), whose bar and club remain open deep into the night, or relax on the wide porch of **El Presidio Bed & Breakfast Inn** (297 N. Main Ave., 520/623-6151, www.elpresidiobbinn.com).

1. Saguaro sunset. **2.** Horseback trail riding at the Tanque Verde Ranch. **3.** Tanque Verde Ranch. **4.** Thrasher on a blooming cactus.

Sequoia and Kings Canyon National Parks

CALIFORNIA

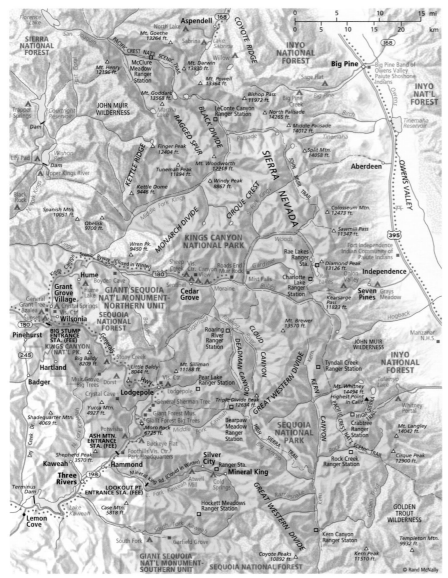

These sister parks in the Sierra Nevada have some of the biggest singular organisms on Earth: giant sequoia trees. You'll also find Mt. Whitney, the highest peak in the lower 48.

Although technically two parks, Sequoia and Kings Canyon are adjacent—with vast tracts of High Sierra wilderness—and managed as one unit. Sequoia is centered on its namesake trees: startlingly massive specimens of the *Sequoiadendron giganteum*. The world's largest trees by volume can grow to more than 300 feet in height and nearly 30 feet in diameter over life spans measured in millennia. Ring counts have shown some have lived more than 3,000 years.

To the north, Kings Canyon is named for a dramatic gorge that was once considered a great site for a reservoir but was instead made parkland in the 1960s. This hiking and backpacking paradise is home to another iconic stand of towering trees at Grant Grove.

Park Basics

Established: September 25, 1890 (Sequoia); October 1, 1890 (General Grant National Park); March 4, 1940 (General Grant renamed Kings Canyon and expanded).
Area: 1,353 square miles; 865,964 acres (total for both parks).

Kings Canyon National Park, CA

Sequoia National Park, CA

Best For: Backcountry Camping, Botany, Hiking.
Contact: 559/565-3341, www.nps.gov/seki.
Getting Oriented: The parks are amid the southern reaches of the Sierra Nevada in central California. CA 198 (aka Generals Highway) runs to the Ash Mountain Entrance

and the **Foothills Visitor Center**, home to park headquarters, on Sequoia's southwest side. It then ascends along hairpin turns to high country, passing the **Lodgepole Visitor Center**. The Mineral King section of Sequoia, which has a ranger station, is accessible via the seasonally open Mineral King Road outside the Ash Mountain Entrance. To the northwest, CA 180 (aka Kings Canyon Scenic Byway) accesses Kings Canyon's Big Stump Entrance and the main visitors center in **Grant Grove Village**. Northeast along the byway is **Cedar Grove Visitor Center**.

The nearest major airport is Fresno Yosemite International, 51 miles west of Kings Canyon's Big Stump Entrance; San Francisco International Airport is 240 miles northwest. Gateway towns include **Three Rivers** (threeriversvillage.com) and **Visalia** (www.visitvisalia.org), situated 7 and 36 miles, respectively, southwest of Sequoia's Ash Mountain Entrance.

Park Highlights

Natural Attractions. In Sequoia, General Sherman Tree in **Giant Forest** is considered the world's largest living tree. It's 275 feet tall, with a 36-foot base diameter—and the 2,100-year-old specimen continues to grow! In Kings Canyon's **Grant Grove**, General Grant Tree (aka The Nation's Christmas Tree), is 267 feet tall and a whopping 103 feet around.

The huge trees are complemented by equally sizable mountains and canyons. Far from any roads on Sequoia's east side, **Mt. Whitney** tops out at 14,494 feet, making it the tallest peak in the contiguous United States. **Kings Canyon** is one of North America's deepest, with a maximum depth of more than 8,000 feet. Carved over eons by glaciers, the granite valley is bordered on the east by the Sierra

Crest and the park's highest peak, 14,265-foot **North Palisade**.

Drives, Trails & Viewpoints. The 36-mile drive from Grant Grove along **Kings Canyon Scenic Byway**—to the so-called Roads End—and the 28-mile drive on Sequoia's **Mineral King Road** offer great scenery in lesser-visited areas. Both roads close from roughly October to May. In Sequoia's Giant Forest, the easy, 2-mile **Congress Trail** takes you to General Sherman and other giant sequoias. Nearby, climb a strenuous 0.25 mile up **Moro Rock** for unparalleled views; add a moderate 4.1-mile hike on the adjacent **Soldiers Loop Trail**.

In Kings Canyon, head to Roads End for a 100-yard walk to **Muir Rock**—a favorite pulpit for Sierra Club founder John Muir to advocate for conservation—then continue on the trail for a moderate, 1.5-mile hike to **Zumwalt Meadow** and back. A stretch of the strenuous, 211-mile **John Muir Trail** between Yosemite Valley and Mt. Whitney runs north–south through both parks. Wilderness permits are required for overnight camping; there's a moderate fee.

Programs, Activities & Sites. Ranger programs include science and nature presentations and guided hikes. There are also campfire talks at Foothills, Lodgepole, and Mineral King in Sequoia and Grant Grove and Cedar Grove in Kings Canyon. In a renovated historic market, the **Giant Forest Museum** (4605 Generals Hwy.) features exhibits on the ecology and history of giant sequoias. Several trails leading to the trees start at this museum.

Located 7 miles northwest of the Generals Highway, near the Ash Mountain Entrance, the intricate subterranean world of **Crystal Cave** (www.explorecrystalcave.com) is accessible via 50-minute guided tours in the summer. Tickets are available for a moderate fee online and at

visitors centers. Allow four hours driving and hiking to the cave plus the tour duration.

Lodging. Fresno and Visalia have lots of chain hotels, and Three Rivers has a mix of independent lodgings and cabin complexes. That said, both parks have a variety of accommodations. Managed by **Delaware North** (866/807-3598, www.visitsequoia.com), Sequoia's **Wuksachi Lodge** (64740 Wuksachi Way) is a newer property with a restaurant and easy access to trails near Lodgepole off Generals Highway. In the Mineral King area, **Silver City Resort** (51490 Mineral King Rd., 559/561-3223, www.silvercityresort.com) offers cabins and chalets, as well as legendary house-made pies (closed in winter).

Kings Canyon has three in-park lodgings (all managed by Delaware North) along Kings Canyon Scenic Byway. In Grant Grove Village, you'll find the cozy **Grant Grove Cabins**, built in the 1920s, and the relatively modern, stone-and-timber **John Muir Lodge**. On the Snake River near Roads End is the motel-like **Cedar Grove Lodge** (closed in winter).

There are 14 campgrounds in the parks; most are first-come, first served. Just off Generals Highway, in the heart of Sequoia, **Lodgepole** (Recreation.gov) is one of the largest and most developed, with a store, showers, and sites for RVs and tents.

1. Grant Grove in Kings Canyon. **2.** Road through Kings Canyon. **3.** The General Sherman Tree in Sequoia is considered the largest living tree on the planet.

Shenandoah National Park

Just one brief sentence—"Let's take a drive in the country"— captures America's love of the road. Take a trip to Shenandoah National Park and that drive can include extras such as mountain climbing, bird-watching, horseback riding, and fly fishing.

More than 100 miles long but just 12 miles wide at most, Shenandoah covers about 200,000 mostly forested acres that wash across mountains and valleys out to the horizon. Topping it off is the 105-mile Skyline Drive, a National Scenic Byway that runs the length of the park on the crest of the Blue Ridge Mountains. While every national park is unique, for motorists and motorcyclists, this scenic road sets Shenandoah apart.

Travel the Skyline Drive and you'll be overwhelmed by the sight of woods and waterfalls, mountains and valleys, and mile after beautiful mile with plenty of places to pause and appreciate the allure of this special corner of Virginia.

Park Basics

Established: December 26, 1935.
Area: 311 square miles; 199,117 acres.

Shenandoah National Park, VA

Best For: Bird-Watching (barred owls, Carolina chickadees, peregrine falcons, red-tailed hawks, wild turkeys); Cycling; Fishing; Hiking; Wildlife Watching (black bears, deer, raccoons, river otters, woodchucks).
Contact: 540/999-3500, www.nps.gov/shen.
Getting Oriented: Shenandoah National Park has four entrances: **Front Royal** (North Entrance), **Thornton Gap**, **Swift Run Gap**, and **Rockfish Gap** (near Waynesboro). The park also has three districts—north, central, and south—and two visitors centers. Mile markers (aka MM and Mile Post or MP) along Skyline Drive, Shenandoah's one public road, start at 0.0 in Front Royal. The **Dickey Ridge Visitor Center** is near MM 5, and the **Harry F. Byrd Visitor Center** is at MM 51. In addition, two east–west roads cross the long, narrow park: US 211 (aka Lee Highway) toward the northern end and US 33 near the southern end.

Major airports close to nearby Washington, D.C., include Ronald Reagan Washington National (70 miles east of Front Royal via I-66) and Dulles International (56 miles east). **Front**

Royal (frontroyalva.com) in the north and **Charlottesville** (www.visitcharlottesville.org), 30 miles east of the park's southern entrance, have lodgings and other amenities.

Park Highlights

Natural Attractions. From Skyline Drive, the most visible attractions are valleys, forests, and the famed Blue Ridge Mountains. Those forests are what color the mountains when they are seen from a distance. Isoprene, an organic compound released by the trees, creates the famous bluish haze across the landscape.

Look closer and you can find rivers and even waterfalls, the most notable of which require a walk in the woods. **Overall Run Falls**, the park's tallest at 93 feet, requires a moderately difficult 6.5-mile round-trip hike from the

parking area near MM 21. The most accessible is 70-foot **Dark Hollow Falls**, a moderate but steep 1.4-mile round-trip near MM 50.7.

Drives, Trails & Viewpoints. The 35 mph speed limit along 105-mile **Skyline Drive** is ideal for stopping and soaking in scenery at 75 overlooks. Some have names reflecting the region's Appalachian roots, such as Hogwallow Flats, Riprap, and Gooney Run. Near Hogback Overlook, the **Elkwallow Wayside** at MM 24 has a coffee shop, grills, and restrooms. Similar waysides are in the central district near MM 51 at **Big Meadows** and the southern district at **Loft Mountain** at MM 79.5.

The road drills a 670-foot-long hole through **Mary's Rock Mountain** (MM 32) and reaches 3,680 feet (the drive's highest point) near MM 42 at **Skyland Resort**. Hint: When driving Skyline Drive, be mindful of bicyclists as well as wild turkeys, bears, and deer. At the road's southern terminus, the scenic **Blue Ridge Parkway** (www.nps.gov/blri) begins, continuing for 469 miles into the Great Smoky Mountains and ending near Cherokee in North Carolina.

Out of view are more than 500 miles of trails—about 100 of them belonging to the **Appalachian Trail**, which runs roughly parallel to Skyline Drive. The rest lead to rivers, waterfalls, mountain peaks, or simply longer trails. The most popular peak is **Old Rag Mountain** (elev. 3,291), whose "rock scramble" summit is accessible via two trails on a strenuous 9.2-mile trek.

Programs & Activities. Rangers lead short hikes, host morning talks, and conduct evening presentations on the park's wildlife and botany. Schedules vary at locations including Dickey Ridge (MM 4.6), Mt. Marshall (MM 15.9), Elkwallow (MM 24), Skyland

(MM 41.7), Big Meadows (MM 51), and Loft Mountain (MM 79.5).

There's a full slate of outdoor activities such as horseback riding, bicycling, rock climbing, and fly fishing. **Trail rides** depart from Skyland and explore a few of the park's 180 miles of horse-friendly trails, and there's **fishing** in 70 mountain streams, including the Rapidan River. For more information, check the park website, Recreation.gov, and www.goshenandoah.com.

Fall foliage is highly anticipated. You can tour Skyline Drive and walk the trails, following hues that change first at higher elevations and roll down the hills in a colorful tide. In season, check the park website for color updates.

Lodging. Though nearby towns such as Front Royal and Charlottesville have many lodging options, so does the park itself. Five main park campgrounds offer more than 600 RV and tent campsites: **Mathews Arm** (MM 22), **Big Meadows** (MM 51), **Lewis Mountain** (MM 57.5), **Loft Mountain** (MM 79.5), and **Dundo Group** (MM 83.4). Not all sites take reservations on Recreation.gov; some are first come, first served.

Shenandoah's **Skyland Resort** (MM 41.7, 855/669-1402) features a 179-room lodge. **Big Meadows Lodge** (MM 51, 855/669-1402) has 96 cabins; there are also several cabins at **Lewis Mountain** (MM 57.5, 855/669-1402). Check Recreation.gov or www.goshenandoah.com for availability. Charlottesville's **Boar's Head Resort** (200 Ednam Dr., 434/296-2181, www.boarsheadresort.com) has restaurants, a spa, and an 18-hole golf course.

1. Dark Hollow Falls. **2.** Shenandoah National Park's Blue Ridge Mountains landscape in fall. **3.** Hikers on Old Rag.

Theodore Roosevelt National Park

NORTH DAKOTA

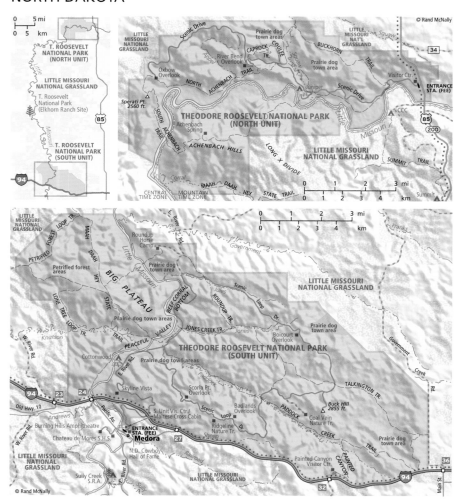

In 1883, Theodore Roosevelt discovered what the local Sioux and Dakota peoples had known for quite some time: that the North Dakota badlands were an incredible natural expanse of buttes, rocks, trees, rivers, and grassland.

The future U.S. president and conservationist took the opportunity during his first visit to establish a ranch. Even though the ranch failed, Roosevelt continued to visit, including a stop in 1903 while he was president. As you tour the same badlands more than a century later, it's clear why he returned.

Stretching out over hundreds of miles, the Little Missouri badlands and grasslands are remote and mostly unpopulated—except for bison, deer, and elk. They also offer some of America's greatest natural vistas. By following the Rough Rider's footsteps through this expanse in and beyond the park, you'll be furthering his legacy as a champion of the American wilderness.

Park Basics

Established: April 25, 1947 (national memorial park); November 10, 1978 (national park).

Area: 110 square miles; 70,466 acres.

Best For: Backcountry Camping, Canoeing, Cycling, Hiking, Horseback Riding.

Contact: 701/623-4466, www.nps.gov/thro.

Getting Oriented: Theodore Roosevelt is just off I-94 in western North Dakota, 600 miles north of Colorado's Denver International Airport. Both Bismarck (North Dakota's capital), 133 miles east of the park on I-94, and Dickinson (North Dakota's oil boomtown), 36 miles east on I-94, have small regional airports, as does Rapid City, South Dakota (239 miles

Theodore Roosevelt National Park, ND

south). Note, too, that Rapid City is a great base from which to explore the Black Hills as well as Theodore Roosevelt, Badlands, and Wind Cave national parks.

The Little Missouri National Grassland connects the park's North and South Units; a quirk of the park is that the North Unit is on Central Time, but the South Unit is on Mountain Time. The main **South Unit Visitor Center** is in Medora; the **North Unit** has one as well (68 miles northeast of Medora). The **Painted Canyon Visitor Center**, 8 miles east of Medora off I-94, is also worth a stop.

For overnight stays, the old railroad town of **Medora** (www.medorand.com) has a small but rather perfect selection of hotels, motels, and eateries.

Park Highlights

Natural Attractions. In one respect, the park really should be considered the northernmost outpost of the famous South Dakota badlands. However, while the color palette of South Dakota's badlands is gold-hued grass and pink sandstone, and the rocks and hoodoos (tall spires of rock) are craggy and pointed, in North Dakota the colors and shapes of these eroded landscapes change rather radically. Rounded rocks, tan- and ash-hued outcroppings, and lush green flood plains are on display. The elegant bends and curves of the Little Missouri River—perfect for canoeing or kayaking—run through the North Unit. Quirkily enough, the similar curves of I-94 weave through the South Unit's southern section.

Trails, Drives & Viewpoints. Since it's impossible to decide which is more beautiful—the 14-mile (one-way) **Scenic Drive** to the **Oxbow Overlook** in the North Unit or the 36-mile **Scenic Loop Drive** in the South Unit—you should spend at least a full day here to do both. Between the two units, **US 85** runs along the eastern edge of (and has turnoffs for) the Little Missouri National Grassland.

Most of the park's signature hikes and viewpoints are quite short, so you can fit several in even on a one-day visit. The North Unit's short walk to the **River Bend Overlook** has spectacular, south-facing views over the badlands and the Little Missouri River. In the South Unit, the moderate 0.6-mile round-trip **Ridgeline Nature Trail** should be your first stop, as you climb to a grass-covered hill overlooking the badlands. The **Coal Vein Trail** is an easy 0.8-mile round-trip walk into the hills to gaze at rusted horizontal coal-vein striations in the rocks.

Museums & Sites. The **Elkhorn Ranch Unit** is a small, third section of the park tucked in the Little Missouri National Grassland halfway between the North and South Units. Roosevelt's first (failed) Dakota ranch was here, although all that remains are the buildings' foundations. Of more interest is the **Maltese Cross Cabin**, steps from the South Unit Visitor Center; Roosevelt used the cabin in the 1880s at the Chimney Butte Ranch, and it's been moved here and restored to period conditions.

Programs & Activities. Ranger-led talks and tours include the daily (in summer) **Maltese Cross Cabin Tour** at the South Unit Visitor Center, and the daily (in summer) **Geology Talk** at the Painted Canyon Overlook. Guided **Full Moon Hikes**, **Night Prowls**, and **Stargazing** programs run occasionally during summer as well.

Biking the South Unit's loop road or the North Unit's scenic drive is a perfect way to access

some short hikes but still get in significant exercise. Horseback riding is allowed only in the backcountry; you'll need a free permit and your own mount. The park's **Roundup Group Horse Camp** (Recreation.gov) can accommodate horse trailers as can **Buffalo Gap Guest Ranch** (3100 Buffalo Gap Rd., Sentinel Butte, 701/623-4200, www.buffalogapguestranch.com).

Lodging. In-park lodging consists of year-round campgrounds and RV pull-through or back-in sites (but no hookups). The 50-site first-come, first-served **Juniper Campground** is in the North Unit; the 76-site **Cottonwood Campground** (Recreation.gov) in the South Unit has 37 sites. Both units offer endless backcountry camping options; pick up free, required permits at the North or South Unit visitors center.

Choices in Medora include the historic **Rough Riders Hotel** (301 3rd Ave., 701/623-4444, medora.com), steps from the **North Dakota Cowboy Hall of Fame** (250 Main St., 701/623-2000, www.northdakotacowboy.com). The log cabin–style **Amble Inn** (425 4th St., 701/623-4345, www.ambleinnmedora.com) features a Western-focused bookstore. In summer, check out the **Medora Musical** (Medora.com), a Western-themed musical variety show.

1. Bison. **2.** Rough Riders Hotel. **3.** Trail through the park's badlands landscape.

Virgin Islands National Park

In the 1950s, philanthropist and conservationist Laurance Rockefeller had the foresight to purchase land in the U.S. Virgin Islands and turn it over to the park service.

Today, this national park covers almost two-thirds of St. John and most of nearby Hassel Island—roughly 9,300 land acres and 5,600 maritime acres. Eco-adventure has always been the draw, and this continues to be true, even after devastation wrought by hurricanes Irma and Maria in 2017.

For a while, it was paradise lost. But, as past storms have shown, renewal is nature's way. The park's foliage has come back, most of its trails and facilities are open, and its swathes of white-sand beach are, once again, inviting. Though the storm toppled some reef formations, the waters are back to their vivid blue hue, clear of sediment and resplendent with marine life. Paradise found.

Park Basics

Established: August 2, 1956.
Area: 23 square miles; 14,948 acres (5,650 underwater).
Best For: Bird-Watching (brown pelicans, hummingbirds, mangrove cuckoos, white-cheeked pintails); Boating; Diving/Snorkeling; Fishing; History.
Contact: 340/776-6201, www.nps.gov/viis.
Getting Oriented: The airport for accessing St. John is Cyril E. King International Airport, near Charlotte Amalie on neighboring St. Thomas; St. John has no airport. Many people also visit the park for a day when their cruise ships dock in St. Thomas. **Varlack Ventures** (340/776-6412, www.varlack-ventures.com) operates passenger ferries to St. John that

Virgin Islands National Park, USVI

depart hourly from Red Hook on St. Thomas's east end (20-minute trip) and hourly or so from Charlotte Amalie (45-minute trip).

All ferries land at Cruz Bay, where the park **visitors center** is just two blocks from the dock. To get around, you can walk, rent a car (drive on the left side of the road), or hire a "safari taxi." Driven by local guides, the taxis depart Cruz Bay and roll into the nearby park along Route 20 (aka North Shore Road) en route to beaches or along Route 10 (aka Centerline Road) into the hills. Many drivers

Museums & Sites. Offerings at the **visitors center** illustrate St. John's natural and cultural resources. Rangers can explain the remains of **Annaberg Plantation**, an 18th- and 19th-century colonial-era sugar-processing works on the north shore east of Mary Point.

Programs & Activities. Among the ranger-led activities are guided hikes (including those highlighting post-hurricane habitat recovery), visits to rock carvings left behind by the Tainos, bird-watching excursions, and forest walks.

The volunteer **Friends of Virgin Islands National Park** (340/779-4940, www. friendsvinp.org) supplements ranger programs seasonally with trips to Hassel Island, kayaking or snorkeling excursions, and other events. **Cruz Bay Watersports** (cruzbaywatersports. com, 340/776-6234) offers diving, snorkeling, sailing, and other aquatic excursions.

Lodging. Many people book lodging elsewhere on St. John or on St. Thomas, and you might have to as well. As of mid-2018, the two in-park resorts were still closed indefinitely owing to severe hurricane damage. Still, it's worth checking on the status of **Cinnamon Bay Resort & Campground** (669/999-8784, cinnamonbayresort.com)—known for its tropical cottages and deluxe eco-tents—and the more luxurious **Caneel Bay Resort** (855/226-3358, www.caneelbay.com), on Laurance Rockefeller's former estate north of Cruz Bay. For more information on these and other lodgings, including those in Cruz Bay, contact the **USVI Department of Tourism** (www.visitusvi.com).

1. Scuba dive trip with Cruz Bay Watersports.
2. Honeymoon Beach. **3.** Sunset cruise from Cruz Bay Watersports. **4.** Trunk Bay.

offer two- or three-hour tours of places both inside and outside the park. Lodgings in and near **Cruz Bay** (www.visitusvi.com), some now open after hurricane damage, are convenient to the park. Although the island is on its way to recovery, check for updates and alerts on the park website.

Park Highlights

Natural Attractions. The national park encompasses more than 60% of St. John, and many of its beaches are considered among the world's best. Two of these are the beach and underwater snorkeling trail at **Trunk Bay**, the only national park beach on the island that requires a fee, and **Cinnamon Bay** beach, the island's longest beach.

Equally inviting beaches are the north shore's **Francis Bay**, great for long swims and long walks; **Hawksnest**, terrific for snorkeling and picnicking; and calm and shallow **Maho Bay**, where sea turtles and stingrays gather. Hike from the visitors center to peaceful **Honeymoon Beach** via the mile-long **Lind Point Trail**. On the island's southeast shore, coral reefs encircling sea grass make **Salt Pond Bay** an enticing snorkeling site.

The Virgin Islands Coral Reef National Monument (www.nps.gov/vicr), off St. John's south shore, protects 12,708 acres of coral reefs and other submerged ecosystems that add to the appeal of scuba diving, snorkeling, and boating. Dive shops, outfitters, and excursion concessionaires are available in Coral Bay in the east and near Cruz Bay in the west.

Trails & Viewpoints. Hiking trails trace the island's history, lead to its highest peaks, and explore environments including salt ponds,

mangrove swamps, dry tropical forests, and moist tropical forests. The easy, half-mile **Cinnamon Bay Nature Loop** leads through the ruins of a sugar plantation operated during the era of Danish settlement (from the 17th century to 1917).

A little more than a mile long, the **Bordeaux Mountain Trail** is a steep climb with overlooks en route to the summit at 1,277 feet. The popular but strenuous 6-mile round-trip **Reef Bay Trail** connects a walk through the forest to the ruins of sugar mills and pre-Columbian Taino petroglyphs. You can also do the hike on a ranger-guided tour with the **Friends of Virgin Islands National Park** (340/779-4940, www.friendsvinp.org; fee and reservations required). The tour includes a bus ride to the trailhead and a 40-minute boat ride back to Cruz Bay.

Voyageurs National Park

MINNESOTA

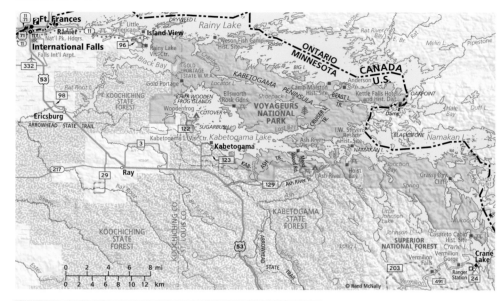

Although Minnesotans began pitching the idea of a national park in 1891, it took more than 80 years to make Voyageurs a reality. But, as Einstein noted, time is relative.

Those 80 years are a fraction of a second compared to what you can find within Minnesota's only national park: rocks half as old as the world, lakes formed by the melting of glacial ice, and visitor-center exhibits that reveal Paleo-Indians were living here 10,000 years ago.

Voyageurs brings to life preconceived images of Minnesota's North Woods. Houseboats float quietly in secluded bays, crisp autumn days are warmed by the fiery spectrum of colorful leaves, and the howl of wolves floats across the purple evening sky. This protected land of woods and waters would be recognizable to the Ojibwe people who lived here, and to the original *voyageurs*—the French-Canadian fur traders who arrived in the 1680s. Today their spiritual heirs are visitors who discover a new world

Voyageurs National Park, MN

on every island, along every shoreline, and when traveling every waterway. *Très magnifique.*

Park Basics

Established: April 8, 1975.
Area: 341 square miles; 218,200 acres (including 83,808 acres of water).
Best For: Bird-Watching (bald eagles, cormorants, loons, owls, warblers); Boating; Canoeing; Cross-Country Skiing; Fishing.
Contact: 218/283-6600, www.nps.gov/voya.
Getting Oriented: Much of Voyageurs is land that clips northeastern Minnesota, but it's the jigsaw-puzzle shorelines created by lakes Namakan, Kabetogama, Rainy, and Sand Point that make this remote park a haven for boaters. Each of the park's three visitors centers, accessible by road, has a boat launch. A few miles southeast of the Canadian border in the western part of Voyageurs, the main **Rainy Lake Visitor Center** near the end of Highway 11 is open year-round. Farther south is the **Kabetogama Lake Visitor Center**, and east of that, the **Ash River Visitor Center**; both are open only in summer.

Minneapolis–Saint Paul International Airport is 310 miles south of the Rainy Lake Visitor Center via I-35 and US 53. Nearby gateway towns include **International Falls** (www.rainylake.org), **Kabetogama** (kabetogama.com), **Ash River** (www.ashriver.com), **Crane Lake** (www.visitcranelake.com), and **Orr** (www.cityoforr.com). East of the park is the famous **Boundary Waters Canoe Area Wilderness** (www.dnr.state.mn.us).

Park Highlights

Natural Attractions. Streams, rivers, coves, inlets, ponds, bays, small inland lakes, and open-water lakes are the park's liquid assets. To explore them, you can rent canoes, kayaks, motorboats, and houseboats from nearby resorts and concessionaires. In International Falls, **Voyageurs Outfitters** (218/244-6506, www.voyageursoutfitters.com) offers services on various lakes. **Anderson's Canoe Outfitters** (800/777-7186, www.anderson-outfitters.com), in the town of Crane Lake, rents canoes and kayaks. In summer, the park service has canoes (Recreation.gov) at the Kabetogama Peninsula's inland lakes.

At this four-season park, fall colors reach their peak between middle and late September. In winter, the lakes freeze and conditions are right for ice fishing, snowmobiling, snowshoeing, and cross-country skiing. Voyageur's remote location and lack of artificial light create a good setting for winter's spectacular aurora borealis, or **Northern Lights**.

Trails & Viewpoints. Voyageurs has more than 50 miles of hiking trails, partly on the Kabetogama Peninsula and partly on islands and the mainland. Ice and snow transform many paths into cross-country skiing and snowshoe trails. Two easy trails from the Rainy Lake Visitor Center are the 1.7-mile **Oberholtzer Trail**, leading to overlooks of forest and wetlands, and the 1.75-mile **Rainy Lake Recreation Trail**, designed for walking, running, and bicycling past woods, rock outcrops, the lake, and marshes. The longest trails, including the 28-mile **Kab-Ash Trail**, are good for snowmobiles. Some trails are accessible only by water.

Museums & Sites. Along with fur trading and gold mining, logging was the area's main industry. Indeed, a lumber baron built the 1910 **Kettle Falls Hotel** (218/240-1724, www.kettlefallshotel.com) on the Kabetogama Peninsula's eastern tip. On the National Register of Historic Places, the restored, summer-only inn is accessible by boat (the park has tours, too) and is one of the few places in the lower 48 that looks *south* into Canada.

On the opposite shore from the Kabetogama Lake Visitor Center and reachable by boat, the **Ellsworth Rock Gardens** feature flowers, rock statuary, and natural rock formations that enhance the dramatic view of the lake. Northwest of the Rainy Lake Visitor Center, **Little American Island** preserves remnants of an abandoned settlement of miners dating from the 1890s gold rush.

Programs & Activities. Most park programs and tours take place in summer and fall. The popular Grand Tour on the ***Voyageur,*** a boat that sails from the Rainy Lake Visitor Center, is a 2.5-hour narrated excursion that delves into the park's human and natural history and looks for active eagle nests and wildlife. The ***Amik***, a pontoon boat, departs from the Kabetogama Lake Visitor Center. All boat tours have fees, and reservations (Recreation.gov) are recommended. During the week, free tours (218/286-5258 for reservations) aboard "voyageurs-style" 26-foot canoes depart from the Rainy Lake and Kabetogama Lake visitors centers.

For **fishing**, you'll need a license (sold at some resorts and service stations near the park) to cast a line for the park's walleye, pike, bass, trout, bluegill, perch, and whitefish.

Lodging. The options in Voyageurs are accessible only by boat, but nearby towns such as Kabetogama, International Falls, Ash River, Crane Lake, and Orr have a variety of woodsy resorts and campgrounds. The park's historic but seasonal **Kettle Falls Hotel** (218/240-1724, www.kettlefallshotel.com) is accessed by boat; boaters can also reach more than 200 park campsites classified as tent, houseboat, or day-use sites. Permits are available at visitors centers and boat ramps.

Near the park boundary is the primitive, 61-site **Woodenfrog State Forest Campground** (County Rd. 122, Kabetogama, 218/235-2520, www.dnr.state.mn.us), along Kabetogama Lake. Also on the lakeshore is the **Pines of Kabetogama Resort** (12443 Burma Rd., 218/875-2000, thepineskab.com), with luxury cabins, RV sites, and a marina.

1. Sunset in Voyageurs. **2.** Paddleboarding.
3. Park landscape.

3

Wind Cave National Park

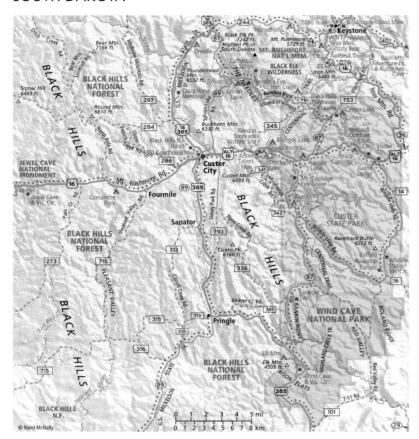

Deep, deep below the surface of the earth, humans walk, climb, or crawl their way through one of the densest, most complex, maze-cave systems in the world.

Yet, on the surface, in an area nestled within South Dakota's craggy Black Hills, bison and deer graze on a seemingly endless mixed-grass prairie, observed by those very same humans and plenty of small, scampering prairie dogs. Is it possible that two such diverse experiences can be found in one national park? The answer is yes.

Wind Cave has been welcoming national park visitors since 1903, when the very first automobiles rumbled through the Black Hills and cave tours were done by candlelight. Amazingly, both the cave system itself and the amount of wildlife on the prairie are greater today than at any point since the park's inception—due to unceasing exploration by cavers as well as a commitment by

conservationists to return this rare ecosystem to its preindustrial roots.

Park Basics

Established: January 9, 1903.
Area: 53 square miles; 33,924 acres.
Best For: Backcountry Camping; Hiking; Horseback Riding; Spelunking; Wildlife Watching (bison, elk, prairie dogs).
Contact: 605/745-4600, www.nps.gov/wica.
Getting Oriented: Wind Cave is one of

Wind Cave National Park, SD

the jewels of South Dakota's justly famous Black Hills, which extend north–south through the southwestern part of the state and also include Mount Rushmore National Memorial, Custer State Park, historic Deadwood, and motorcycle-happy Sturgis (during the weeklong rally in August, lodging is hard to come by). Colorado's Denver International Airport is about 350 miles south of the **Wind Cave Visitor Center** via either I-25/US 85 through Wyoming or I-76/NE 71/US 385 through Nebraska; the mileage is essentially identical. Rapid City Regional Airport is another fly-in option, about 70 miles north of the park via either SD 79/US 385 or scenic US 16/385 through the Black Hills.

The park has a northern entrance on SD 87 and two southern entrances on US 385, closer to the visitors center. US 385 runs through the park between Pringle on the west side and the amenities-filled town of **Hot Springs** (www.hs-sd.org), 11 miles south of the visitors center.

Park Highlights

Natural Attractions. A sacred site to the Lakota and other Native American tribes, **Wind Cave** attracted exploration after two brothers, settlers Jesse and Tom Bingham, came upon it in 1881—when Tom's hat blew off from gusts emanating from a small hole in the ground, the cave's only natural opening. (Rangers can predict the local weather due to barometric changes in cave pressure.) The stunningly intricate boxwork patterns in several of the cave walls and ceilings are formed from thin slices of calcite. They resemble honeycombs or bizarre giant waffles and are the most elaborate formations in this maze cave's 147 miles of mapped, interconnected passages.

The **prairie** covering the top of this giant cave is another visual feast. Bison and deer graze on open, grassy plains as prairie dogs burrow underground, occasionally popping up to check the scene. Hills and stands of pine dot the landscape, producing one of the Black Hills' most pastoral settings.

Trails, Drives & Viewpoints. All the aboveground attractions lie along a 13-mile stretch of US 385 and SD 87 between the south and north park entrances. The drive itself is magnificent, and you may see bison, deer, and prairie dogs along the way. The road has more than a dozen scenic lookouts where you can stop. The farther north you go, the more varied and hilly the landscape becomes; but the vast expanse of open prairie is equally evocative.

In the park's southern area, explore the prairie by hiking part or all of the somewhat strenuous 3.7-mile (one-way) **East Bison Flats Trail**. In the north, don't miss the easy 1-mile-loop **Rankin Ridge Trail**; the expansive view east from the base of the fire tower at the top of the ridge is one of the park's best viewpoints. If you'd rather see the prairie on **horseback** (on your own horse, of course), the park's open prairie is free (with a permit) to wander through, John Wayne–style.

Programs & Activities. Guided tours, the only way to see the cave, are the park's only cost. Tours must be reserved in person on the day you wish to visit; tickets go on sale when the visitors center opens at 8 am.

Summer has the most tour options, with both the 1-hour **Natural Entrance Tour** (easy, 300 steps) and the 1.5-hour **Fairgrounds Cave Tour** (moderate, 450 steps) winding their way through the boxwork-encrusted cavern; a highlight is when rangers plunge the cavern into its natural total darkness. Also fun is the 2-hour **Candlelight Tour** (moderate, summer only); you carry a "candle bucket," the way visitors did in the early 20th century.

Lodging. Camping at the 75-site **Elk Mountain Campground** (first-come, first-served) or in the backcountry is the only option for staying within the park. The campground is a mile north of the visitors center; backcountry

③

camping is limited to the northwest section of the park; get permits (required but free) at the visitors center.

Historic Hot Springs is a lovely town, high in the hills, with early-20th-century red sandstone buildings. Its **Red Rock River Resort** (603 N. River St., 605/745-4400, www.redrockriverresort.com) is a great example of this architectural style. Another appealing choice is the **Historic Log Cabin Motel** (500 Pacific Ave., 605/745-5166, historiclogcabins.com), with 18 stand-alone cabins dating from the 1920s. Breakfast at **Dale's Family Restaurant** (745 Battle Mountain Ave., 605/745-3028) is how everyone starts their day; say hello for us.

1. Prairie landscape. **2.** Prairie dog. **3.** Cave interior. **4.** Bison in the park.

④

Wrangell–St. Elias National Park & Preserve

ALASKA

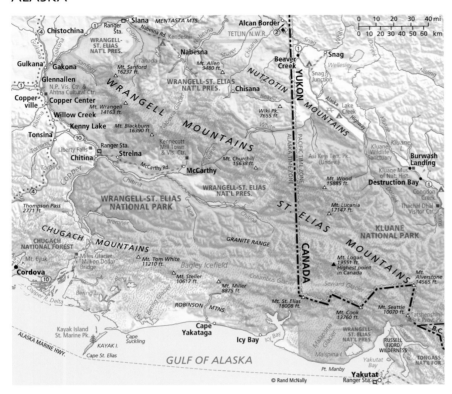

Try fitting a national park the size of six Yellowstones—or one Yellowstone, one Yosemite, *and* the nation of Switzerland—into one state. Then again, when that state is five times larger than Germany, it's a cinch.

Size—more than 13 million acres—is key to the splendor of Wrangell–St. Elias, but it's not the only thing that places America's largest national park on travelers' wish lists. The park's astounding environmental diversity

and remarkable geologic composition add to its allure. Although a handful of parks can claim active volcanoes, Wrangell–St. Elias will match those volcanoes and then raise the stakes as a World Heritage Site where glaciers are larger than entire states, four mountain ranges contain more than half of America's highest 16 peaks, and park terrain starts at sea level and reaches an 18,000-foot summit.

A glimpse of the Last Frontier only whets your appetite for more.

**Wrangell–St. Elias
National Park & Preserve, AK**

Immerse yourself in Wrangell–St. Elias and enjoy a feast.

Park Basics

Established: December 1, 1978 (national monument); December 2, 1980 (national park).
Area: 20,587 square miles; 13,175,790 acres.
Best For: Backcountry Camping; Bird-Watching (great horned owls, hairy woodpeckers, northern flickers, robins); Botany; Geology; Wildlife Watching (bears, beavers, caribou, foxes, moose, sea lions, seals, wolves).
Contact: 907/822-5234, www.nps.gov/wrst.
Getting Oriented: Wrangell–St. Elias is in southeastern Alaska; the closest major airport is Ted Stevens Anchorage International, 190 miles west of Copper Center; Fairbanks International is 250 miles north. About 200 miles northeast of Anchorage, AK 1 (aka Glenn Highway) meets AK 4 (aka Richardson Highway) in the town of Glennallen.

Ten miles south on AK 4 is the **Copper Center Visitor Center Complex**, including the nearby Ahtna Cultural Center. It's another 50 miles southeast to the summer-only ranger station on Edgerton Highway in **Chitina**, and from there another 65 miles east via gravel McCarthy Road and a shuttle (or hike) to the **Kennecott Visitor Center**. The park's airstrips are primarily for air taxis and sightseeing planes. Small towns near the park with amenities include **Copper Center** and **Glennallen**, near the Copper Center complex (www.traveltoalaska.com).

Park Highlights

Natural Attractions. Ranger programs, wilderness hikes, and aerial tours introduce you to the park's wonders: glaciers, mountain peaks, icefields, rivers, wetlands, and alpine and subalpine environments. One convenient place to see wildlife is along the Copper River, where waterfowl live and where bears and eagles go to fish.

Well over half of Alaska's glacial ice is within the park, where major glaciers include **Nabesna**, the longest non-polar valley glacier; **Malaspina**, which is larger than Rhode Island; and North America's largest tidewater glacier, **Hubbard**. In Kennecott (aka Kennicott), outfitters rent poles and crampons so you can hike onto **Root Glacier**. Flying services such as McCarthy's **Wrangell Mountain Air** (907/554-4411, www.wrangellmountainair.com) and Glennallen's **Copper Valley Air** (907/822-4200, www.coppervalleyairservice.com) let you see glaciers and mountains from above.

From the Copper Center complex you can see three major volcanic peaks: **Mt. Drum** (12,010 feet), **Mt. Sanford** (16,237 feet), and **Mt. Wrangell** (14,163 feet); steam plumes often cap Mt. Wrangell. Wrangell–St. Elias has four major **mountain ranges**: the eastern part of the Alaska Range, Chugach, St. Elias, and Wrangell.

Drives, Trails & Viewpoints. Only two gravel roads enter the park. The ranger station in Slana, in the park's northwest, is at the park entrance along **Nabesna Road**. To travel its 42 miles, allow 90 minutes each way. The rough but scenic route has trailheads mixed in among private property and an old mining facility. When you reach the end, turn around and return.

In Chitina, narrow and winding **McCarthy Road** heads east into the park. Conditions might include rough surfaces and washouts. Allow 2 hours each way for the 60-mile trip to McCarthy. From there, it's a 5-mile hike (or shuttle ride) to the historic mining town of Kennecott.

Hiking trails that branch off both roads range in difficulty from the moderate 1.5-mile **Rambler Mine Trail** at the end of Nabesna Road to multiday backcountry hikes.

Museums & Sites. The **Copper Center Visitor Center** has interactive exhibits on wildlife and tributes to those who helped preserve this land. A short walk away, the **Ahtna Cultural Center** (907/822-3535) displays clothing, tools, and ceremonial items used by the indigenous Ahtna, who entered the region about 2,000 years ago.

The **Kennecott Visitor Center** highlights the town's mining history with photographs and tools. Another way to explore Kennecott, a National Historic Landmark District and a premier example of early 20th-century copper mining, is on a two-hour tour with **St. Elias Alpine Guides** (907/554-4445, www.steliasguides.com).

Programs & Activities. Between mid-May and mid-September, rangers at Copper Center Visitor Center present programs, including an evening guided walk. Programs are also offered at the Kennecott Visitor Center and Kennecott Glacier Lodge. The **Wrangell Mountains Center** (907/554-4464, www.wrangells.org) in McCarthy has talks about science and the environment.

Independent outfitters can expand your Wrangell–St. Elias experience by arranging or hosting excursions including river rafting, hiking, glacier trekking, fishing, kayaking, and more. Check the Plan Your Visit section of the park website for companies.

Lodging. Despite its remote location, the area near the park has an impressive variety of options, primarily RV parks and campgrounds, with a few motels and hotels. Most are near Glennallen and Copper Center; others are inside the park along McCarthy and Nabesna roads. Some campers and RVers park near scenic overlooks along the roadside; it's free for 24 hours.

The only park service–managed campground is 10-site **Kendesnii** at Mile Marker 28.2 on Nabesna Road. Nearby hotels include **Kennicott Glacier Lodge** (15 Kennecott Millsite, Kennecott, 907/258-2350, www.kennicottlodge.com), inside the park, and the 85-room **Copper River Princess Wilderness Lodge** (1 Brenwick Craig Rd., Copper Center, 907/822-4000, www.princesslodges.com), just outside the park boundary.

1. Backpacker crossing a stream on the surface of Root Glacier. **2.** Snowcapped peaks. **3.** You can explore the historic district in Kennecott (aka Kennicott) with St. Elias Alpine Guides.

Yellowstone National Park

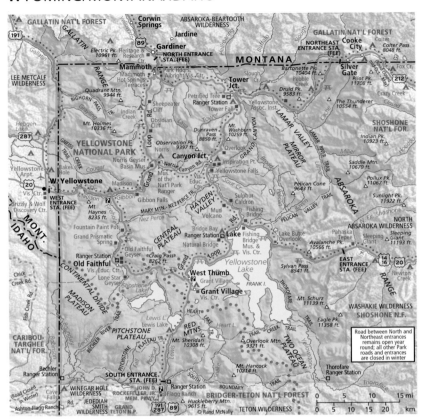

Home to grizzly bears, geysers, jaw-dropping canyons, rugged mountains, and the largest high-altitude lake in the West, Yellowstone is arguably the nation's most iconic park.

Not only was it the first national park, but it's one of the largest and most visited, and it remains a model for the system in terms of balancing recreation and conservation. Make no mistake, though. Despite its hotels and other visitor amenities (as well as its peak-season traffic jams), it's still notably wild: 98% is designated wilderness. And it's utterly unique. Yellowstone could have earned park status for its mountains and waterfalls, or its wildlife, or its bubbling hot springs. But it's got all of these—and much more.

Be sure to go on a hike. Few visitors to Yellowstone make it a mile beyond the roadside, meaning it's easy to have a slice of this unique wilderness to yourself along a trail less traveled.

Park Basics

Established: March 1, 1872.
Area: 3,468 square miles; 2,219,790 acres.
Best For: Fishing; Geology; Hiking; Wildlife-Watching (bald eagles, bears, big-horn sheep, bison, elk, gray wolves, moose).
Contact: 307/344-7381, www.nps.gov/yell.
Getting Oriented: Measuring roughly 50 by 60 miles, Yellowstone is in Wyoming's far northwestern corner; the park's northern fringe extends into southern Montana, its western edge into Idaho. Wyoming gateway towns include **Cody** (www.yellowstonecountry.org), 64 miles from the East Entrance, and **Jackson** (www.jacksonholechamber.com), 57 miles from the South Entrance. In Montana, **West Yellowstone** (www.destinationyellowstone. com), **Gardiner** (www.visitgardinermt. com), and **Silver Gate/Cooke City** (www. cookecitychamber.org) are the gateways nearest to the West, North, and Northeast entrances.

Many visitors fly into Salt Lake City, 329 miles from the West Entrance, or Denver, 521 miles from the South Entrance. There are also regional airports in Bozeman and Billings, Montana, and small airports in Jackson, Cody, and West Yellowstone. US Highways 14/16/20, 89/191/287, and 212 converge from different

Yellowstone National Park, WY/MT/ID

directions on the figure-8-shaped Grand Loop, a drive that hits most of the park's major attractions, including the Grand Canyon of the Yellowstone, Yellowstone Lake, and Old Faithful.

Visitors centers are at Mammoth Hot Springs (Albright), Canyon, Fishing Bridge, Old Faithful, and Grant; **information stations** are at Norris, West Thumb, Madison, and in the town of West Yellowstone. Several of these facilities also have museums.

The park's primary season is summer (roughly May through mid-October); few roads and facilities are open in other seasons. The

1. Lower Falls, Grand Canyon of the Yellowstone.
Opposite Page: Old Faithful geyser.

North Entrance is open year-round as are the portion of the Great Loop between it and the Northeast Entrance (whose visitors center is closed in winter), the campground at Mammoth, and hotels there and at Old Faithful. The only access to Old Faithful in winter, though, is by snowcoach or snowmobile.

Park Highlights

Natural Attractions. Yellowstone comprises one of the world's only undeveloped **hydrothermal areas**. Underlying volcanism heats snowmelt to a boil; the water then bubbles, seeps, and explodes up through the ground via hot springs, fumaroles, mud pots, and geysers that represent half of the planet's hydrothermal features.

Old Faithful—perhaps the most famous and predictable geyser on Earth—is the centerpiece of an entire geyser basin near the center of the park. Other must-sees for geyser gazers are **Norris Geyser Basin** in the park's northwest quadrant, and **West Thumb Geyser Basin** on the shore of Yellowstone Lake.

Near the North Entrance are **Mammoth Hot Springs**, a series of otherworldly terraces created over the eons by mineral deposits, and **Boiling River**, where geothermally heated water flows into the Gardner River at the only place you're allowed to soak in the park. (Warning: The rest of the hot springs are extremely dangerous.) The **Yellowstone Caldera**, in the heart of the park, is a supervolcano that erupts in a very, very big way every 700,000 years or so. But don't worry: It's only been 630,000 years since

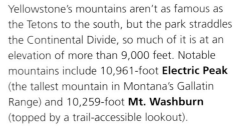

its last eruption, and scientists don't expect another anytime soon.

The park's volcanic activity is matched by its biodiversity, from the microscopic thermophiles that thrive in its thermal features to the bison grazing in its meadows. The Lamar Valley, near the Northeast Entrance, is known as "The Serengeti of North America" for its **wildlife**, which includes grizzly and black bears, gray wolves, elk, deer, moose, bighorn sheep, cutthroat trout, and bald eagles, to name a few. (Another warning: Maintain at least 25 yards between yourself and most wildlife; 100 yards if the wildlife is bears or wolves.) Lamar Valley's southern rim is also home to a petrified forest along **Specimen Ridge**. The fossilized trees were formed by volcanic activity nearly 50 million years ago.

Yellowstone's mountains aren't as famous as the Tetons to the south, but the park straddles the Continental Divide, so much of it is at an elevation of more than 9,000 feet. Notable mountains include 10,961-foot **Electric Peak** (the tallest mountain in Montana's Gallatin Range) and 10,259-foot **Mt. Washburn** (topped by a trail-accessible lookout).

With 136 miles of surface area, **Yellowstone Lake** is North America's largest freshwater lake at an elevation above 7,000 feet. Like the park's surface, the lakebed has geysers and other thermal features. The longest free-flowing river in the lower 48, the **Yellowstone River** runs from the park's southwest side and flows in and out of Yellowstone Lake before cutting through the spectacular **Grand Canyon of the Yellowstone. Upper and Lower Falls** are iconic sights: The latter is 308 feet high—twice the height of Niagara Falls—and is the highest-volume waterfall in the Rockies.

Other major bodies of water include **Shoshone Lake**, the largest backcountry lake in the continental United States, and **Lewis Lake**, connected to Shoshone Lake via the Lewis River Channel. In-park fishing destinations include the **Madison River** and **Soda Butte Creek** in Lamar Valley.

Trails, Drives & Viewpoints. Some of the most rewarding hikes are the **boardwalks** that explore the geysers and other thermal features at Old Faithful, Mammoth, Norris, and West Thumb. **Artist Paintpots Trail** is another good pick, an easy 1.1-mile loop around a thermal area featuring multihued hot springs and belching mud pots. From **Old Faithful**, the easy, 4.8-mile round trip to **Lonestar Geyser** offers the chance to glimpse an eruption well off the beaten path.

About 5 miles south of Mammoth, it's a strenuous 2.3 miles to the summit of **Bunsen Peak**. From the top, you can return the way you came or make a loop that includes a steep descent to **Osprey Falls** for a strenuous, 8.7-mile round trip. In Lamar Valley, **Slough Creek Trail** is a moderate hike that ascends about 400 feet before leveling out in the postcard-perfect mountain valley. From the trailhead, it's 10.6 miles one way to the park boundary.

The north and south rims of the **Grand Canyon of the Yellowstone** have scenic trails. For the best look at Lower Falls, try the short (0.7-mile) but strenuous **Uncle Tom's Trail**, which includes a staircase bolted to the canyon wall culminating in a viewing platform. Near Yellowstone Lake, **Elephant Back Trail** is a moderate, 3.5-mile round-trip hike with stellar lake views.

Although you could spend just a day driving the 140-mile **Grand Loop** (fully open only seasonally) and stopping at some of the major attractions, a multiday trip is much better. There are numerous **scenic overlooks** at Canyon, Tower, Lake, and other areas. Two interesting one-way routes veer off (and then return to) the main roads: 3-mile **Firehole Lake Drive** takes you to a popular swimming hole on the Firehole River north of Old Faithful; 6-mile **Blacktail Plateau Drive**, a less-trafficked dirt road, has nice views and wildlife-watching opportunities east of Mammoth.

Museums & Sites. Museum-worthy exhibits are at a number of Yellowstone's visitors centers: **Old Faithful** covers the park's hydrothermal activity, **Canyon** covers volcanism, and **Albright** at Mammoth covers the park's human history and cultural heritage. The last of the three is part of **Historic Fort Yellowstone**, dating back to the U.S. Army's control of the park in the early 1900s.

Just north of the Norris Information Station, the **Museum of the National Park Ranger** is dedicated to telling the story of its namesake profession. In the park's northeast corner, the old **Lamar Buffalo Ranch**, where hardy wranglers helped rebuild the decimated buffalo population from 1907 until the 1950s, now serves as a field campus for the Yellowstone Forever Institute.

Programs & Activities. Yellowstone offers a variety of mostly free **ranger programs** at Old Faithful, Canyon, Mammoth, and other areas, including guided hikes, campfire talks, photography workshops, and narrated boat tours. In winter, rangers lead snowshoe walks and evening programs at Mammoth and Old Faithful.

Operating from Gardiner, Montana, and the Lamar Buffalo Ranch in the park, the **Yellowstone Forever Institute** (406/848-2400, www.yellowstone.org) has a long list of workshops on everything from geology and bison biology to photography and history. It also offers Learning & Lodging packages that include stays at park hotels and tours with naturalist guides.

Guided **horseback rides** are available through Yellowstone National Park Lodges (see Lodging, below) at Roosevelt and Canyon. The park's primary concessionaire also offers a variety of tours, including **fishing charters** on Yellowstone Lake. In winter, it operates **snowcoaches** to and from Old Faithful as well as **cross-country skiing and snowshoeing** excursions.

Lodging. There's a wide range of historic in-park hotels and cabin complexes. You'll also find plenty of lodging and dining in the gateway communities of Jackson, Cody, Silver Gate/Cooke City, Gardiner, and West Yellowstone.

Yellowstone National Park Lodges (307/344-7311, www.yellowstonenationalparklodges.com) operates eight different lodgings inside park boundaries. Open since 1904, the summer-only Old Faithful Inn, with a lobby that's a wooden work of art, was the prototype for all the national park lodges that followed. Nearby, stylish Old Faithful Snow Lodge & Cabins is one of two lodgings that are open for the summer and winter seasons; the other is the historic Mammoth Hot Springs Hotel & Cabins.

Other (summer-only) in park options include Lake Yellowstone Hotel & Cabins, a luxurious, Victorian-era gem; Canyon Lodge & Cabins,

with newly built lodges; the very cowboy Roosevelt Lodge Cabins; Lake Lodge Cabins; Old Faithful Lodge Cabins; and Grant Village, near West Thumb.

Established in Cody in 1902, the **Irma Hotel** (1192 Sheridan Ave., 307/587-4221, www.irmahotel.com) is town founder "Buffalo Bill" Cody's historic hostelry (named for his youngest daughter), with historic suites and a newer, motel-style annex. Buffalo Bill's one-time hunting lodge, just outside the park's eastern boundary, the **Pahaska Tepee Resort** (183 North Fork Hwy., Cody, 307/527-7701, www.pahaska.com) features cabins with one to seven bedrooms, along with a restaurant, bar, and well-stocked gift shop.

In Gardiner, the **Absaroka Lodge** (310 Scott. St. W., 406/848-7414, www.yellowstonemotel.com) is a solid independent motel with private balconies and patios fronting the Yellowstone River. Just outside the Northeast Entrance, **Silver Gate Lodging** (109 US 212, Silver Gate, 406/838-2371, www.pineedgecabins.com) offers nicely renovated cabins (in three different locations) with fully equipped kitchens and easy access to Lamar Valley.

Moose Creek Inn (119 Electric St. and 220 Firehole Ave., West Yellowstone, 406/646-7952, www.moosecreekinn.com) mixes comfort, convenience, and charm in its cabin complex and nearby motel. Set on 200 acres, **Bar N Ranch** (890 Buttermilk Creek Rd., West Yellowstone, 406/646-0300, bar-n-ranch.com) has New West style to spare in its lodge rooms and cabins.

Between Yellowstone and Grand Teton National Park, along the John D. Rockefeller, Jr. Memorial Parkway, **Headwaters Lodge & Cabins at Flagg Ranch** (307/543-2861, www.gtlc.com) features cabins (from bare-bones to upscale), a restaurant, and a store.

The park has **12 campgrounds** (307/344-7311, www.yellowstonenationalparklodges.com), five of which accept reservations. All accommodate tents and RVs, except **Fishing Bridge RV Park** (the only campground with hookups), where tents aren't permitted. Of the first-come, first-served campgrounds, **Mammoth** is the park's only year-round facility. Lamar Valley's **Slough Creek** campground is in a notable wolf-watching area. Shoshone Lake and Heart Lake are circumnavigated by popular backpacking routes; a backcountry camping permit is required.

1. Fly fishing on Soda Butte Creek in Lamar Valley. **2.** Chromatic pool at West Thumb Geyser Basin with Yellowstone Lake in the background. **3.** Roosevelt Lodge horseback riding.

Yosemite National Park

1

If you can visit only one national park in your life, make it Yosemite. Its iconic granite peaks, plunging waterfalls, giant trees, and alpine meadows will be forever burned in your memory.

Although more than 5 million visitors make it their park of choice each year, never fear. With nearly 1,200 square miles to explore, it's easy enough to get away from the crowds of Yosemite Valley . . . once you've seen the valley for yourself, that is. Three or four days there, a day or two wandering the giant sequoia groves, and a couple of days in the high meadows would be the perfect week in one of the world's most perfect places.

A few notes: Yosemite's popularity means that its lodgings fill up, so book in-park stays well in advance. And although the park is open year-round, restoration and conservation projects, dry-season forest fires, and the High Sierra's renowned snowfall (or snowmelt) can result in road and other closures. Always check ahead.

Park Basics

Established: October 1, 1890.
Area: 1,190 square miles; 761,347 acres.
Best For: Backcountry Camping, Cross-Country Skiing, Hiking, Rafting, Rock Climbing.
Contact: 209/372-0200, www.nps.gov/yose.
Getting Oriented: Tucked into eastern California's Sierra Nevadas and surrounded by national forests, Yosemite is roughly 200 miles (a 4- to 5-hour drive) east of San Francisco International Airport. It has three western entrances, one in the south, and one in the east.

CA 120 (E. Yosemite Ave.) leads to the **Big Oak Flat Entrance**, whose namesake road continues east toward Yosemite Valley and Village, site of the main **Yosemite Valley Visitor Center and Theater**. To access

Yosemite National Park, CA

Yosemite's remote northwestern hikes and sites, turn off CA 120 just before entering the park and head north on Evergreen Road to the **Hetch Hetchy Entrance**. South of Big Oak Flat, CA 140 leads to the **Arch Rock Entrance** and Yosemite Valley via El Portal Road.

The **South Entrance** is on CA 41/Wawona Road, north of the town of Fish Camp and close to the Mariposa Giant Sequoia Grove and Pioneer Yosemite History Center. From the town of **Lee Vining** (www.leevining.com), 25

1. Yosemite Falls. **Opposite Page:** View of Yosemite Valley and Half Dome.

miles from the Nevada border, CA 120/Tioga Road leads to the **Tioga Pass Entrance**, the park's only eastern gateway and the best way to access Tuolumne Meadows. Note, though, that Tioga Road is closed between November and mid-May or June. (Once, it didn't open until July 1!)

Park Highlights

Natural Attractions. "Granite rocks" might sound boring—until you gaze upon **El Capitan**, a colossal cliff rising 3,000 feet from the Yosemite Valley floor, or massive **Half Dome**, the sliced-in-half, rounded rock that has become a symbol of the park. Also awe-inspiring are the countless waterfalls, including 1,000-foot **Horsetail Fall** on the east side of El Capitan and three-tiered **Yosemite Falls**, one of the world's tallest, plunging a total of 2,400 feet into Yosemite Valley. Completing the scene is the glittering **Merced River** snaking its way through the Valley en route to Merced, California.

All that should be enough to make Yosemite one of America's greatest parks . . . but there's more—including the wildflower-covered slopes of **Tuolumne Meadows**, 8,600 feet above the Valley in the park's northeastern quadrant, and the giant sequoias in **Merced Grove** and **Tuolumne Grove**, each with a couple of dozen big trees near the park's western border, and the majestic **Mariposa Grove**, with several *hundred* sequoias in the park's southern reaches.

Trails, Drives & Viewpoints. There's no way to prepare for the sheer beauty of the **Tunnel View**, the awesome sight of the entire Yosemite Valley—its green meadows, waterfalls, El Capitan, and Half-Dome—stretched out before you as you emerge from the tunnel on **Wawona Road** en route from the South Entrance to the Valley.

On a drive along the **Valley Road**, be sure to stop for the 0.5-mile round-trip (easy) hike to

620-foot **Bridalveil Fall**, which flows year-round, or the 1-mile (easy) loop to **Lower Yosemite Falls**. Escape (some) of the crowds by taking the **Mist Trail** (strenuous, 2.4 miles round trip) to the top of powerful, 318-foot **Vernal Fall**; it's one of the Valley's best hikes.

Then there's the drive to, and view from, 7,200-foot **Glacier Point**. It's about 30 miles from Yosemite Valley, with 17 or so miles along winding **Glacier Point Road** (open seasonally, depending on conditions). Shuttles run to the point during the day, but you can drive yourself at sunrise and sunset. The light is different, yet equally stunning, during the day and at twilight; try to go twice.

Museums & Sites. The Valley's excellent **Yosemite Museum**, a National Park Service Rustic–style structure completed in 1925, offers changing exhibits and a fascinating look into the history of both the park and the Native Americans who lived in the area for thousands of years before the trappers and traders arrived. Don't miss **The Ansel Adams Gallery** (650/692-3285, www.anseladams.com), also in the Valley. Prints by the great American landscape photographer are both on view and on sale; his winter imagery is especially evocative.

In the south, near Mariposa Grove, you cross a covered bridge to reach the **Pioneer Yosemite History Center**, a collection of historic structures built in different eras throughout

the park and moved here in the 1950s and '60s. Wander amid the buildings year round; in summer, explore their interiors or sign up for carriage rides and other programs.

Programs & Activities. Yosemite has many programs on tap. A free, hour-long **Naturalist Stroll** is a good way to learn about the park; it's also a good warm-up for an art or photography class, a guided hike, or a **Yosemite Valley Floor Tram Tour**. There's also the fun 2.5-hour **Bike to Hike Tour**, the **Ask a Climber** program, and frequent presentations about John Muir—founder of the Sierra Club and a tireless advocate for conservation at Yosemite.

MAJESTIC MEADOWS

If anything can top the view of Yosemite Valley from Glacier Point, it's the High Sierra panorama that is **Tuolumne Meadows**. It's home to crystal-clear mountain lakes, impossibly green wildflower-filled meadows, and solitary granite peaks (sometimes featuring lone, windswept pine trees) from which you can gaze south and west down to Yosemite's other majestic formations, including Half Dome itself.

From Yosemite Valley, you can access "The Meadows" by shuttle bus (209/372-0200 for information). The best way to get here in your own car is through the eastern Tioga Pass Entrance, along Tioga Road (CA 120), which runs between the town of Lee Vining and the Big Oak Flat Road in Yosemite Valley. It features the **Tioga Pass**, situated at 9,943 feet—making it California's highest highway pass. Given the snowfall at this elevation, Tioga Road is open only for a brief time in summer.

Along the way, stop for a hike to pretty Lukens Lake, a short, easy trek beginning 2 miles east of **White Wolf Road**. Alternatively, follow the longer, more difficult route from **White Wolf Lodge** (888/413-8869 or 602/278-8888, www.travelyosemite.com), which has 24 canvas-tent cabins, to soak in the views at **Tenaya Lake**. Or spend an afternoon among the birds and bees at hidden **Gaylor Lakes**, accessible via a strenuous 3-mile round-trip hike to and from the Tioga Pass Entrance. The trail climbs a 10,000-foot ridge before descending into meadows with lakes on the other side. Incredible.

If you've made reservations well in advance, your day will end with a fabulous, gourmet-style camp meal at **Tuolumne Meadows Lodge** (see White Wolf Lodge contact info, above) and a restful night under the High Sierra stars in one of 69 canvas-tent cabins (complete with wood-burning stoves, a necessity at this elevation). If Tuolumne sounds like paradise, you're right.

Rafting a stretch of the Merced River is a pastoral way to take in Yosemite Valley; rentals are available when the water is high, typically June and July. **Canoeing** and **kayaking** are also permitted at other of the park's myriad waterways. The **Yosemite Mountaineering School & Guide Service** (209/372-8344) provides guided rock climbs and classes—from free-form to fixed-rope to everything in between. In winter, **cross-country skiing** through the Valley will put you *inside* an Ansel Adams photograph. Sublime.

Lodging. Although Yosemite has several in-park lodging options, showing up without reservations is not a good idea. Book hotels and campsites through **Aramark** (888/413-8869 or 602/278-8888, www.travelyosemite.com), the park's primary concessionaire. Yosemite Valley's **Majestic Yosemite Hotel**

(formerly the Ahwahnee Hotel; open year-round) is a historic stone-and-timber building with 123 rooms, several cottages, a heated outdoor pool, a bar, and a stunning dining room.

The Valley is also home to the family-friendly, year-round, 205-room **Yosemite Valley Lodge** near Yosemite Falls; to the seasonal **Half Dome Village**, near Half Dome and Glacier Point, with 403 motel rooms, cabins (some with private baths), or canvas-tent cabins; and to the seasonal **Housekeeping Camp**, with 266 concrete-and-canvas units near sandy beaches along the Merced River. There are also lodgings at Mariposa Grove and Tuolumne Meadows (see "A Grove of Giants" and "Majestic Meadows").

Nine of the **13 park campgrounds** allow RVs. Four campgrounds are open year-round, including two in Yosemite Valley; the rest open as early as March or April and as late as May or June, depending on the location and the snowmelt. It can be just as hard to secure an in-park campsite as a hotel room. Some campgrounds allow reservations; others are first-come, first-served (arrive before 8 am).

To book a spot in one of the park's five **High Sierra Camps**, equipped with tents and cooking gear, you must enter a lottery. Even getting a permit for **backcountry camping** is a competitive sport (best chance of success: fax a request to the permit office, 209/372-0739).

Don't despair about the lack of in-park lodging availability. There are plenty of nearby hotels, motels, lodges, and B&Bs. In Fish Camp,

just south of the park, the stunning **Tenaya Lodge** (1122 Hwy. 41, 559/683-6555, www.tenayalodge.com) has upscale hotel rooms and cottages, restaurants, pools, a spa, and many on-site activities.

Just outside the park's Arch Rock Entrance in El Portal, the quiet, adults-only **Yosemite Blue Butterfly Inn** (11132 Hwy. 140, 209/379-2100, www.yosemitebluebutterflyinn.com) features five uniquely decorated rooms and gourmet breakfasts. The privately owned **Yosemite West Cottages** (559/642-2211, www.yosemitewestreservations.com), within the park a mile or so from the junction of Badger Pass/Glacier Point and Wawona roads, rents hundreds of fully-equipped cabins, condominiums, and cottages.

1. Lupine and Indian paintbrush, Tuolumne Meadows. **2.** El Capitan. **3.** Mariposa Grove. **4.** Tenaya Lodge.

Zion National Park

UTAH

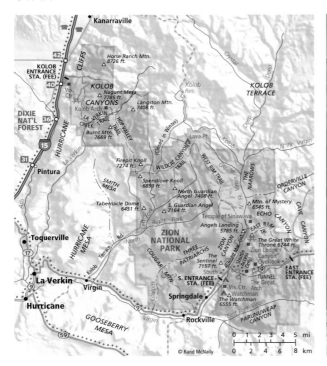

Burnished red Navajo sandstone cliffs rise from the Colorado Plateau, forming a series of majestic outcroppings illuminated by the sun and backlit by the deep blue Utah sky.

Welcome to Zion Canyon, one of the plateau's most striking formations, featuring 2,000-foot-high walls carved over countless millennia by the snaking Virgin River. On any given day, thousands of people gaze up at the canyon's walls and its intrepid rock climbers. Actually, *many* thousands of people; with more than 4 million visitors annually, Zion is one of America's most popular national parks. It has even considered introducing an online reservation system to address overcrowding and potential environmental damage.

But whether you choose to wade in the icy waters of the Virgin River on your way upstream, climb up to a bird's-eye viewpoint above the canyon, or escape to a less-visited corner of the park in search of giant sandstone arches, Zion National Park will be there to welcome you.

Park Basics

Established: July 31, 1909 (national monument); November 19, 1919 (national park).
Area: 230 square miles; 147,237 acres.
Best For: Backcountry Camping, Climbing, Cycling, Geology, Hiking.
Contact: 435/772-3256, www.nps.gov/zion.
Getting Oriented: Zion sits in Utah's southwest corner, near both the Nevada and Arizona borders. McCarran International Airport in Las Vegas is 160 miles southwest of the park's South Entrance, mainly via I-15; Salt Lake City International Airport is 313 miles northeast, also via I-15. It's 40 miles on UT 9 and I-15 between the **South Entrance**, where most folks enter the park, and the much less-trafficked **Kolob Canyons Entrance** to the northwest. (If you're tired of the crowds, this is your answer.) Both entrances have visitors centers. The **East Entrance**, on UT 9, is also less visited; it accesses the scenic Zion–Mount Carmel Highway.

Motels and inns line UT 9 outside the South Entrance in **Springdale** and **Rockville** (www.zionpark.com for both), but many visitors choose **St. George** (www.visitstgeorge.com), 41 miles west of the South Entrance, or **Kanab** (www.visitsouthernutah.com), 40 miles east, as bases from which to explore not only Zion but also Bryce Canyon and the north rim of Arizona's Grand Canyon.

Zion National Park, UT

Park Highlights

Natural Attractions. The sheer walls of **Zion Canyon** and many other mesas, buttes, and rusty red outcroppings are the park's main draws. You can see formations like the **Court of the Patriarchs** and **Weeping Rock** as you move in to the canyon, and it's impossible to say whether the canyon itself is more spectacular seen from its floor looking up or from its top looking down.

Zion displays a more desert-style landscape in its southwest corner (accessible by two trailheads off UT 9); the varied landscape of the high-elevation Kolob Canyons area in the northwest, however, is worth a full extra day. Few explore Kolob's hikes and views or the stunning 287-foot span of **Kolob Arch**, a strenuous 14-mile (round-trip) hike that is one of the park's hidden treasures.

Trails, Drives & Viewpoints. The 7-mile (one-way) **Zion Canyon Scenic Drive** from the South Entrance visitors center, which ends at the natural amphitheater called the **Temple of Sinawava**, and the 12-mile (one-way) **Zion–Mount Carmel Highway**, connecting the park's South Entrance to the East Entrance, are unmissable. Zion Canyon can be visited only via park shuttle bus mid-March through October (and weekends in November), but the spectacular narrowing and rising of the canyon's walls inspires awe as you travel farther in. The winding Zion–Mount Carmel Highway is one of America's most beautiful roads, with striated mesas and canyon views.

The Narrows begin at the north end of Zion Canyon; here, the canyon's walls are sometimes only 20 or 30 feet wide. The easy 2.2-mile round-trip **Riverside Walk Trail** is where you can examine The Narrows for yourself. For a spectacular bird's-eye view of Zion Canyon, the strenuous, 5.4-mile round-trip **Angels Landing Trail** from the Grotto trailhead, with its cliff-hugging stone steps and helpful (and necessary) chain handholds, is one of Zion's greatest experiences.

Programs & Activities. Rangers lead a great mix of summer programs, including a moderate 2.5-hour, 3.3-mile round-trip hike on the **Watchman Trail** that climbs to a great view of Zion Canyon. In mornings and afternoons, rangers conduct **Patio Talks** on Zion's wildlife and geology, while evening programs generally feature more personal stories.

Zion Canyon Scenic Drive is open for cycling, as is the pedestrian-and-bike-only Pa'rus Trail (3.5 miles round-trip). Zion Canyon's sheer cliffs and narrow slot canyons draw thousands

for climbing every year, and **canyoneering** (a combination of climbing, rappelling, and scrambling) is becoming increasingly popular. Permits for canyoneering and overnight climbs are required.

Lodging. The park has limited lodging options; there are, however, many choices in nearby Springdale and Rockville or farther afield in St. George and Kanab. **Zion Lodge** (888/297-2757, www.zionlodge.com) has 122 rustic rooms and 28 cabins; it's 4 miles from the South Entrance along Zion Canyon Scenic Drive. You must book 9 to 12 months ahead to stay in this classic lodge.

Zion's camping choices include the 184-site **Watchman** and 117-site **South** campgrounds (reserve on Recreation.gov) and the 6-site first-come, first-served **Lava Point Campground** in

the Kolob Canyons section, 7,890 feet above sea level. The park's 50 or so backcountry campsites are also popular, especially in The Narrows; you can reserve permits online 3 months in advance.

Zion Canyon Bed and Breakfast (101 Kokopelli Circle, Springdale, 435/772-9466, www.zioncanyonbnb.com) has four comfortable rooms just outside the South Entrance; in St. George, the adobe-style **Inn at Entrada** (2588 Sinagua Trail, 435/634-7100, www.innatentrada.com) is a polished golf and spa resort. The **Aikens Lodge** (79 W. Center St., Kanab, 435/644-2625, www.aikenslodge.com) has a seasonal outdoor pool where you can cool off after a day's hiking.

1. View of Zion Canyon from Angels Landing.
2. The Narrows. **3.** Sandstone landscape.

Index of National Parks by State & Territory

Contributors

Vice President, Publishing: Joan Sharp

Editorial Director: Laura M. Kidder

Writers: Gary McKechnie, Eric Peterson, Rob Tallia

Editor: Linda Cabasin

Design Director: Joerg Metzner

Art Director: Jodie Knight

Photo Editor: Cherie Cincilla

Cartographers: Greg Babiak, Robert Ferry (Project Manager), Justin Griffin, Steve Wiertz, Tom Vitacco (Director)

Production: Carey Seren

National Parks
Explore America's 60 National Parks

©2018 RM Acquisition, LLC d/b/a Rand McNally.
Rand McNally and the globe logo are registered trademarks
of RM Acquisition, LLC. All other trademarks appearing in
this publication are trademarks of third parties and are the
responsibility of their respective owners.

Published in U.S.A.
Printed in Canada

ISBN 13: 978-0-528-02082-7

For licensing information and copyright permissions,
contact us at permissions@randmcnally.com
If you have a comment, suggestion, or even a compliment,
please visit us at randmcnally.com/contact or write to
Rand McNally Consumer Affairs
P.O. Box 7600
Chicago, Illinois 60680-9915

1 2 3 FC 20 19 18